DATE DUE

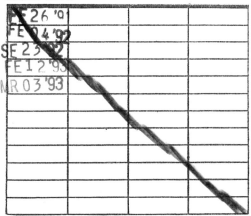

FE 26 '91		
FE 04 '92		
SE 23 '92		
FE 12 '93		
MR 03 '93		

NEW THREATS

RESPONDING TO THE PROLIFERATION OF NUCLEAR, CHEMICAL, AND DELIVERY CAPABILITIES IN THE THIRD WORLD

An
Aspen Strategy Group
Report

Published by
The Aspen Strategy Group
and
University Press of America
1990

University Press of America®, Inc.
4720 Boston Way
Lanham, Maryland 20706

3 Henrietta Street
London WC2E 8LU England

Co-published by arrangement with
The Aspen Institute.

The Aspen Institute and its logo are
trademarks of The Aspen Institute.

Library of Congress Cataloging-in-Publication Data

New threats, responding to the proliferation of nuclear, chemical, and
delivery capabilities in the third world : an Aspen Strategy Group
report.
       p.   cm.
1. Nuclear nonproliferation.   2. Chemical warfare (International
law)   3. Developing countries—Foreign relations.   I. Aspen
Strategy Group (U.S.)
JX1974.73.N48   1990   327.1'74—dc20   89–29096 CIP

ISBN 0–8191–7670–2 (alk. paper)
ISBN 0–8191–7671–0 (pbk. : alk. paper)

 The paper used in this publication meets the minimum requirements of
American National Standard for Information Sciences—Permanence
of Paper for Printed Library Materials, ANSI Z39.48–1984.

The Aspen Strategy Group

The Aspen Strategy Group is a bipartisan committee organized under the auspices of The Aspen Institute. The Group's primary goal is to help advance thinking and practice in the areas of international security and East-West relations. It aims to relate differing perspectives about the long-term direction of American security to current policy debates. As a standing body, the Group acts as a source of private policy advice; it contributes to the public debate through reports and other publications; and it encourages the study of broad conceptual issues that shape security but are sometimes hurried over in debates regarding immediate policy choices.

CONTENTS

About this Report   vii

Executive Summary   ix

1 Nuclear, Chemical, and Missile Proliferation
   in a Global Context   1

2 Responding at the Global Level:
   International Regimes and Proliferation   11

3 Proliferation in a Regional Context   19

4 Recommendations for American Action   23

Endnotes   31

Appendix 1: Nuclear Proliferation in the 1990s:
The Storm After the Lull – *Leonard S. Spector*   35

Appendix 2: Chemical Weapons Proliferation:
Current Capabilities and Prospects for Control –
Elisa D. Harris   67

Appendix 3: Ballistic Missiles in the Third World –
Janne Nolan and Albert Wheelon   89

Appendix 4: Feasibility of a Chemical Weapons
Regime – *Kyle B. Olson*   129

Appendix 5: Policy Issues in Chemical Weapons
Control – *Paul Doty*   143

Appendix 6: Solving Proliferation Problems in a
Regional Context: South Asia – *Stephen Philip Cohen* 163

Appendix 7: "Solving" the Proliferation Problem
in the Middle East – *Geoffrey Kemp*   197

Appendix 8: Four Decades of Nuclear Non-
Proliferation: Some Lessons from Wins, Losses,
and Draws – *Lewis A. Dunn*   233

Appendix 9: Rethinking Non-Proliferation Policy:
Increasing Efficiency and Enhancing Stability –
Thomas W. Graham   255

ABOUT THIS REPORT

This study is part of a series of reports prepared under the auspices of the Aspen Strategy Group, a program of The Aspen Institute. As a bipartisan standing committee, the Group aims to relate differing perspectives about the long-term direction of international security to current policy debates in the United States. Its members are drawn from the American academic, policy and business communities.

This report was written and prepared by the directing staff: Bobby Inman and William Perry (cochairmen), Joseph Nye (director), and Roger Smith (executive officer). Many of the ideas in this report were presented and discussed at the Aspen Strategy Group workshop on "Responding to the Proliferation of Nuclear, Chemical, and Ballistic Missile Capabilities," held on August 13–18, 1989, in Aspen, Colorado. Participants from the Aspen Strategy Group included Antonia Chayes, Kenneth Dam, John Deutch, Paul Doty, Tom Graham, Bryan Hehir, William Hyland, Bobby Inman, David Jones, Lawrence Korb, Jan Lodal, Joseph Nye, William Perry, George Rathjens, Roger Smith, John Steinbruner, Strobe Talbott, Albert Wheelon, James Woolsey, and Charles Zraket.

Guests at the workshop included Ruth Adams, Reginald Bartholomew, Stephen Cohen, Lewis Dunn, Richard Gardner, Elisa Harris, Geoffrey Kemp, Kent Kresa, Frederic Mosher, Janne Nolan, Kyle Olson, David Robinson, Amy Sands, Thom Shanker, Lawrence Scheinman, Leonard Spector, and William Webster. We are very grateful for their participation and contributions. We are especially indebted to those who prepared major background papers and delivered detailed presentations:

Stephen Cohen, Paul Doty, Lewis Dunn, Tom Graham, Elisa Harris, Geoffrey Kemp, Kent Kresa, Janne Nolan, Kyle Olson, Leonard Spector, and Albert Wheelon.

Generous support for this project was provided by the Carnegie Corporation of New York and the MacArthur Foundation. The authors of this report would also like to thank Lisa Grumbach for all her detailed comments, criticisms, and editorial assistance. Finally, we would like to express our appreciation to W. Daniel Wright and his colleagues at The Aspen Institute for computer services and production support.

Readers should take careful note that the contents of the report are the sole responsibility of the directing staff of the Aspen Strategy Group. Other group members and workshop participants, as well as sponsoring organizations and The Aspen Institute, are not responsible for the views or opinions expressed in this report.

EXECUTIVE SUMMARY

At the very moment when East and West are beginning to make significant progress in nuclear and conventional arms control, there has occurred an unparalleled intensification in the military competition in the Third World. More important than the increased tempo of Third World arms acquisitions is the growing lethality of the arsenals at the disposal of states often locked in bitter and violent conflict. Simply put, a growing number of countries are on the threshold of acquiring and deploying the full panoply of man's most sophisticated instruments of mass destruction.

The slow and steady diffusion of nuclear capabilities has not only continued, but it has become more sophisticated in both political and technical terms. Nations intent on acquiring a nuclear weapons capability have been able to operate elaborate networks of clandestine trade to supply them with the needed nuclear materials; moreover, this second generation of aspiring nuclear weapon states has not been content with possession of simple atomic devices, but are now crossing the thresholds into "boosted" and thermonuclear weapons. Iraq's use of chemical weapons against Iranian troops and its Kurdish minority has cast into stark relief the quiet but accelerating spread of chemical weapon capabilities across the globe. Any country with a petrochemical, pesticide, fertilizer or pharmaceutical industry has the potential to produce some chemical weapons. By themselves, either of these sets of developments would be disturbing to American national decision-makers. Given the dynamic that chemical and nuclear proliferation often feed on one another, as in the Middle East, the problem becomes more disturbing still.

The proliferation of ballistic missiles in the Third World acts to exacerbate the trends in nuclear and chemical proliferation. Ballistic missiles operate as more than combat multipliers for Third World countries, they act as proliferation multipliers. Most of the nations which have ambitious and advanced missile programs also have a prior interest in acquiring nuclear and chemical (and biological) weapons. Unchecked, the dangerous synergism between these three forms of proliferation will significantly alter America's future security environment. What can the United States do?

Two basic courses of action are open to the United States. On one level, the United States must pursue a global policy against proliferation. The centerpiece of this global effort should be the creation and maintenance of international regimes to control the proliferation of nuclear, chemical, and delivery capabilities. At present there are regimes in place to deal with nuclear and missile proliferation. While the nuclear non-proliferation regime is generally regarded as a stable and effective institution that only requires improvements on the margin, there are mounting concerns over its counterpart's ability to deal with missile proliferation. The missile technology control regime is hampered principally by the absence of such key missile suppliers as the Soviet Union, China, India, Argentina, and Brazil. Currently under negotiation is a chemical weapons convention, which seeks a total and complete ban on chemical weapons possession and production in all countries. Although considerable progress has been made in the negotiations, U.S. leadership will be as critical to the endgame of the convention's negotiation and institutionalization as it will be to the broadening of the missile regime.

As important as international regimes are to U.S. efforts at non-proliferation, they are only necessary, not sufficient, responses. What is also needed are region and country specific policies to complement those pursued at the global level. U.S. success at stemming proliferation will hinge on policies which are sensitive to the dynamics of regional politics and the motivations of key states. For example, any attempt at non-proliferation in the Middle East, which is divorced from efforts at political settlement of the major conflicts in the region, is unlikely to meet with much success; likewise, any non-proliferation effort in South Asia which does not acknowledge India's great power aspirations is unlikely to generate significant progress.

Although the reconciliation of regional security objectives with non-proliferation goals is by no means impossible, it cannot be accomplished without changes in how the United States formulates its policy both at home and executes it abroad. Specifically, the United States must make a greater visible commitment to non-proliferation, establish greater policy coordination with the Congress and within the executive branch, and rationalize its research and development program on verification arrangements and technologies. Beyond better organization, the United States must actively engage the Soviet Union, Western Europe and Japan in a more concerted and comprehensive approach to non-proliferation. And most fundamentally, the United States must begin to match its rhetoric with diplomatic action on non-proliferation.

1

NUCLEAR, CHEMICAL, AND MISSILE PROLIFERATION IN A GLOBAL CONTEXT

I. INTRODUCTION

In April 1986 Libya fired two *Scud*-B missiles at the U.S. Coast Guard station on the island of Lampedusa, off the coast of Italy, in retaliation for U.S. air raids on Tripoli and Benghazi. Both missiles failed to hit the island. This incident should have been dismissed and forgotten, a curious bit of trivia in the annals of strategic affairs. Instead, it has come to be regarded as the harbinger of a new, emerging and more dangerous security environment.

The six week "War of the Cities," in which Iran and Iraq fired nearly 600 hundred missiles at one another, the unabashed resort to chemical warfare by Iraq in its struggle with Iran and its Kurdish minority, and the near-certainty that Pakistan has mastered the technology of building nuclear weapons and Israel has begun developing "boosted" nuclear weapons has compelled national security decision-makers to rethink assumptions about Third World weapons programs. Projects once thought to be without promise or danger are now seen to possess both. With the exception of biological weapons, the steady diffusion of scientific knowledge, technological innovation, and engineering/manufacturing skills has engendered a situation in which a

1

growing number of countries are on the threshold of acquiring and deploying the full panoply of man's most sophisticated instruments of mass destruction.

While the development and spread of biological weapons, particularly those employing living organisms (anthrax, lassa fever, typhus, etc.) as opposed to genetically manipulated toxins, has been slow and uncertain, the same cannot be said of nuclear and chemical weapons development nor of ballistic missile capabilities. The purpose of this chapter is to review what is new in the proliferation of nuclear, chemical, and delivery capabilities and explain why this evolving technological diffusion compels serious attention by policymakers. The most recent develpment is the dangerous synergism linking all three forms of proliferation. When taken together, the interaction of all three forms of proliferation is greater than the sum of the individual changes in each area. This chapter will be divided into three sections. The first will focus on changes in the nature and dynamism of nuclear proliferation. The second will examine the emerging capacity in a host of countries to produce chemical weapons. The third and final section will explore the implications behind the manufacture and acquisition of ballistic missiles in the Third World.

II. NEW TRENDS
IN NUCLEAR PROLIFERATION[1]

The last time a group under the auspices of the Aspen Institute examined the problem of nuclear proliferation, the focus was on the then pressing issues of the international fuel cycle, the possible misuse of commercial deals, and the diversion of special nuclear material from civilian facilities.[2] That concern with nuclear proliferation was a response to the Indian nuclear test of 1974 and the sale of reprocessing technology by Germany and France to Brazil and Pakistan. This study is a response to new but equally troubling circumstances.

The fears of the mid-1970s about the widespread commercial use of plutonium have been replaced by a set of new concerns. Because of economic trends and tightened export controls by nuclear suppliers, it now appears that the preferred method of nuclear proliferation is by the uranium enrichment route, not the plutonoium path, and by secret facilities dedicated to the military production of nuclear material, facilities designed, constructed and maintained by extensive and intensive webs of nuclear smuggling. The example par excellence of a state which has moved up to and quite probably beyond the nuclear threshold is Pakistan. After France suspended work on a plutonium reprocessing plant in 1977, after the United States expressed concerns over Pakistan's possible misuse of the plant, Pakistan increased its efforts to develop a clandestine uranium enrichment facility using technology stolen from the Netherlands and imports through dummy corporations and trans-shipments via third countries. Pakistan's clandestine approach to gaining a nuclear weapons capability has led to violations of export control laws in both North America and Western Europe. However, Pakistan is not alone in orchestrating a secret line of nuclear supply. There is mounting evidence that both India and Israel have resorted to heavy water smuggling and safeguard violations in order to expand their nuclear weapon manufacturing capabilities.

As troubling as the nuclear smuggling may be, it is only part of the new nuclear proliferation equation. Another component is the growing number of facilities, quite possibly dedicated to weapons production, which are outside the system of international safeguards. In addition to the now publicized Kahuta enrichment facility in Pakistan, there are three other facilities worthy of note. First, North Korea appears to be constructing a plutonium extraction plant. This plant has little civilian justification but immense military potential. Though North Korea signed the Nuclear Non-Proliferation Treaty (NPT) in 1985, it has not yet signed an International Atomic Energy Agency (IAEA) safeguards agreement. Also not under IAEA safeguards are uranium enrichment plants in both Argentina and Brazil. Indeed, Brazil has not only constructed a uranium enrichment facility, but has established two "parallel" nuclear programs, one civilian, one military, with only the former under international safeguards.

The cumulative effect of this transformation in how nations "go" nuclear has been twofold. It has made the monitoring of nuclear progress by proliferating nations much more difficult, and it has accelerated the movement of additional nations toward the nuclear threshold. By the mid 1970s, there were two "*de facto*" nuclear powers in addition to the five designated in the NPT: Israel and India. In the 1980s two more covert proliferators emerged: South Africa and Pakistan. Three more states may be on the verge of attaining that status in the 1990s: Argentina, Brazil, and North Korea. The recent developments in North Korea could complicate immensely the strategic situation in Northeast Asia, as both South Korea and Japan might then feel pressure to reduce their current policies of restraint and exercise their latent nuclear capabilities.

The development of a second generation of nuclear powers (the first generation being the five declared nuclear powers: the United States, USSR, Britain, France and China) has also led to the development of a second tier of nuclear suppliers. These second-tier-suppliers are nations which are neither members of the Nuclear Suppliers Group nor parties to the NPT, nations such as Argentina, Brazil, India, and Pakistan. It has been reported that Argentina and Pakistan have established nuclear trade links with Iran, which may be renewing its drive for a nuclear weapons capability now that the war with Iraq has ended. It has been said that while every nation wants a nuclear weapon, once it gets one it tries to deny others the same capability; but before that nation becomes committed to the cause of non-proliferation it makes a mistake. For example, the United States helped the British, and the French helped the Israelis, and the Soviets helped the Chinese, who in turn helped the Pakistanis. In a complicated, more opaque world, the likelihood for more "mistakes" grows. And since many of the states acquiring new nuclear capabilities lack the political and technological capabilities for command and control of nuclear weaponry, the danger of further leakages to terrorist groups or of unauthorized use in time of political turmoil will increase.

III. THE GROWTH OF CHEMICAL WEAPONS CAPABILITIES IN THE THIRD WORLD[3]

Unlike nuclear weapons proliferation, the threat posed by the diffusion of chemical weapons is a relatively old problem. Chemical agents were used as long ago as 600 BC by the Greeks. Modern chemical weapons have been around since the turn of the century. Mustard gas was used along the Western Front in World War I, and by the Japanese in their military operations in China during World War II. However, it is an old problem with a new saliency. Iraq, in its war with Iran and in its counterinsurgency operations against its Kurdish population, resorted to large scale and frequent use of chemical munitions. In fact, it is widely believed that the Iraqi threat of using chemical weapons in a strategic role, in attacks against Iranian cities, was ultimately the decisive factor in Iran's eventual decision to accept United Nations Resolution 598 calling for a ceasefire.

Iraq's use of chemical weapons cast into stark relief the quiet, but accelerating spread of chemical weapon capabilities across the globe. Prior to the mid-1980s, the United States regarded chemical proliferation primarily in terms of the East-West conflict; the U.S. 1984 draft treaty on chemical weapons was largely concerned with the Warsaw Pact chemical threat to NATO. Iraq's use of chemical weapons, reports about Libya's possible use of chemical weapons in Chad, and the probable development of a chemical weapons plant at Rabta changed all that.

In a number of key respects chemical proliferation differs from nuclear proliferation. First, and foremost, any country with a petrochemical, pesticide, fertilizer or pharmaceutical industry has the potential in terms of equipment, raw materials, and technical expertise to produce some chemical warfare agents. It is this daunting problem of "dual use" technology that makes the danger of commercial misuse much more of a problem in chemical proliferation than in nuclear proliferation. Because of the wide accessibility through dual use technology, there is significantly less hard data on chemical proliferation than there is on nuclear proliferation; most discussions about chemical proliferation speak of numbers of states (usually 20), rather than actual states, which is the case in nuclear proliferation. The problem of dual use technology and materials means that the chemical proliferation watchlist is quite different than the one for nuclear proliferation. While most of the emerging nuclear powers have achieved a significant level of economic development, some of the world's poorest countries are among the "probable" chemical weapon states, countries such as Burma, Ethiopia, and Vietnam; and among those "possible" chemical weapon states are Angola, Laos and Somalia.

What Iraq's use of chemical weapons and the pattern of chemical proliferation suggests is a second and potentially far more disturbing difference between nuclear and chemical proliferation. States which seek to acquire chemical weapons do so primarily for military reasons and plan on using those weapons in combat. With nuclear proliferation there has always been a strong element of political prestige in the motivations of states; one need only to think of why Britain and France went nuclear, and why Argentina, Brazil, and India have moved to the nuclear threshold. For countries to derive some prestige value from a chemical weapons capability they would have to acknowledge in some way such a capability; in the nuclear realm, India held a test, while Argentina and Brazil have publicly announced their achievements in uranium enrichment. Yet virtually all the probable and possible chemical weapon states deny any such capability. Even Iraq, which first used mustard gas and cyanide agents to repel Iranian attacks in 1984, did not openly acknowledge its use until the summer of 1988. In contrast to chemical weapons, nuclear weapons have always possessed a certain mystique of "non-usability," the only military utility lay in non-use or deterrence. Because of Iraq's use of chemical weapons, their effectiveness on the battlefield,[4] and the weak international reaction to Iraq's use,[5] the usability quotient for chemical weapons has been enhanced.

While chemical weapons proliferation is distinct from nuclear weapons proliferation in both its form and scope, there can be a tight interaction between the two. One of the military rationales for acquiring chemical weapons is to counter a foe who possesses superior conventional strength. For example the development of chemical weapons capabilities in a number of Arab nations can be attributed in part to Israel's military superiority on the battlefield. However, Arab acquisition of an ability to wage chemical warfare has led Israel, in an attempt to retain some qualitative edge, to enhance its nuclear capability by developing "boosted" weapons. The linkage of chemical and nuclear weapons was evident at the Paris Conference on chemical weapons in January 1989 when a number of Mid-Eastern countries joined steps to control nuclear proliferation with agreements on the elimination of chemical weapons.

IV. BALLISTIC MISSILES
AND THE THIRD WORLD[6]

Like chemical weapons, the Iran-Iraq war has put the problem of ballistic missile proliferation high on the agenda of pressing national security issues. The effect of the "War of the Cities" in highlighting the dangers posed by the spread of ballistic missiles was reinforced by several other developments. In March 1988, the People's republic of China (PRC) sold medium-range surface to surface missiles (SSMs) to Saudi Arabia. A year earlier, Israel tested an indigenously developed missile, the *Jericho* II, with a range of approximately 900 miles, and in September 1988 used the *Jericho* II as the basis for a satellite launching rocket, raising the spector of an eventual Israeli missile with truly intercontinental range. And in May 1989, India successfully tested the *Agni*, a SSM with a range of 1500 miles; only a year earlier the Indians had flight tested a missile with a range of just 150 miles. Some 14 less developed countries now possess ballistic missiles. A dozen of them are also on the list of suspected chemical weapon states; and half of these states have missiles with ranges greater than 200 miles.

The accomplishments of Indian and Israeli science in successfully developing an indigenous ballistic missile capability is the exception not the rule thus far in ballistic missile proliferation. The Chinese sale to Saudi Arabia, while unusual in the type of rocket system sold and the partners involved, is a much more typical example of how missiles proliferate into the Third World.

Most of the ballistic missiles in the Third World were designed and manufactured somewhere else, most likely in the Soviet Union. The USSR has transferred thousands of SSMs to the Third World; most are of relatively short range, such as the *Frog-7*, the SS-21, and the *Scud*-B with ranges of 40, 75, and 190 miles respectively. While many countries have not gained the technological and engineering skills to design and manufacture from scratch a reliable ballistic missile, they possess more than enough expertise to significantly modify and upgrade what their military patrons have supplied them. For example, the Iraqis have produced two upgraded versions of the *Scud*-B: the al-Husayn and the al-Abbas with ranges of 385 and 560 miles respectively.

What makes this independent ability to modify and improve existing missile systems strategically significant is that what has been done for range can also be done for accuracy. Until now most of the short-range SSMs at the disposal of Third World militaries have been relatively inaccurate; for instance, the *Scud*-B has a circular error probable (CEP) of about 1000 yards at a range of 190 miles. Such accuracy limits the *Scud*-B to a strictly countervalue role. However, by adapting the inertial navigation systems built for commercial and military aircraft, it may become possible to get CEPs of 40 yards at 200 miles and 70 yards at 500 miles. With such accuracies, the *Scud*-B can be transformed into a potent counterforce weapon. Thus, the strategic problem of the 1990s is not the proliferation of countervalue intercontinental ballistic missiles (ICBMs) in the Third World—such a problem remains one for the next century—but highly accurate, short-range SSMs capable of being effectively coupled with nuclear, chemical, or high explosive warheads.

At first glance, this might be of some comfort to an American decision-maker, because the continental United States will remain for most of the next decade out of range of most missile systems in the Third World. However, a more discerning look will reveal a troubling future. Any increase in the accuracy of such a system as the *Scud*-B will increase the demand for such systems (which are currently produced in a number of countries outside the Eastern bloc) regardless of the security environment. The development of a ballistic missile force puts very little demands on a military infrastructure, in terms of training or manpower, especially one that has a modern air defense component. In fact, the acquisition of a ballistic missile force may actually lessen the burden placed on any military structure, because such a force will lessen the training and competence required of military pilots. The substitution of SSMs for manned aircraft in the performance of deep strike missions will be welcome not only because of its man power savings but also on the basis of military efficiency; ballistic missiles offer a relatively cheap way to break the stalemate which has developed between strike aircraft and layered air defenses.

The acquisition of accurate SSMs will do more than place at risk American efforts at power projection; it will fundamentally accentuate international insecurities and jeopardize efforts at preserving regional crisis stability. A prompt, hard-target kill capability will add to the inherent pressure to preempt in moments of crisis. The erosion of crisis stability in regions such as the Middle East will make more likely superpower intervention and conflict. What makes the prospect of further missile proliferation particularly worrying is the fact that most of the nations which have ambitious and advanced missile programs also have a prior interest in acquiring nuclear, chemical and biological weapons. Ballistic missiles then operate as more than a combat mutiplier; they act as a proliferation mutiplier as well. It is the simultaneous and interactive diffusion of nuclear, chemical and delivery capabilities that has significantly altered the security environment. There is more than a little irony in the fact that at the very moment when East and West are beginning to make significant progress in nuclear and conventional arms control, there is an intensification of the military competition in the Third World. The question of "what is to be done?" will be addressed in the remainder of this report.

2

RESPONDING AT THE GLOBAL LEVEL: INTERNATIONAL REGIMES AND PROLIFERATION

I. INTRODUCTION

Perhaps the most readily agreed upon response to the dangers of nuclear, chemical and ballistic missile proliferation is the need to respond at the global level, to create and sustain international regimes in each issue area. An international "regime" is a set of principles, norms, rules, and decision-making procedures around which the expectations of states converge.[7] While regimes can be either implicit or explicit, more often than not, the most important have their norms and rules codified in a formal treaty arrangement. An excellent example of a regime that guides international economic behavior is the one based on the General Agreement on Trade and Tariffs. In the realm of security, there are two regimes that currently exist which seek to control nuclear and ballistic missile proliferation, and a third currently under negotiation which would deal with the spread of chemical weapons. The purpose of this chapter is to examine each of these regimes in turn, with particular attention being given to the critical questions confronting each one.

II. THE NUCLEAR NON-PROLIFERATION REGIME

The nuclear non-proliferation regime is an elaborate yet simultaneously patchwork set of unilateral, bilateral, and multilateral institutions. Its origins can be traced back to Eisenhower's Atoms for Peace proposal in 1953 and the creation of the IAEA four years later. The regime includes a number of treaties that exclude nuclear weapons from certain geographical boundaries: Antarctica, outer space, Latin American and the seabed. The heart and soul of the regime is the Nuclear Non-Proliferation Treaty which spells out the basic bargain between the nuclear "haves" and the "have nots." The NPT divided the world into two classes of states, those with nuclear weapons and those without as of 1968; in return for foregoing the acquisition of nuclear weapons, the non-nuclear weapon states extracted from the nuclear states a commitment to provide the former with nuclear technology suitable to the development of peaceful nuclear energy and to restrain the vertical spiral in nuclear armaments.

By and large the nuclear regime is regarded as a success. The NPT has nearly 140 signatories and has reduced the number of problem states to just about a dozen; and because of safeguards and export controls only four of those twelve problem states can be considered *de facto* nuclear states. However, the very success of the non-proliferation has driven potential proliferators underground and into covert and illegal actions. The existence of these problem states is a source of constant tension for the regime, for it was premised as a global arrangement. The critical question as the NPT heads for renewal in 1995 is how long can the regime's legitimacy endure when a handful of countries are able to circumvent the rules and acquire a nuclear weapons capability without any significant political cost.

The consensus among the experts is that despite the "success" of countries such as India, Pakistan, Israel, and South Africa, the norm against non-proliferation remains quite strong. With the possible exception of India, no state is attacking the inherently discriminatory nature of the NPT. Even when India does try to foment dissatisfaction with the NPT, it is careful to not to attack the notion of a non-proliferation regime; in fact, Indian attacks against the NPT, it was noted, are usually balanced by the offer of an alternative non-proliferation regime. The consensus at the conference was that the regime was widely adhered to and that it required no major initiatives, such as the Nuclear Suppliers Group (NSG) and the International Fuel Cycle Evaluation (INFCE) in the late 1970s, to shore up international support of the regime. Nonetheless, the question of extending the life of the treaty must be agreed upon by a majority of signatories in 1995, and the dangers of erosion may present a more subtle threat.

III. THE MISSILE TECHNOLOGY CONTROL REGIME

The Missile Technology Control regime (MTCR), unlike the nuclear non-proliferation regime, is quite new, far less elaborate, and less comprehensive in both its membership and scope. The MTCR's roots can only be traced back to the short-lived Conventional Arms Talks of the late 1970s. The regime was formally created in April 1987 with the simultaneous announcement by the United States, Canada, France, West Germany, Italy, Japan, and Britain of a new policy to restrict exports that could contribute to the acquisition of nuclear capable missiles. Like the NPT, the MTCR is an inherently discriminatory regime; it attempts to divide the world into two classes of states, those with missiles with a range of 190 miles or more and a payload of 1,100 pounds and those without such missiles. The MTCR is unlike the nuclear non-proliferation regime in that it is not a treaty; indeed, it does not even have the force of an executive agreement. Moreover, there is no international organization to monitor missile-related exports; each national government is expected to regulate the exports from its country. In many ways the MTCR is akin to the 1977 Nuclear Suppliers Group and the 1949 Coordinating Committee of Multilateral Export Controls (COCOM) on East-West trade; all three are based on lists of sensitive items which require some form of export control. The MTCR has two components: 1) a "strong presumption" against exports of complete missile systems and 2) a less rigorous set of restrictions on production technologies that could be used in the development of ballistic missiles. As with the NSG and COCOM, there is no mechanism to apply sanctions to signatories or non-signatories who act against its prescriptions.

The two central questions which concern this nascent regime are effectiveness and legitimacy. Missile proliferation is an issue area in which a suppliers cartel could be quite effective. For example, in order for the Pershing II missile to function properly, a hundred thousand precision-crafted moving parts must function perfectly; this is no mean feat for even the most developed of countries. Consequently, missile programs in the developing world are vulnerable to supplier disruption. The MTCR has experienced some success already. The MTCR is generally credited with impeding access to critical components and developmental technologies necessary for the *Condor II*, an Argentine missile that was reportedly being developed in concert with Egypt, Iraq, and Saudi Arabia. While the *Condor* project may not be stalled forever, the MTCR has bought a precious commodity, time.

However, the MTCR is plagued by a number of problems. First, Some MTCR governments have at times applied the export restrictions in a rather loose manner in order not to shut off profitable commercial deals. Second, and more importantly, the future effectiveness of the MTCR is cast very much in doubt because of its limited membership. Though the MTCR countries have raised the problem of missile proliferation with other missile developers, such as the USSR, the PRC, Argentina, and Brazil, they have not been able to gain the cooperation of any additional state. Without widespread cooperation, many of the items that the MTCR countries refuse to export will be sold by countries outside the regime. To a certain extent, an effective counter to the MTCR is already being developed by the Third World. Increasingly, there is intra–Third World cooperation on ballistic missile development. Moreover, the rather robust black market in arms that grew to maturity during the Gulf War offers another way to circumvent the MTCR's export controls. Closely related to the issue of effectiveness is the question of legitimacy. There is no international taboo against ballistic missiles. Unlike nuclear and chemical weapons, there is no great moral stigma attached to the use of ballistic missiles (unless they are topped with nuclear warheads). How effective can a regime function, if the weapon it is trying to discourage is not perceived as illegitimate?

IV. THE CHEMICAL WEAPONS CONVENTION[8]

At present, the United Nations Conference on Disarmament is engaged in negotiating a chemical weapons convention (CWC) that goes well beyond what the non-proliferation regime and the MTCR have attempted. In contrast to the discriminatory nature of the NPT, the CWC would institutionalize a complete and total ban on chemical weapons in all states; this ban would prohibit the production or stockpiling of chemical weapons and would require the destruction of all existing chemical weapon stocks. In contrast to the MTCR, there would be no exceptions for particular types of weapons or technology (the MTCR permits technology transfers for missiles with ranges under 190 miles and for space launch technology); the entire world-wide chemical industry would be "captured" by the CWC in one form or another. Also in contrast with the MTCR, an international authority charged with the global monitoring of the treaty's implementation would be established. In regard to monitoring, the verification measures and procedures required and proposed for the CWC would be on such a scale that they would dwarf all previous inspection regimes, including those under the IAEA, the Intermediate-range Nuclear Forces (INF) treaty, or those considered for the Strategic Arms Reduction Treaty (START). As noted earlier, chemical weapons have been around for a long time. Likewise, proposals to control and prohibit the use of chemical weapons have been around almost as long. In 1675 French and German armies agreed to prohibit the use of poisoned bullets in combat. At the Hague peace conferences of 1899 and 1907, agreement was reached on the prohibition of artillery shells containing poison gas. After World War I, the 1925 Geneva Protocol was signed which permitted the production and stockpiling of chemical weapons, but prohibited the "first use" of chemical weapons. Although the Geneva Protocol remains the principal international legal constraint on chemical weapons, and hence the basis for constructing a chemical weapons regime, it has been complemented in recent years by an informal institution: the so-called "Australia Group." In 1985, under Australia's auspices, nineteen chemical suppliers met to discuss the implementation of tougher export controls on chemicals that are precursors to the manufacture of chemical weapons. The Australia Group has agreed to require formal licenses on eight specific chemicals and has issued a warning list for thirty more, in the hope that the chemical industry will voluntarily alert national governments to any foreign interest in acquiring those substances.

At this stage of the chemical regime's development (negotiations on the CWC began in 1980 and the most optimistic assessment about conclusion is for early 1991), the most pressing issue concerns verification. How the question of verification is answered will determine whether the CWC becomes a viable means to controlling a dangerous class of weapons or a curious footnote in the history of arms control. Verification of the CWC needs to be examined on several different levels, two technical and one political. The first level of technical concern on the issue of verification concerns the destruction of chemical weapon inventories and the cessation of chemical weapons production (Articles III–V in the "rolling text" of the CWC). The key issue at this level is less the confirmation of the size of stockpiles and the monitoring of their destruction,[9] than the question of illegal and undeclared stocks and production facilities. There are two ways a country, intent on preserving a chemical warfare capability, can beat the system. First, limited production of modern chemical weapons requires neither a lot of space nor a lot of equipment; consequently, a small chemical weapons plant could be hidden within the larger industrial infrastructure of country, especially if the country in question has a reasonably well-developed industrial base. Second, a country can do what Libya attempted: build a chemical weapons plant in a remote area, which is unlikely to attract foreign surveillance. The Rabta facility was located nearly 50 miles from Tripoli and American intelligence was alerted to the facility, not only by distant national technical means (NTM), but also by human sources. One of the ways that delegates at the Conference on Disarmament are trying to address this problem is through "ad hoc" inspections of non-declared facilities.

The second technical level of verification which raises concern relates more to monitoring rather than detection. Under the provisions of the CWC (Article VI), a number of precursor chemicals (Schedule 2) and commercial chemicals which have the potential to be used in the manufacture of chemical weapons (Schedule 3) must be monitored at both the production and consumption ends of the product cycle. The burden of monitoring precursor production will fall on the proposed international authority and the inspection teams from its technical secretariat. The cost of visiting all declared production and consumption facilities for at least the first ten years, when both military and civilian plants must be monitored, is projected to be anywhere between $150–$300 million per year. In comparison, approximately $25 million is budgeted annually for the IAEA's inspection role. The problem with monitoring the vast array of chemicals with potential to be used in chemical weapons production is that it can only be done through very basic accounting methods, methods which can be easily defeated through falsification. Even if falsification were not a potential problem, there are inherent difficulties in reliance on accounting as the principal means of monitoring. In the Third World there is generally a much lower premium placed on adherence to rigorous accounting procedures than in the West; and in the Eastern bloc there is a tendency to make the books conform with the projected outcomes regardless of the reality of production.

A third level at which verification for a comprehensive chemical weapons regime becomes a daunting prospect is the level of political expectations. Without ratification, signatures on a CWC will be meaningless, and the politics of ratification in the United States, as in a number of key countries rests on expectations about the degree of verification. The experience of the U.S. in ratifying nuclear arms control treaties with the Soviet Union does not bode well for the CWC. While the second Strategic Arms Limitation Treaty (SALT II) may ultimately have been lost in the "sands of the Ogaden," as Zbigniew Brzezinski claims,

Soviet intervention in the Third World was not the only cause for the treaty's demise. SALT II was in deep trouble with the Senate over the issue of verification, especially in regard to telemetry encryption. The experience of INF supporters before the Senate offers little comfort as well. INF witnesses encountered serious difficulty in explaining "pinholes" in the INF verification regime, such as omissions concerning canisters large enough to hold SS-20 missile stages (a "pinhole" is a potential verification shortcoming that is smaller than the proverbial "loophole"). What may be true for the United States may be doubly true for other countries. Whatever verification measures are eventually agreed upon for the CWC, they will still be a supplement to America's full-range of technical and human sources of intelligence. Consequently, the United States (at least in the abstract) can afford to accept a CWC with considerably less than 100% verification. However, for an Iraq or an Israel, with considerably fewer intelligence assets than the United States, a 75% verification regime might be too low to accept, regardless of domestic politics. This then raises the question that the nuclear non-proliferation regime has wrestled with: how does a regime, which is premised on universal participation, deal with and survive the existence of key states outside of the regime.

The issue of hold-outs tangentially raises another key issue which dogs the delegates to the Conference on Disarmament: sanctions. There are a number of unresolved issues regarding sanctions. First, how will a determination of non-compliance be made and who will make it? If the international authority will make decisions about compliance, what will be its voting procedures, how politicized will the process be? Second, should a determination be made that an instance of non-compliance exists, against whom will the sanctions be levied: the importing country, the exporting country the companies responsible, or all of the above? Third, if the noncompliance involves a non-signatory, how does that change things?

3

PROLIFERATION
IN A REGIONAL CONTEXT

I. INTRODUCTION

Although there is a general consensus on the need to build and sustain effective international regimes in order to slow nuclear, chemical and missile proliferation, there is also the recognition that global norms and rules are only a necessary, not sufficient, response. While regimes may reduce transaction costs of doing business and conducting diplomacy by establishing clear and stable expectations and by increasing the flow of accurate and reliable information, they provide very little help in dealing with the exceptional case, the extraordinary circumstance. There are two regions where proliferation developments have advanced so far that they are largely beyond the influence of global rules. Moreover, these two regions are areas where American strategic interests run deep and, consequently, pose a sharp challenge to the pursuit of non-proliferation objectives. Despite the basic similarities, these two regions require fundamentally different policy responses from the United States. These two regions are South Asia and the Middle East. The purpose of this chapter is to ex-amine the dynamics which push the United States to embrace a region-specific non-proliferation policy in addition to a global one.[10]

II. SOUTH ASIA[11]

In a number of respects America's global approach to non-proliferation in South Asia has worked. Despite the fact that

19

India tested a nuclear device in 1974, there have been no subsequent tests; not has there been any move to configure and deploy overt nuclear forces in either Pakistan or India. While U.S. efforts to block Pakistani access to a nuclear weapons capability have failed, American efforts to thwart Pakistan's movement via the plutonium route forced Pakistan on to the more costly and more complicated path of uranium enrichment; in the end this rearguard action purchased nearly a decade in which Pakistan was without nuclear weapons. However, this globalist approach has reached a point of diminishing marginal returns. Pakistan and India are both de facto nuclear weapon states. Any further adherence to a global approach will blind American decision-makers to important factors which may help stem further proliferation in South Asia.

Given the power of India and Pakistan to make both nuclear weapons and ballistic missiles, South Asia has become the focal point for nuclear proliferation. One of the most important factors in South Asian proliferation that is often misunderstood concerns motivation. It is widely assumed, because of the wars that have been fought by the two former British colonies, that the Indian and Pakistani nuclear programs are driven by the logic of a tightly interlocked arms race. What is forgotten or neglected is the fact that India's pursuit of a nuclear capability initially began in the 1940s and had nothing to do with Pakistan. By the 1960s, it had everything to do with the Sino-Indian conflict. It was only in the late 1970s that Pakistan's nuclear program belatedly entered into India's strategic calculations. Beyond the Chinese dimension to India's nuclear program, there is a larger element. If neither Pakistan nor China had nuclear weapons, there is an excellent chance India would have still embarked on a nuclear weapons program. One of the most enduring motivations behind Indian foreign policy is the aspiration for great power status. Just the reverse is true for Pakistan. While there is a desire to gain stature in the Islamic world by being the first to possess atomic capabilities, the primary motive for Pakistan's nuclear program is India's program. A second and equally important factor that is often missed is that neither state has the military or the public pressing for a nuclear weapons capability. In both states, the military and the general public are ambivalent at best about nuclear weapons; the primary push for obtaining a nuclear weapons capability in both states came from a small coterie of scientists and bureaucrats working with political leaders. The cumulative effect of these two misperceptions is the belief that nuclear proliferation in South Asia is inevitable. While it is true that technology denial or offers of economic or military aid will not roll back either nuclear program, there is reason to believe that less traditional non-proliferation policies, policies that conflict with the global approach, can bring a measure of stability to South Asia and retard further nuclear progress. Specifically, a "freeze" or nuclear standstill (no tests or deployments), if taken in conjunction with a number of other steps, could be extremely useful. In return for a freeze the United States would have to continue providing aid to Pakistan and acknowledge India's great power aspirations by involving it more directly in the reconciliation of global not just regional issues, such as disarmament. If poorly managed, however, a freeze would legitimize and reward Pakistan and India for their nuclear accomplishments, thereby contravening the norms and rules which the United States has tried to institutionalize.

III. THE MIDDLE EAST[12]

The Middle East is to chemical proliferation what South Asia is to nuclear proliferation. In addition to Iraq—the only non-NATO/Warsaw Pact country known to possess nuclear weapons—five of the eleven "probable" chemical weapon states are located in the Middle East: Egypt, Iran, Israel, Libya, and Syria (the other "probables" are Burma, China, Ethiopia, North Korea, Taiwan and Vietnam). Moreover, each of these countries possess long-range strike aircraft and short-range ballistic missiles, and virtually all are in the process of developing long-range missiles. Three factors, however, serve to make the situation in the Middle East more complicated than that prevailing in South Asia: 1) nuclear proliferation is bound up with chemical and missile proliferation in a very direct way (at the Paris Conference on chemical weapons the Arab nations linked any ban on chemical weapons to progress on restraining Israel's nuclear program); 2) unlike other regions the countries in the Middle East are locked into a series of cross-cutting and violent conflicts, such as the Arab/Palestinian-Israeli conflict, the Iran-Iraq war, and the many intra-Arab disputes; and 3) the taboo against use of chemical weapons has been broken in the region.

These three factors should have an impact on how the United States approaches the issue of non-proliferation in the region. The relative priorities discussed for South Asia should be reversed for the Middle east. In South Asia an initially limited approach stressing arms control (the "freeze") could open doors on the sources of proliferation. In contrast, an arms control initiative separate from and prior to any peace settlement will achieve little. Because the Arab world sees their chemical weapons as a deterrent counter to Israel's nuclear capability, and because Israel sees its nuclear capability as the most durable of its qualitative advantages over the Arabs, a fundamental deadlock exists on arms control. Consequently, a more political approach must be taken initially. In short the dangers of future proliferation might be used to propel the various parties to some gradual settlement of their differences; only then will a proliferation settlement have a reasonable chance for success. Again such a wait and see attitude runs contrary to the global norms of non-proliferation that the United States has tried to foster through its regime-building efforts.

The Middle East also highlights the need to tailor proliferation policies not only to different regions but to different countries within various regions. For example the differences between Israel and Iraq's missile programs mandate different goals. In the Israeli case the goal should be to prevent Israel from deploying a missile with the range to threaten Moscow; in Iraq's, the goal would be to prevent the development of longer-ranged missiles. Different goals require different policies: in the case of Israel, quiet political consultations; for Iraq, policies of technology denial.

4

RECOMMENDATIONS
FOR AMERICAN ACTION

I. INTRODUCTION

While it may be true that political prediction is a very uncertain science, we can, as one of Ibsen's characters in *Hedda Gabler*, say "a thing or two . . . about [the future] all the same." The slow, steady, and silent spread of nuclear capabilities has been joined in recent years by a far faster and much more overt proliferation of chemical weapon and ballistic missile capabilities. These changes pose a quantitatively and qualitatively different security environment than the United States has ever confronted. The diffusion of these instruments of mass destruction constitute new threats to the security of the American continent, to U.S. forces stationed abroad, and to the projection of U.S. power. Although much is still to be gained by pursuing traditional U.S. responses to the problem of proliferation, these new threats require new responses.

First, the United States must complement its "global" policies—export controls and regime-building—with region-specific and country-specific policies. In particular, the United States needs to avoid the tendency to think in dichotomous terms when it comes to proliferation: either working actively to prevent proliferation or quietly accepting it when it occurs. Instead, proliferation policy should be organized around three goals: prevention, containment, and management, with the selection

23

determined by individual circumstances. For example, in regard to Israel, the United States should seek to prevent the development of a chemical weapons capability, contain Israel's development of an intercontinental ballistic missile, and manage Israel's nuclear program to the extent that neither testing nor deployment occurs. More broadly, the United States must adopt policies tailored specifically for the so-called "opaque" or "covert" nuclear proliferators: India, Israel, Pakistan, and South Africa. The principle which should guide U.S. policy toward these states can be neatly summed up in the aphorism "a bomb in the basement is better than a bomb in the frontlines." The United States must work to insure that none of those states embarks on a testing or military deployment program.

The second element of any U.S. "new thinking" on proliferation would be the recognition that greater policy integration will be required. This policy integration will have to take place on two levels. On one level, it will be necessary to deal with all three types of proliferation together, not in a piecemeal fashion. The proliferation multiplier effect of ballistic missiles, when joined with the perception that chemical weapons constitute an adequate counter to a nuclear capability, makes such integration imperative. On another and more fundamental level, American non-proliferation policy must be integrated more closely with broader U.S. foreign policy goals. As the consideration of the proliferation problem in South Asia and the Middle East reveals, it is very difficult to unpack the proliferation issue from other issues which dominate the region. This second level of integration will pose a number of dilemmas for U.S. policymakers. For example, should the United States openly provide permissive action link (PAL) technology to a *de facto* nuclear weapon state in order to prevent unauthorized use or theft by terrorists? If yes, then the United States will, in effect, be visibly rewarding the *de facto* state for its proliferation and undercutting the nuclear non-proliferation regime; if no, then the United States increases the risk that a stolen weapon could fall into terrorist hands. A failure to make discrete adjustments to changing circumstances in order to preserve a consistent policy makes the best an enemy of the good.

II. SPECIFIC RECOMMENDATIONS[13]

The fate of the various non-proliferation regimes depends in part on U.S. leadership. While the United States must persuade others of its interest in joining efforts to stem proliferation, it must be clear about its own objectives and consistent in the implementation of its policies. What is critical for U.S. leadership is not only diplomatic action, but how the United States organizes itself for action.

1. Long-Term Research and Development Program for Verification

There was strong agreement among the Aspen Strategy Group membership on the need for a more sustained and significant research, development, testing and evaluation program on verification schemes and technologies than currently exists. As it now stands most of the research within the U.S. government is being done by the Department of Defense, and is focused on the technologies and procedures necessary to monitor strategic arms agreements with the Soviet Union. With the prospect for a wide-ranging chemical weapons convention being signed in the near future and the need for more and better nuclear monitoring techniques as the number of Third World facilities grows, there is a pressing need for a broader and more intensive effort in this field. There was also a strong consensus on the need to involve many departments and agencies in this work, while having it coordinated by just one agency.

2. Concerted Action with the Soviet Union.

While better organization, coordination, and more research will make the United States a more effective actor in any non-proliferation campaign, it would be for naught if such a campaign was unsupported by other key supplier states. The acknowledgment of the inherent limits of unilateral U.S. action led the Strategy Group to strongly endorse exploring closer cooperation with the Soviet Union on non-proliferation.

There is a widely shared assumption that the Soviet Union, after its experience with the Chinese nuclear program, has been a "good citizen" on the issue of proliferation. By and large this is a well-founded assumption in the realm of nuclear and chemical proliferation, though the USSR could still be more forthcoming in discussing some sensitive client states. It is in the realm of delivery capabilities that the USSR has been less forthcoming. In just the last two years the Soviets transferred advanced strike aircraft and in-flight refueling technology to Libya, SS-21 missiles to Syria and cruise missile nuclear attack submarines to India. The primary reason for this ambivalence on proliferation is that restraint on the transfer of delivery capabilities, unlike nuclear and chemical technology, cuts quite close to the heart of Soviet influence in the Third World. The relationships of military supply that Moscow has forged with developing countries are the primary instruments of its influence. The consensus at the conference was that the United States should make increased Soviet cooperation on controlling missile proliferation a major issue in discussions of Gorbachev's "new thinking" on international security.

Despite the fact that the Soviet Union has been reluctant to discuss problem countries in the bilateral talks which the two superpowers hold on missile proliferation every six months, there was general agreement that the USSR could be drawn into greater cooperation. One key to unlock Soviet cooperation on missile proliferation is not to insist that the USSR formally join the MTCR. It was deemed highly unlikely that the USSR could be enticed to join a Western technology control regime from which they had initially been excluded. While achieving de facto Soviet participation in the MTCR's restrictions would be worthwhile and possibly attainable, a better and still realizable goal would be the negotiation of a new and tighter missile control regime. An ambitious but probably unattainable new regime would be one that placed restrictions on missile systems with a range of 100 kilometers or more, as opposed to the current limit of 300 kilometers. The consensus of the conference was that a more profitable approach would be to concentrate diplomatic resources at building a stringent regime that prevented the proliferation of missiles with a range of 500 kilometers or more.

Beyond eliciting greater Soviet cooperation on missile proliferation, it was felt that the United States should challenge or invite the Soviets to be more active in constraining nuclear proliferation. There were two areas in particular that Soviet pressure could be quite instrumental. In East Asia, the Soviet Union should reciprocate the pressure that the United States has put on South Korea and Taiwan to adhere to the norm of non-proliferation; specifically, Moscow should persuade Pyongyang to promptly sign an IAEA safeguards agreement for its nuclear facilities. In Latin America, Soviet pressure on Cuba to sign and ratify the Treaty of Tlatelolco. Cuban adherence to the treaty would remove an obstacle to Argentinean and Brazilian participation.

3. Encourage Greater European and Japanese Engagement on Proliferation.

It is often forgotten that the most important nuclear non-proliferation successes have not been in the Third World, but in Europe and Japan. While countries such as West Germany and Japan have gone on to become members of the NSG, the MTCR, and the Australia Group, they need to be more actively involved at home (in terms of tighter export controls) and abroad in the campaign to slow the diffusion of weapons of mass destruction. Given that both Germany and Japan were subjected to massive campaigns of strategic bombardment during World War II and that it is unlikely that either will seek to acquire nuclear, chemical or missile forces of their own, their presence on the front line against proliferation would be potentially quite valuable and non-threatening to allies and neighboring states. A more active and visible diplomatic effort by Japan could be especially rewarding, given its growing role in the economic development of the Third World. Greater European involvement will become critical to sustaining the non-proliferation regimes after the move to create a single market within the European Community in 1992. To gain greater European and Japanese involvement will not cost the United States anything in terms of financial resources. However, it will require a significant investment of the most precious commodity in Washington: the time and energy of senior officials over a long period.

4. Strengthen the IAEA and Conclude a CWC

There is a complementarity between strengthening the nuclear non-proliferation regime and institutionalizing a similar one for chemical weapons. The IAEA performs a critical role in the nuclear non-proliferation regime by implementing the NPT's verification safeguards. There is a pressing need to review, update, and expand the IAEA's capabilities; more nuclear facilities will be coming on line in the Third World and the verification agreements reached on the INF treaty and those proposed for the CWC offer ways in which the IAEA can better meet its mission. The success or failure of the CWC will ultimately rest on the effectiveness of the international inspection agency that is to be established. In large measure, the IAEA will serve as a template for that inspection agency. A stronger IAEA will improve the prospects for a successful CWC. And the quicker a CWC is concluded, the greater will be the willingness to strenghten the IAEA's monitoring capabilities and use its practical experience as a verification laboratory. The United States must not only push for a successful conclusion to the CWC negotiations, but must also continue to insure that the IAEA remains a depoliticized agency with strong international support, both financial and diplomatic.

5. Matching Actions with Words

Over time, the United States has acquired a credibility problem in the area of non-proliferation. In terms of rhetoric, the United States is without an equal in the strength and the consistency of its opposition to proliferation. However, in terms of backing up that commitment with diplomatic action, the United States has a record of uncertain and ambivalent leadership. For example, in regard to Pakistan, India, and South Africa, the United States has denied military aid and nuclear exports and then later arranged for transfers of military equipment and nuclear fuel. U.S. silence on Israel's nuclear program has been deafening. The test for American leadership will be to accept some diplomatic costs in its pursuit of constraining the spread of nuclear, chemical, and missile capabilities. Without a closer match between what the United States says and what the United

States does, the regimes that the United States has tried to create and sustain will inexorably erode.

There is no easy or simple way to reconcile non-proliferation goals with regional security objectives. One way not to think about such a reconciliation is to think solely in terms of either/ or. The United States needs to think in terms of proportional responses to a country's development and deployment of nuclear, chemical, or ballistic missile systems. In particular, the United States must begin to tailor more closely its military and economic assistance to Pakistan's restrain in nuclear and missile development; while deliveries of additional F-16s should not be "lost" on the docks, they should be phased over a number of years. A necessary complement to a commitment to accept costs is a commitment not to complicate delicate balances by opening up new avenues for intensified military competition; for example, the temptation to export or assist in the development of sophisticated weapons systems, such as anti-tactical ballistic missile systems, should be resisted.

There are also a number of positive steps that the United States can take in order to improve its international credibility and effectiveness on non-proliferation matters. First, the United States needs to make better use of the resources at its disposal through better coordination among the executive departments and agencies. The Bush administration has made progress in fostering greater coordination among the various bureaus that have responsibility for non-proliferation matters by giving the Under Secretary of State for Science, Technology, and Security Assistance primary responsibility for coordinating policy, but more can be done. Specifically, there needs to be greater coordination between the Department of Energy, which has substantial resources focused on non-proliferation problems, and the State Department, which consumes most of that information but has no formal ability to set priorities.

In addition to improved coordination within the executive branch, there needs to be closer cooperation with the Congress. Non-proliferation is an issue that should inherently enjoy bipartisan support. However, that support is not automatic; rather it must be nurtured and cultivated. Where coordination between the two ends of Pennsylvania Avenue will become increasingly critical is in the crafting of a durable, effective sanctions policy. The issue of sanctions creates a critical dilemma for policy makers. On the one hand, there is the desire to make sanctions strong enough to penalize the violator and strengthen the regime by deterring others from taking similar action. On the other hand, there is the desire not to ruin U.S. relations so completely with the violator that any future cooperation is foreclosed. One concrete step that can help foster a bipartisan and coordinated approach is to energize the long dormant General Advisory Committee (GAC) to the Arms Control and Disarmament Agency, by appointing congressmen interested in proliferation matters to its membership rolls. Because the GAC reports directly to the president, a new avenue would be opened up for private executive-legislative consultations on non-proliferation policy. Closer coordination between executive and legislature can also prevent states from trying to exploit differences between the two.

ENDNOTES

1. This section is based in large part on the presentation and paper delivered by Leonard Spector to the Aspen Strategy Group on August 14, 1989. A revised and edited version of that paper is reproduced as Appendix One.

2. The Aspen Strategy Group's predecessor was the Aspen Arms Control Consortium, and in the summer of 1976 its meeting was devoted to nuclear proliferation; see Thomas A. Halsted, *Nuclear Proliferation: How to Retard It, Manage It, Live with It* (Aspen Institute for Humanistic Studies, 1976).

3. This section is based in large part on the presentation and paper delivered by Elisa Harris to the Aspen Strategy Group on August 14, 1989. A revised and edited version of that paper is reproduced as Appendix Two. For an earlier treatment of this subject by the Aspen Strategy Group, see *Chemical Weapons and Western Security Policy* (Lanham, MD: University Press of America, 1987).

4. By most accounts Iraq's use of chemical weapons was decisive in stopping the Iranian counter offensive in 1984, in halting subsequent Iranian assaults, and in aiding the Iraqi recapture of the Faw pennisula. For a brief review of the conditions under which chemical weapons can be effective battlefield weapons, see *Chemical Weapons and Western Security Policy*, op. cit., pp. 4–8.

5. Iraq's use of chemical weapons engendered considerable condemnation but very little action from the international

community; and as time went on, even condemnation was hard to come by. The January 1989 chemical weapons conference in Paris was convened in large part becasue of Iraq's resort to chemical weapons; however, there was very little specific reference to the Iraqi case during the conference and no specific mention in the conference's final declaration.

6. This section is based in large part on the presentation and paper delivered by Janne Nolan and Albert Wheelon to the Aspen Strategy Group on August 14, 1989. A revised and edited version of that paper is reproduced as Appendix Three.

7. See Stephen D. Krasner, ed., *International Regimes*, (Ithaca, NY: Cornell University Press, 1983).

8. This section is based in large part on the presentations and papers delivered by Kyle Olson and Paul Doty to the Aspen Strategy Group on August 15, 1989. A revised and edited version of those papers are reproduced as Appendices Four and Five.

9. Most of the concern in this area originally involved Soviet reluctance to accept "anywhere, any time" on-site challenge inspections in order to alleviate suspicions about declared sites and facilities. However, since 1986 the USSR's position on intrusive verification has under gone a radical transformation, and it has come to accept almost all of the West's verification demands.

10. This is not to imply that there are no proliferation problems in Latin America or Africa. On the contrary, both Argentina and Brazil have extensive nuclear programs and South Africa, like Brazil and Argentina, has a well-developed nuclear and ballistic missile infrastructure. However, for the purposes of the conference, there was a need to focus the group's efforts, and consequently, the group selected two regions where the problems of proliferation were the most complex and immediate.

11. This section is based in large part on the presentation and paper delivered by Stephen Cohen to the Aspen Strategy Group on August 16, 1989. A revised and edited version of that paper is reproduced as Appendix Six.

12. This section is based in large part on the presentation and paper delivered by Geoffrey Kemp to the Aspen Strategy Group on August 16, 1989. A revised and edited version of that paper is reproduced as Appendix Seven.

13. This section is based in large part on the presentations and papers delivered by Lewis Dunn and Thomas Graham to the Aspen Strategy Group on August 16, 1989. Revised and edited versions of those papers are reproduced as Appendices Eight and Nine.

Appendix 1

NUCLEAR PROLIFERATION IN THE 1990s: THE STORM AFTER THE LULL

Leonard S. Spector

For much of the past decade, and particularly after Israel's destruction of Iraq's Osiraq research reactor in 1981, the fear that nuclear arms might spread rapidly to numerous new states—a major concern of policy-makers in the 1970s—appeared to subside. Certainly in Congress, in the foreign policy community at large, and probably within many corridors of the Reagan administration, there appears to have been an increasing complacency on this point and a readiness to assume that, for the foreseeable future, nuclear weapons would probably be confined to four regional states: Israel, India, South Africa, and Pakistan.

The first three already possessed undeclared nuclear capabilities by 1980, and although throughout the Reagan years their capabilities were dramatically increasing, these developments went largely unremarked. Rather, U.S. non-proliferation attentions were concentrated on dissuading Pakistan from acquiring a nuclear capability of its own. U.S. efforts ultimately proved unsuccessful, but the pace of Pakistani nuclear advances was slow, and when the country silently crossed the nuclear threshold on a *de facto* basis—apparently in 1986—Washington, and the international community, absorbed this blow to non-proliferation calmly.

Obviously, the restraint shown by each of the four nuclear-capable regional states in not undertaking nuclear tests or otherwise brandishing its nuclear potential helped to create the impression that proliferation, if not entirely under control, was remaining within manageable bounds. The fact that none of the four countries at issue was hostile to the United States also undoubtedly contributed to this atmosphere of relative equanimity in Washington, as did the efforts of the Reagan administration and elements of Congress to downplay nuclear differences with Israel and Pakistan for strategic reasons.

There was also much to suggest in the mid-1980s that the threat of proliferation elsewhere had eased. Though Argentina announced the partial construction of an unsafeguarded uranium enrichment plant in 1983, the country's new civilian president, Raul Alfonsín, appeared genuinely committed to nuclear disarmament. And it was by no means clear that Brazil would seek to develop a matching capability, especially given the absence of external threats to its security and Argentina's proposals for confidence building in the nuclear area. In the Middle East, with no end in sight to the Iran-Iraq War, the prospect that either of these states might develop nuclear arms also appeared remote. And, in East Asia, concerns about North Korea's construction of a large, unsafeguarded research reactor appeared to be assuaged when the country, with Soviet encouragement, joined the Non-Proliferation Treaty in 1985. Nor were there publicly available indications that South Korea or Taiwan were interested in pursuing nuclear weapon options.

Whatever validity there may have been for the widespread perception of calm during the mid-1980s, today the dangers from the continuing spread of nuclear arms have greatly intensified, creating the need for a new sense of urgency in addressing this issue. The magnitude of the problem is not always apparent from snapshot surveys of the capabilities and intentions of the nuclear threshold states. But the trends are unmistakable when developments in these nations are examined over a period of years.

- *First, the pace of proliferation—the spread of the bomb to new states—appears to be quickening.* In the wake of Pakistan's acquiring a nuclear capability in 1986, it now appears that North Korea is moving aggressively to follow suit—a step that will likely stimulate parallel ambitions in South Korea. Brazil and Argentina, meanwhile, are primed to cross the nuclear threshold if political winds should shift, and Iran and Iraq have launched new weapons efforts. (Taiwan and Libya apparently remain interested in similar capabilities but are, for now, unable to pursue their ambitions.)

* *Second, it is now clear that Israel, India, Pakistan, and South Africa do not intend to "hover" at the nuclear threshold by limiting themselves to rudimentary nuclear capabilities.* In recent years, all of these countries have increased their stocks of nuclear weapons material dramatically, and most of them appear to be developing advanced delivery systems and thermonuclear capabilities. Moreover, the spread of chemical weapons and ballistic missiles in the Middle East and South Asia is increasing the risk of nuclear weapons being used in a future regional conflict and is introducing serious nuclear tensions between some regional nuclear powers and extra-regional nuclear weapon states.

Unfortunately, new challenges to the non-proliferation regime—and even to the concept of nuclear non-proliferation, itself—are likely to make it all the more difficult to address these burgeoning nuclear dangers in the developing world.

I. THE QUICKENING PACE OF PROLIFERATION

North Korea
North Korea is now believed by some U.S. officials to be constructing a plutonium extraction plant near the large research reactor, noted earlier, that it completed between 1985 and 1987 at Yongbyon. Relatively little detailed information has been published about these North Korean facilities. It appears, however, that the reactor is of the "gas/graphite" design, which is particularly well suited to the production of plutonium, and that

it has been operating for some time, though probably well below full capacity. Theoretically, if the reactor is rated at 40 to 60 megawatts, as some reports indicate, it could produce enough plutonium for one or two devices per year.

The status of the possible plutonium extraction plant is not clear from the open literature, and some U.S. government analysts are said to question whether the facility, which is apparently still under construction, is intended for this purpose. If it is indeed a plutonium facility, and if it were ready to operate by 1991, Pyongyang by that time could have accumulated several years worth of spent fuel. This could give North Korea the wherewithal for several nuclear weapons early in the next decade and could permit the country thereafter to add to its stockpile at a rate of one or two weapons per year. The particular combination of facilities would be a clear indication of the country's intentions to move in this direction, since it would bear little relationship to the legitimate needs of a peaceful nuclear research program, while being ideally matched to military applications.

Although North Korea joined the Nuclear Non-Proliferation Treaty (NPT) in 1985, three and a half years later it still has not concluded the required subsidiary safeguards agreement with the International Atomic Energy Agency (IAEA). Thus neither the research reactor nor the alleged plutonium plant are currently subject to IAEA inspections. Many believe that Pyongyang is deliberately stonewalling to delay the application of safeguards as long as possible.

The emergence of a North Korean nuclear capability would raise a host of disturbing issues. Given its diplomatic isolation, history of hostile acts against South Korea, support for international terrorism, and unbridled arms transfers to Iran and others, North Korea could emerge as the quintessential nuclear renegade state. Its continued resistance to IAEA safeguards, for example, could be a signal of its intention to withdraw from or abrogate the NPT, and if it were to take this action, there would be little reason to expect it to refrain from nuclear testing. Either step would be a severe blow to current international nonproliferation norms.

Far graver is the risk that Pyongyang might threaten to use nuclear weapons against South Korea. Among other scenarios, it might attempt to smuggle a nuclear device into a major South Korean city and, through nuclear blackmail, attempt to topple the Seoul government or obtain the expulsion of U.S. forces, hoping to create conditions conducive to reunification of the country under Northern control. Even if Pyongyang were to use its nuclear capability more benignly as a deterrent against U.S. nuclear weapons, the development would drastically alter the security equation on the Korean Peninsula. Such a step could largely neutralize the security benefits to Seoul of the U.S. nuclear presence and, by exposing U.S. forces to a new class of threat, could reduce South Korea's confidence in U.S. readiness to come to its defense. At a minimum, a North Korean nuclear option would trigger powerful pressures in the South for the development of a comparable capability.

Indeed, even if Pyongyang were to accept IAEA safeguards on the Yongbyon facilities—assuming that a plutonium plant is being built—Seoul's concerns would remain, since the North would be legally entitled to stockpile plutonium and, having built the necessary facilities, would presumably do so. This would leave the North with a ready nuclear option. In 1981, Israel was so concerned that Iraq might acquire just such an option, notwithstanding IAEA supervision, that it destroyed the Osiraq facility. Given North Korea's air defenses and retaliatory capabilities—including possible strikes against South Korean nuclear power reactors—it is unlikely that the South would risk an Israeli-style preventive attack. This handicap, too, will likely produce intensified pressures on Seoul to develop an indigenous countervailing nuclear force.

Today, South Korea possesses a sizeable and advanced nuclear infrastructure, but, largely because of U.S. pressure and security guarantees, it has not built the facilities necessary to produce nuclear weapon materials. Renewed calls in the U.S. Congress for the withdrawal of U.S. forces from South Korea— calls which so far have not taken into account the possibility of a nuclearized North Korea—could lead to added to pressures for a South Korean nuclear option.

In the immediate term, averting the risks of a nuclear-armed North Korea—risks that include the danger that Pyongyang might transfer sensitive nuclear technology or materials to others—means ensuring that it does not construct a plutonium facility. In theory, the Soviet Union, which has demonstrated considerable commitment to non-proliferation over the years, would appear to be in the best position to dissuade North Korea from this path, and the United States is apparently urging Moscow to pursue the issue. Unfortunately, the fact that the North has resisted IAEA safeguards for over three years, despite presumed Soviet interventions, suggests that even Moscow may not have the necessary influence in this arena.

Brazil

Brazil is a second state that appears to be rapidly approaching the nuclear threshold, with Argentina poised to follow suit. With respect to the former, there is increasing evidence that the Brazilian military has been engaged in a slow but steady effort to build a nuclear weapons option. The vehicle for this effort has been Brazil's so-called "parallel" nuclear program, *i.e.*, a classified, unsafeguarded, supposedly indigenous nuclear research and development program, which has operated largely under military control along side the country's safeguarded nuclear energy program. The safeguarded program is based on imported facilities and technology, especially those transferred under the massive 1975 Brazil–West Germany nuclear deal.

Since the late 1970s, a component of the parallel program controlled by the Brazilian Navy had been attempting, with little apparent success, to develop a uranium enrichment capability using centrifuges. In September 1987, however, Brazilian President Jose Sarney announced that Brazil had succeeded in using this technology to enrich uranium on a laboratory scale, and in April 1988 Brazil commissioned a pilot-scale enrichment facility at Ipero. The plant is believed to be producing uranium enriched to only 5 percent—not usable for weapons—but Brazil has since announced that it reached the 20 percent enrichment level in its laboratories. A recently disclosed West German intelligence report, moreover, stated that as early as 1987 Brazil had sufficient mastery of the uranium enrichment process to produce 70 percent enriched material, virtually weapons-grade.[1]

According to published reports, by late 1988, the Ipero plant had 300 operating centrifuges; some 2000 to 3000 are planned. When this level is reached the facility will have the capacity for producing enough weapons-grade uranium for 2 to 3 weapons annually, according to the best published estimates.[2]

Brazilian officials claim the facility is intended for the production of 20 percent enriched uranium to fuel research reactors and future nuclear submarines. However, a number of factors suggest that the overall goal of the parallel program is the development of a nuclear device. The most telling indicators have been:

- repeated statements by Brazilian military leaders describing nuclear arms in positive terms and highlighting Brazil's emerging capabilities in this field;

- the construction by a Brazilian Army unit of an apparent nuclear test site in the Amazon jungle;

- the construction—and apparent operation—of a pilot plutonium extraction facility at a Navy-run research facility (plutonium would have no utility in a nuclear submarine program);

- the development by military-backed research institutes of designs for two different plutonium production reactors;

- the use of secret bank accounts to fund the parallel program;

- the use of clandestine purchasing operations to obtain key components for enrichment centrifuges in Western Europe; and, it appears,

- the deliberate circumvention of controls on safeguarded West German technologies in order to use them in the unsafeguarded parallel program.[3]

It seems highly unlikely that Brazil would have gone to these lengths simply to obtain research reactor fuel or to improve its maritime capabilities in the next century.

Given Brazil's accomplishments in other high technology areas, it is likely that the country could by now have manufactured nuclear weapons if it had chosen to do so. Budgetary constraints and the lack of an urgent security need for nuclear arms have undoubtedly contributed to the more deliberate pace of developments. On the other hand, progress has been consistent and, in light of the evidence cited above, there appears to be a powerful pro-bomb constituency within the military that favors the acquisition of a nuclear capability for reasons of national and institutional prestige.

Whether this constituency will ultimately push Brazil across the nuclear threshold will depend in large measure on domestic political factors and on developments in Argentina. Brazil's current president, Jose Sarney has been dependent on the military for political support and has shown little inclination to curb its nuclear ambitions, although he has supported limited nuclear confidence building with Argentina, as discussed below. Sarney's successor will be elected later this year, in Brazil's first direct presidential election in more than 20 years; right now the race is wide open. It is too early to predict whether the country's new leadership will be more inclined to reduce the military's behind-the-scenes political role or to curb its discretion in nuclear matters, specifically. Popular sentiment appears to be decidedly anti-nuclear, but the question seems unlikely to become a campaign issue.

Argentina

Like Brazil, Argentina has not yet produced the material needed for nuclear weapons, but it, too, has built a uranium enrichment plant that is free from IAEA safeguards and other international non-proliferation controls. The Argentine facility, at Pilcaniyeu, was built in secret between 1978 and 1983 by the country's military regime and was disclosed only weeks before the inauguration in December 1983 of Argentina's first democratically elected president in over a decade, Raul Alfonsín. The military government's nuclear aides insisted at the time that the plant had been built to produce nuclear reactor fuel that could not be used for nuclear weapons. There are strong grounds for believing, however, that the secret project, which was begun at a time of growing Argentine militarism, was initiated to provide Argentina with a nuclear weapons capability. Alfonsín brought the country's nuclear program under civilian control, however, and during his tenure appeared to be firmly opposed to developing this potential.

If completed according to its original design, the Pilcaniyeu facility would be able to produce 500 kilograms of 20 percent enriched uranium per year. In theory, this means that the plant could also be operated to produce weapons-grade uranium enriched to 90 percent or more, possibly enough for several weapons annually. However, budgetary limitations have slowed work on the facility, and it is likely to be a number of years before such a production goal could be met. The installation is now believed to be producing material enriched to less than 5 percent, although small quantities of 20 percent material have also been obtained.

Soon after taking office, Alfonsín initiated a series of dramatic bilateral initiatives with Brazil through which the two countries have sought to reassure each other that their respective nuclear activities would not lead to the manufacture of nuclear explosives. The high points of these confidence building efforts were a visit by President Sarney to Argentina's classified uranium enrichment plant in July 1987, and a reciprocal visit in April 1988 by Argentine President Alfonsín to the inauguration of Brazil's uranium enrichment facility.

Unfortunately, these confidence building initiatives do not permit either country to monitor the quantities and enrichment level of uranium produced at these plants or to account for its disposition. Today, neither country is producing weapons-grade uranium, but both will soon be able to do so as the Pilcaniyeu and Ipero facilities become fully operational. Indeed both states have already reached the 20 percent level, at least on a laboratory scale. Unless additional verification mechanisms are adopted, neither country could then be confident that the other was not enriching uranium to higher levels in a secret bid to develop a nuclear weapons option.[4] Argentina has proposed more stringent bilateral verification measures, but so far Brazil has been unwilling to embrace such enhanced controls.

In June of this year, Peronist Party candidate Carlos Menem succeeded Alfonsín as Argentina's president. During Alfonsín's tenure, Peronist parliamentarians had expressed reservations about the nuclear rapprochement with Brazil and had criticized the budget cuts Alfonsín had forced on the country's nuclear program, which for many years had been promoted as a symbol of national accomplishment. Indeed, during his campaign for the presidency, Menem himself declared that he did not see a need for nuclear weapons "at the moment" but did not rule them out for the future.[5] Given this background and the nationalistic fervor long associated with Peronism, many observers anticipated that Menem would appoint a staunch advocate of open-ended nuclear development to head the country's nuclear program.

Rather unexpectedly, however, Menem rejected a highly visible champion of such policies and appointed a little-known technocrat to the post. He also expressed his intention to maintain cordial nuclear relations with Brazil. It thus appears for the moment that Argentina is likely to remain at some distance from a weapons capability. The country's economic crisis is also likely to be a restraining factor.

On the other hand, given the numerous demands on Argentina's new leadership and the pending elections in Brazil, it is unlikely that existing confidence building measures will soon be broadened. Moreover, recent reports of Brazil's production of 20 percent enriched uranium, circumvention of controls on West German technology, clandestine nuclear purchasing efforts, and secret activities related to plutonium production could cast a long shadow. In the months ahead, these developments may lead some elements of Menem's party to agitate for a more assertive nuclear stance. The Pilcaniyeu plant would allow Argentina to move rapidly toward the nuclear threshold if it ultimately chose this course.

Iraq

It is clear from the foregoing analysis that the seeds for the potential emergence of North Korea, Brazil, and Argentina as new nuclear states began to sprout earlier in the decade, although few observers appeared to pay much attention to these developments. In contrast, nuclear programs in Iraq and Iran seem to have been largely dormant for most of the 1980s. With the end of the Iran-Iraq War, however, both states have begun massive rearmament programs, including, it appears, efforts to develop nuclear arms.

There is now considerable evidence that during the late 1970s Iraq was building a nuclear infrastructure intended to provide it with a nuclear weapons capability by the end of the current decade. The Iraqi effort was centered on the Osiraq research reactor, purchased from France. In June 1981, Israel destroyed the reactor in a surprise air strike, crippling Iraq's nuclear program.

That facility has not been rebuilt, and it appears unlikely that it will be any time soon. However, Iraq is beginning to revitalize its efforts to acquire nuclear arms by pursuing another route. Apparently, Baghdad has initiated a program to obtain components for the construction of a facility to enrich uranium to weapons-grade. A March 1989 *Washington Post* article stated that Iraq might be able to build nuclear arms within two to five years.[6] This appears, however, to have overstated the threat.

A better estimate is that it will probably be ten years before Iraq could manufacture nuclear arms. In effect, the Iraqi program appears to be comparable to the Pakistani nuclear effort of the early 1970s, when the latter country had a plan to produce nuclear weapons and little more, rather than to the Pakistani program of the late 1970s, when Islamabad had a major uranium enrichment facility well under construction. Iraq is thought to be advancing its program by using clandestine purchasing networks in Europe that it set up during the Iran-Iraq War to support its secret chemical weapon and missile development programs.

Iraq is a party to the Non-Proliferation Treaty and is obligated to place any facility containing nuclear materials under IAEA oversight. If Baghdad constructed a uranium enrichment plant, it could place the facility under safeguards and could then legally stockpile weapons-grade uranium if it chose to—as long as IAEA inspectors were able to verify that the material was not being diverted to non-peaceful purposes. In effect, this would provide Iraq a ready nuclear weapons option, which it could exercise quickly by abrogating safeguards or withdrawing from the NPT. Another alternative, of course, would be for Baghdad to attempt to avoid safeguards by denying the existence of the facility, a step that would directly challenge the IAEA system.

Today, Iraq almost certainly is building this nuclear capability as a response to the long-term threat it perceives from Iran, although Israel, too, has need to be concerned about Iraq's nuclear ambitions. For either of these states to thwart Iraq's efforts through military action, however, will be far more difficult than it was in 1981. Iraq has, for example, built up significant air defenses and reportedly has located key laboratories underground to protect them from possible air strikes. More important, however, is that Iraq's extensive ballistic missile forces now give it the ability, which it lacked in 1981, to retaliate powerfully against any future attack on one of its nuclear installations. Thus neither Iran nor Israel could assume that if it mounted such an attack today, it would escape unscathed, as Israel did eight years ago.

This said, there is still some question as to whether Iraq's missiles can shield its nuclear program against all external threats. Baghdad would, itself, have to calculate very carefully before taking retaliatory action—such as launching a missile attack against an Israeli city—for fear that this might, in turn, trigger a still more devastating counter-retaliation. Nonetheless, the advent of a potent Iraqi missile capability has clearly increased the risks to its adversaries of a pre-emptive strike and may ultimately be the key factor that leads to the emergence of a second nuclear power in the Middle East.

Iran

Less has been published about Iran's nuclear intentions. Iran's revolutionary government inherited a useful nuclear research base from the Shah, which is thought to have included some work on the design of nuclear weapons and some analysis of the steps needed for their manufacture. But with only one small research reactor, the country remains far from possessing a nuclear infrastructure to support a nuclear weapons effort.

Nonetheless, Iran opened a new nuclear research center in Isphahan in 1984 and has attempted to restart work on two partially completed German-supplied nuclear power reactors at Bushehr, so far without success. It has also established useful nuclear trade links with Argentina, which is to supply Iran with 20 percent enriched uranium for its research reactor. In addition, there have been reports of discussions of nuclear technology transfers with Pakistan, which is also said to be training a number of graduate-level Iranian students in nuclear engineering, some supposedly in sensitive technologies.[7] Given these efforts to resuscitate the country's nuclear program and the continuing armaments race with Iraq, it is not unreasonable to surmise that a long-term program to obtain nuclear weapons has also been launched. So far, however, little has emerged publicly about any such effort.[8]

Iran, too, would have to be concerned about a pre-emptive attack. During the Gulf War, Iraq repeatedly attacked the Bushehr reactor construction site, presumably to forestall further work on the units. Iran is also a party to the NPT and, like Iraq, would have to take into account its obligation to place all of its nuclear activities under IAEA inspection.

Taiwan and Libya

Weapons related nuclear activities in Taiwan and Libya, both long considered to be potential proliferants, appear to be dormant for the moment.

During 1987, Taiwan is believed to have secretly began construction of a small-scale plutonium extraction unit. In March 1988, under U.S. pressure, it agreed to halt work on the facility—probably a laboratory with a number of radiologically shielded "hot cells"—and to dismantle a 40-megawatt Canadian-supplied research reactor. The incident recalled an almost identical episode in 1976, when the United States had discovered that work on a secret plutonium extraction unit was under way; after that confrontation, Taiwan formally pledged not to resume plutonium research.

Why Taiwan decided in 1987 to reactivate a clandestine plutonium extraction program is puzzling, since at the time, Taiwan's president, Chiang Ching-kuo, was successfully pursuing a policy of rapprochement with the mainland. Chiang may have reasoned, however, that as Beijing pursued the on-going liberalization of its economy and political structures, the rationale for an independent non-Communist Taiwan might erode, leading to reduced U.S. support for Taiwanese autonomy.

Chiang died on January 13, 1988, but the reprocessing initiative continued under his immediate successor, Lee Teng-hui— possibly because of bureaucratic momentum—until blocked by U.S. intervention in March. Since that date there have been no new indications of Taiwan's interest in a nuclear option. Recent developments in the PRC have no doubt caused additional anxieties in Taipei, but so far these have not manifested themselves in the nuclear sector.

Turning to Libya, for the moment, this country does not appear to be a proliferation threat. Despite repeated pronouncements by Libyan leader Muammar Khadafi calling for the development of nuclear arms—and a number of attempts to purchase them from other states or on the black market—the country's nuclear capabilities remain very rudimentary.

Libya's chemical weapons capabilities and its efforts to acquire long-range delivery systems, including 600-mile range missiles being developed by Brazil, could increase the threat to Israel from unconventional weapons. As discussed below, this growing threat could increase the risk of Israel's using nuclear arms in a future Middle East war.

II. SURGING BEYOND THE NUCLEAR THRESHOLD

The accelerating movement of additional nations toward the nuclear threshold has been accompanied by a second trend: horizontal proliferation is going vertical, as the regional states that have already crossed this barrier strive to increase their stocks of weapons material, develop advanced delivery systems, and acquire thermonuclear options. At the same time, these growing capabilities—and in the Middle East, the growing military capabilities of some non-nuclear states—are increasing the risk of nuclear weapons being used in a future regional conflict and introducing serious nuclear tensions with extra-regional nuclear weapon states.

Israel

The revelations in late 1986 by former Israeli nuclear technician Mordechai Vanunu—which have now been widely accepted as genuine—have confirmed the existence of Israel's nuclear arsenal beyond serious doubt and have provided a number of significant new details about it.

Israel's nuclear stockpile probably consists of 60 to 100 devices. The precise number is less important than the fact that with 50 or more weapons, Israel would have a sufficient arsenal to permit it to use nuclear arms against military targets in wartime while maintaining a strategic deterrent against basic threats to national survival.

According to Vanunu, Israeli capabilities grew substantially between 1977 and 1985, when he worked at the Dimona nuclear complex. He stated that during this period, facilities there were producing 40 kilograms of plutonium per year, enough for up to ten weapons annually, given the apparent sophistication of Israeli nuclear weapon designs. If Israel has continued to produce plutonium at this rate, the estimate of its current capabilities may be low. Even if production tapered off after 1985, as some U.S. government analysts believe, the bulk of the Israeli stockpile—perhaps 50 to 60 percent—would have been produced during the 1980s.

Vanunu also stated that between 1980 and 1982 Israel constructed a facility for the production of lithium deuteride, and his photos apparently show weapon components made from the material. Theodore Taylor, in analyzing the photos, stated that Israel may be building "superboosted" weapons with yields of perhaps 100 kilotons, the size of some warheads in multiple-warhead U.S. strategic missiles. "Boosted" weapons are devices that rely principally on the fissioning of plutonium or highly enriched uranium for their yield, but in which this reaction is enhanced by the presence of tritium or lithium deuteride. The tritium or lithium deuteride undergoes an atomic fusion reaction when the device is detonated, releasing a stream of neutrons that greatly improves the efficiency of the fission reaction. (Israel's design uses lithium deuteride in an unusual configuration for which Taylor coined the term "superboosting.") Presumably, the manufacture of full-fledged, multi-stage thermonuclear weapons would require an extensive nuclear testing program and currently remains beyond Israeli abilities.

Israel also appears to have advanced its nuclear program in a third area in recent years, the development of improved ballistic missile delivery systems. Israel is thought to have developed the short-range, nuclear-capable *Jericho* ballistic missile with French assistance in the 1960s and to have deployed a more advanced version, with a 400-mile range, in the early 1980s. (Some place the range of this missile at 900 miles.) The latter rocket is sometimes referred to as the *Jericho* II. It is widely assumed that these missiles carry or can be rapidly equipped with nuclear warheads. Israel has never acknowledged the existence of either of these systems.

Since 1987, the country has apparently been testing a new missile, sometimes referred to as the *Jericho* IIB, which has usually been estimated to have a range of 900 miles. Such a system would place Riyadh, Benghazi, Baghdad, and major cities in Iran within range, as well as the Soviet cities of Baku, Tbilisi, and Odessa. In 1988, Soviet radio issued a series of warnings to Israel against building such a missile.

In September 1988, Israel publicly demonstrated its rocket capabilities for the first time by orbiting its first space satellite, using a powerful launcher, which it has named the *Shavit* II. It appears that this is the same rocket as the *Jericho* IIB, but with a third stage added.

Based on the details of the satellite launch, an analysis performed by a researcher at Lawrence Livermore Laboratories has estimated that a two-stage version of the *Shavit* II—which would be, in effect, the *Jericho* IIB—could have a range of 3,500 to 5,000 miles, far beyond the earlier estimates of 900. This would make it possible for Israel to reach Moscow. A separate analysis prepared for the Aspen Strategy Group indicated that the missile could travel approximately 2,500 miles with a 1,000 pound payload.[9] Having voiced objections to tests of what was thought to be a 900-mile range version of the missile, the Soviet Union can only be the more concerned about this newly revealed Israeli potential.[10]

Why Israel would want a missile with an extra-regional reach is not clear—but it does appear to be pursuing this capability. Some observers have speculated that Israel may want to build a long-range missile—which might be coupled with a "super-boosted" warhead—in order to make the Soviet Union think twice before coming to the aid of Syria with massive reinforcements in a future Arab-Israeli war.

For the United States the dangers of a long-range Israeli missile could also be great: even a veiled Israeli nuclear threat against the Soviets would greatly increase the risk of a U.S.–Soviet nuclear confrontation in a future Middle East conflict. An Israeli deterrent against the Soviet Union would also affect the Middle East military balance significantly by opening the possibility that Israel might be able to use a portion of its growing nuclear forces against regional military targets without fear of Soviet nuclear retaliation.

As Israel expanded its nuclear capabilities during the 1980s and as it apparently pursued the ability to threaten a major power beyond the region, the risk of Israel's using nuclear weapons in a Middle East war has also grown because of the intensifying threat posed by the missile and chemical weapon capabilities of its adversaries.

Syria, Iraq, Iran, Saudi Arabia, and Egypt today all possess missiles that can reach Israel and against which Israel currently has no defense. Libya is also seeking to acquire such a capability. All of these countries, moreover, with the exception of Saudi Arabia, could equip these missiles with chemical warheads. In most cases, these weapons, because of their lack of accuracy, could be effectively used only against Israel's cities, causing heavy casualties and sowing terror. Syria's more accurate Soviet-supplied SS-21s, however, could probably also be used against Israeli military targets, such as mobilization points and airfields. Israeli officials have repeatedly expressed the concern that if the system were used in this way, the country might be prevented from responding effectively to a Syrian thrust in the Golan.

To meet these challenges, Israel is improving civil defense measures, working on strategies to destroy enemy missiles during an unfolding crisis before they can be used, and with U.S. assistance, developing the Arrow anti-ballistic-missile system. In the meantime, however, the country is relying increasingly, and more explicitly than ever before, on deterrence. Since early 1988, Israeli leaders have been openly alluding to the country's potent retaliatory capabilities. Last July, for example, Defense Minister Yitzhak Rabin, declared:

> One of Israel's fears is that the Arab world and its leaders will mistakenly believe that the lack of an international response to the use of rockets and gas [in the Iran-Iraq War] affords them a legitimization of sorts to employ them. They know full well that in regard to Israel this is an entirely different matter. If heaven forbid, they dare to employ these means, the response will be one hundred times stronger.[11]

Prime Minister Yitzhak Shamir, Shimon Peres, and other senior Israeli aides have made comparable statements. Although the word "nuclear" is never used, there can be little question—particularly given the wide publicity that the 1986 revelations of Israeli nuclear technician Mordechai Vanunu have received—that the invocation of Israel's ability to retaliate "one hundred times" over is intended as a reminder of the country's nuclear might.

How Israel would respond in an actual crisis if deterrence were to fail cannot be predicted. Although it has possessed a nuclear capability for many years, few believed that this capability would ever be used unless the very existence of the country were at risk. The missile and chemical threat to Israel has now grown so serious, however, that it is possible to imagine circumstances short of threatened national annihilation in which Israel might consider escalation to the nuclear level. As a result, the stakes in any future Arab-Israeli conflict have increased dramatically.

India

Although India, unlike Israel, has not deployed a nuclear force, it, too, has advanced well beyond a rudimentary nuclear weapons capability. During the 1980s it completed a string of unsafeguarded nuclear facilities that vastly increased its ability to produce plutonium. These included the 100-megawatt Dhruva research reactor, several Canadian-style heavy water power reactors, and a plutonium extraction plant at Tarapur with a nominal output of 100 kilograms of plutonium per year. In addition, India refurbished and enlarged the plutonium plant at the Bhabha Atomic Research Center, which serves the Cirus and Dhruva reactors and where the plutonium for India's 1974 test was produced. Even if these facilities are exploited at only half of their total capacity, New Delhi could easily have more than 50 nuclear devices by 1991.

India has announced that it is accumulating plutonium for its breeder program and hopes to have two tons of the material by the turn of the century—enough for hundreds of weapons, if used for this purpose. There have also been repeated reports that it is working on a variety of nuclear weapon designs, including those for thermonuclear devices; indeed, earlier this year CIA Director William Webster told a congressional committee that the country was pursuing work in this area. Annual reports of the Department of Atomic Energy indicate that India has conducted research into separating isotopes of lithium, a key step in producing lithium deuteride or tritium for advanced nuclear weapons.

It is also clear, however, that India has not deployed a nuclear force, although stories are beginning to appear that the Indian military has identified the specific Air Force units that will be responsible for nuclear missions. What is not publicly known is whether India has manufactured nuclear weapons or is merely stockpiling needed materials. In early 1988, U.S. officials testified that India had not "actually taken the final step to acquire nuclear weapons"[12] and in off-the-record interviews other administration and congressional sources have stated that they believe that India is not developing an undeclared stockpile of nuclear devices or their components. Whatever the precise state of Indian nuclear readiness, there is no question that the country could deploy nuclear arms in a future war, a strategic factor well recognized by Pakistan.

Like Israel, India is also developing nuclear-capable ballistic missiles, although it is not yet able to deploy such systems. In February 1988, it tested the *Prithvi*, a 150-mile range missile, and apparently it is working to ready the system for use as quickly as possible, though this is still probably several years away. The missile will be able to reach major targets in Pakistan, including Lahore, Rawalpindi, and Islamabad. New Delhi insists that the system is intended to be used with conventional warheads.

With its test of the 1500-mile *Agni* intermediate-range missile in May of this year, however, India appears to have exposed its long-term intentions to become a nuclear power. Though it insists that this system, too, will be conventionally armed, the missile will be useful militarily only as a nuclear-armed system, even if it is relatively accurate. Moreover, no other nation has ever undertaken the enormous expense of building such a missile except for use with nuclear warheads. The fact that New Delhi chose to present the system as a *missile* rather than as a space launch vehicle, as it could easily have done, is all the more provocative and is one of several recent examples of Indian muscle-flexing.

India's pursuit of the *Agni* seems certain to alter relations with the People's Republic of China. Since the latter tested its first nuclear weapon in 1964, India has been concerned over this potential threat to its security. Today China's nuclear status remains a major reason for New Delhi's reluctance to enter into comprehensive non-proliferation understandings with Pakistan that might require India to renounce the option of building nuclear arms.

Nonetheless, the nuclear threat from China has not been in the forefront of Indian security concerns. The best evidence for this is the fact that in the fifteen years since India's first and only nuclear test in 1974, the country has not deployed nuclear weapons, a step it surely would have taken if it had perceived an urgent need for a deterrent against China's nuclear might. Most observers, in turn, believe that China has not targeted its nuclear missiles against India, since Beijing perceives its principal antagonist to be the Soviet Union and has only a limited nuclear arsenal to counter vastly greater Soviet nuclear forces. Indeed, on his return from his historic summit in Beijing in December 1988, Indian Prime Minister Rajiv Gandhi declared that China had not targeted its missiles against India, challenging assertions to the contrary by some Indian hawks.

The *Agni* test could lead to a dramatic and dangerous change in this relationship. Currently, India lacks the ability to deliver nuclear warheads confidently to major military and civilian targets within China, since it would have to rely on manned bombers, which, over the long distances involved, would be vulnerable to Chinese air defenses. In effect, India now poses only a nominal nuclear threat to its neighbor.

If it were to deploy the 1500-mile range *Agni*, however, much of China would become vulnerable to Indian nuclear attack. Deployment of the system would thus inevitably lead China to target India with its own nuclear missiles, a step it has apparently refrained from taking so far. It thus requires little imagination to appreciate that the *Agni* appears destined to trigger an era of unprecedented nuclear tensions between the two Asian giants.

The more immediate concern for Indian nuclear policy-makers remains Pakistan, however. Since the election in November 1988 of Benazir Bhutto as Pakistani Prime Minister, relations between the two states appear to be improving, and tensions over the Punjab and the Siachen Glacier have eased noticeably. On the nuclear front, the signing in December 1988 of an agreement prohibiting attacks on nuclear facilities was also a step forward, although the pact has yet to be ratified by either country. Implementing the accord will raise new issues. By next January each country is supposed to provide the other with a list of all of its nuclear facilities, but both states are believed to have installations that they have not publicly acknowledged. How this issue will be dealt with remains to be seen.

Little progress on easing nuclear tensions was made during Indian Prime Minister Rajiv Gandhi's visit to Islamabad in July. Gandhi maintained India's long-standing opposition to Pakistan's proposals for mutual arms control arrangements and undercut Ms. Bhutto's protestations of good faith by asserting that Pakistan's military continued to run the country's nuclear program. With the Indian leader facing national elections this fall, it appears unlikely that for the remainder of 1989 he will consider major new nuclear accords with Islamabad, which could be highly controversial at home. As noted below, new opportunities for improved nuclear relations may arise, however, if recent reports that Pakistan is slowing its nuclear advances are correct.

Pakistan

With a capacity since 1986 to produce enough highly enriched uranium free from international non-proliferation controls for one to four nuclear weapons per year, Pakistan today probably has the essentials for five to ten devices. Various press reports quoting U.S. officials state that the country is also manufacturing most if not all of the non-nuclear components for nuclear arms, indicating that like its rival to the east, Pakistan could deploy a small nuclear force in a future conflict.

Like Israel and India, Pakistan is developing a ballistic missile with nuclear capabilities and appears to have taken steps towards advanced nuclear weapons. In January 1989, it conducted its first tests the *Hatf* I and II missiles. Although the former has a range of only 48 miles, the latter can carry a payload of 1,100 pounds to a range of 180 miles and could be equipped with nuclear warheads when deployed.

Investigations of Pakistani smuggling activities in West Germany indicate that since the mid-1980s, Pakistan has been pursuing the capability to produce tritium, used in "boosted" nuclear weapons. Between 1985 and 1987, it obtained a tritium purification and storage plant from a West German concern and subsequently sought to purchase lithium, from which tritium is produced, from the same source. Although the tritium plant was apparently built at a military installation some 150 kilometers south of Rawalpindi, Pakistan is not known to have obtained other necessary components for tritium production. Given the complexity of designing boosted nuclear devices and expectations that Pakistan will continue to refrain from nuclear testing, it appears unlikely that it will be able to produce advanced nuclear weapons for a number of years.

From the time he took power in 1977 until his death in a suspicious plane crash in August 1988, Pakistan's military president Mohammed Zia ul-Haq aggressively advanced the country's nuclear capabilities, despite repeated pledges to the Carter and Reagan administrations that he would restrain these activities. After the Soviet invasion of Afghanistan in late 1979, Washington became reluctant to enforce nuclear sanctions against Islamabad because of growing U.S. reliance on Pakistan as a strategic ally in the region. Pakistan's nuclear capabilities advanced throughout the 1980s and in July 1988, Zia went so far as to tell U.S. visitors that the country's program had reached the point that a system of rudimentary nuclear deterrence had emerged in South Asia.

The election of Benazir Bhutto in late 1988 and the withdrawal of Soviet troops from Afghanistan earlier this year have opened a new chapter in U.S.–Pakistan nuclear relations. Ms. Bhutto has declared that she will slow the country's nuclear program, but her true intentions are by no means clear, and many question whether, as a newly elected civilian leader with an uncertain mandate, she has the authority to control Pakistan's military-dominated nuclear weapons effort.

Pakistan's nuclear intentions came under sharp scrutiny earlier this summer when Ms. Bhutto visited Washington. Some six months earlier, President Reagan had certified to Congress that Pakistan did not "possess a nuclear explosive device," a finding required under the U.S. Foreign Assistance Act to permit U.S. aid to be distributed to Islamabad. In a letter accompanying the certification, however, the president also made clear that if the Pakistani nuclear program continued on its current course, it would be difficult for his successor to make the required annual certification of "non-possession" in late 1989.

At the time of Bhutto's visit, a number of press stories appeared suggesting that—perhaps as part of a deal under which Pakistan is to receive 60 F-16s—Ms. Bhutto had agreed to restrain the country's nuclear program sufficiently to ensure the non-possession finding. Although details remain murky, it may be that Pakistan will stop short of fabricating certain key bomb components so that it can claim that it does not possess a weapon, while at the same time continuing to enlarge its overall production capabilities and stockpiles of weapons-usable material. This trade-off might allow Benazir Bhutto to placate Washington, while maintaining enough of a *de facto* nuclear counter to India to assuage nuclear hawks at home.

For the United States, this would represent only a modest step forward, but it could provide a basis for urging India to pursue a more serious dialogue with Pakistan in the future. Indeed, after Benazir's visit, President George Bush is said to have telephoned Rajiv Gandhi to encourage such discussions.

South Africa

Since 1980 or 1981, South Africa has been able to produce two to three bombs' worth of weapons grade uranium per year that is free from international non-proliferation controls. By this point, it probably has a stockpile of material for about 20 weapons, but Pretoria has not deployed a nuclear force and, indeed, may not have fabricated complete nuclear devices.

Its capabilities are expanding dramatically, however, as it brings on line a semi-commercial scale uranium enrichment facility at Valindaba. The low-enriched uranium output from this plant is slated to be used to fuel South Africa's Koeberg nuclear power plants, but it could also be used as the feed material for a smaller enrichment plant at Valindaba, which has been the source of the country's presumed stocks of weapons-grade material accumulated to date. By starting with low-enriched, rather than natural uranium, the smaller facility's output could be increased by at least a factor of three.

Whether or not Pretoria takes this step, it is clear that, as is true for Israel, India, and Pakistan, the bulk of the country's reserves of nuclear weapons material were accumulated during the 1980s. Also, like these countries, South Africa has moved to develop ballistic missiles during this period. Though few details have been published, most observers assume the program has been pursued in close cooperation with Israel and is based on the *Jericho* systems.[13] There have been repeated allegations, for example, that the two states operate joint test facilities, permitting rockets to be fired from the South African mainland into the South Atlantic and tracked at a down-range installation on Marion Island in the Antarctic. Medium-range nuclear-capable missiles would help ensure South Africa's strategic reach at a time when its traditional air superiority in the region is seriously eroding.

Threatened with expulsion from the IAEA, in 1987 South Africa agreed to begin negotiations on joining the NPT with the treaty's three depository states, the United States, Britain, and the Soviet Union. Little has come of these talks, however. The South African government is said to be internally divided over whether to join the pact. The foreign ministry supposedly supports accession because of the diplomatic benefits that would result, while elements of the country's security establishment are said to oppose joining because of a desire to preserve South Africa's nuclear options. (One factor in the negotiations is South Africa's desire for guarantees that after its accession, Western economic sanctions banning imports of South African uranium would be lifted.)

It is difficult to predict how the pending settlements in Angola and Namibia and the retirement of President P.W. Botha will affect decision-making on this and related nuclear issues. The NPT question can be expected to come to a head once again at the IAEA General Conference next month.

* * * * *

Addressing the challenges described above will be increasingly difficult because as the 1980s draw to a close, the non-proliferation regime is also coming under stress. Recent years, for example, have seen:

- the advent of Pakistan as a new *de facto* nuclear state, despite considerable and highly publicized efforts, particularly by the United States, to block its nuclear advances;

- revelations of a wide-spread black market in nuclear equipment and unimproved nuclear materials (though fortunately not involving nuclear arms or weapons-grade nuclear materials);

- the clear disregard of past non-proliferation commitments by at least one emerging nuclear country (Israel's circumvention of Norwegian heavy water controls);

- the advent of new "second-tier" nuclear supplier states that are hostile to strict export norms; and

- increasing non-nuclear-weapon-state interest in nuclear-powered submarines, whose fuel is often suitable for nuclear weapons but not subject to international controls.

Many also fear that the centerpiece of the regime, the Non-Proliferation Treaty, will come under increasing pressure at the 1990 NPT Review Conference and, possibly, may not be extended in 1995, when it must be renewed.

Despite the unprecedented progress that is being made in U.S.–Soviet arms control, certain parties to the NPT, including Mexico, Yugoslavia, and Sri Lanka—as well as several nonparties that are prominent in the Non-Aligned Movement, including India and Argentina—argue that Washington and Moscow have not lived up to their obligations under Article VI of the pact. This provision requires the superpowers to negotiate in good faith for an end to the nuclear arms race. Lobbying by these developing nations could block a statement endorsing the treaty at the 1990 review conference and might lead to the adoption by the conference participants of a timetable that conditioned extension of the treaty in 1995 on the superpowers' acceptance of specific arms control measures in the interim. Since certain arms control measures that have wide support with the Non-Aligned Movement, in particular a comprehensive ban on nuclear testing, are known to be unacceptable to the United States, such "countdown to 1995" could trigger a crisis of potentially grave proportions for the treaty.[14]

At the same time, the very concept of nuclear non-proliferation may be losing some of its legitimacy. The concept assumes that the spread of certain weapon systems is inherently undesirable because of the threat they pose to international security and peace. The concept also assumes that even if some countries have these systems, it is per se legitimate to attempt to stop their spread to others. This is the idea behind the NPT, which permits the five countries that had detonated nuclear devices before 1967 to retain such weapons but requires others to forego them. This arrangement has stuck so far and—despite several major exceptions—some 133 non-weapon states have joined the treaty and renounced nuclear arms.

But with the emergence of new forms of proliferation on the international scene the validity of this approach is being increasingly challenged. First, nuclear weapons have for many years been one of a cluster of advanced weapons systems whose spread has been largely restricted, on a *de facto* basis to a limited number of major powers. The existence of this wider band of restricted weapons has buttressed the taboo against the spread of the most dangerous systems, nuclear arms. In effect, nuclear non-proliferation was part of a larger pattern of global military stratification.[15]

In recent years, however, the extensive use of chemical weapons in the Iran-Iraq War, the unprecedented sale by the People's Republic of China of conventionally armed intermediate-range ballistic missiles to Saudi Arabia, and the Soviet Union's nuclear submarine transfer to India, have tended to legitimize the unrestrained acquisition by regional powers of increasingly sophisticated and lethal weapons that had previously been restricted to the major powers. In this environment, nuclear arms may appear to be no more than the next rung on the ladder. As the traditional stratification of armaments breaks down, the taboo against the acquisition of nuclear arms is likely to be perceived increasingly as an isolated exception, making it more difficult to sustain.

Efforts to establish regimes to limit the spread of ballistic missiles and the manufacture and stockpiling of chemical weapons inevitably raise further questions about the validity of nuclear restrictions. In the missile area, there never has been an international norm against proliferation and indeed, the United States and the Soviet Union have been transferring such systems to their regional allies for years, albeit with conventional warheads. Now the United States is trying to establish a regime to limit these transfers—the Missile Technology Control Regime. But only seven Western governments have signed on and only missiles with a sufficient range and payload to make them potentially usable by a developing country for nuclear delivery are covered. The countries that are the target of the regime—India, Argentina, Brazil, Iraq, and others—claim that these weapons should no more be subject to special international controls than warplanes or other standard military items. These controversies about the legitimacy of one technology control regime inevitably invite questions about the basis of others, including that to curb the spread of nuclear arms.

Where chemical weapons are concerned, the principal international effort to limit them is through a comprehensive ban—one that would apply to all states equally, without exception.[16] This approach contrasts sharply to the two-tiered system of the Non-Proliferation Treaty. The chemical arms convention is obviously the fairer approach, and the more attention it receives, the more the inherent discrimination of the nuclear treaty stands out. India has been particularly vocal in stressing the discriminatory aspects of the NPT in various international fora, promoting a three-tiered nuclear arms control plan as a substitute to the treaty that would tie restrictions on nuclear programs in the emerging nuclear states to steps towards the elimination of nuclear arms by all of today's five declared nuclear powers.

In addition, as advanced non-nuclear weapons have spread, they have been increasingly portrayed as legitimate deterrents to similar or more potent capabilities in the hands of rival states. This logic—that advanced weapons in the hands of regional powers should be thought of in traditional security terms rather than as forbidden objects of international non-proliferation regimes—is spilling over into the nuclear realm. Israel's nuclear capabilities have surely gained added legitimacy in this way as Israel's regional antagonists have acquired chemical weapons and ballistic missiles.[17] And there is increasing recognition that

Pakistan's quest for a nuclear capability is an understandable response to the conventional and nuclear threat it perceives from far more powerful India.[18]

* * * * *

Given the magnitude and diversity of the problem of nuclear proliferation today, specifically tailored initiatives will be needed to address the nuclear ambitions of each of the countries discussed above. Many of these appear to have been incorporated already into current U.S. policy, although more focused attention is needed to restrain North Korea's nuclear advances, Israel's possible deployment of a long-range missile, and the nuclear ambitions of the Brazilian military.

Most urgently required, however, is a strong, *public* commitment to nuclear non-proliferation by top U.S. policy-makers and by President Bush, in particular, to ensure a high priority for the issue on the U.S. foreign policy agenda. Such a high-profile stance would provide needed reinforcement for behind-the-scenes U.S. diplomacy in foreign capitals, help ensure that country-specific nuclear initiatives are not displaced within the U.S. bureaucracy by other bilateral issues of the moment, and buttress the increasingly fragile institutions of the non-proliferation regime.

Stated simply, the multi-front proliferation dangers of the 1970s are returning. High-visibility, 1970s-style, American leadership is needed to meet this challenge.

NOTES

1. Mark Hibbs, "Germans Say Brazil Developing Two Production Reactors," *Nucleonics Week*, July 27, 1989.
2. David Albright, "Bomb Potential for South America," *Bulletin of the Atomic Scientists*, May 1989, p. 16.
3. Hibbs, "Germans Say Brazil Developing Two Production Reactors."
4. The situation could be greatly complicated if the nuclear submarine programs that Brazil, and possibly Argentina, are pursuing ultimately require weapons-grade uranium fuel. In this case—even if additional verification procedures were implemented—it would be difficult to be certain that weapons-usable material produced to run submarine propulsion reactors was not being diverted for nuclear explosives.

5. Hugh O'Shaughnessy, "People's Choice for New Peron," *Observer*, October 16, 1988.
6. Glenn Frankel, "Iraq Said Developing A-Weapons," *Washington Post*, March 31, 1989.
7. Farzad Bazoft, "Iran Signs Secret Atom Deal," *The Observer*, June 12, 1988; "Nuclear Cooperation with Iran Reported," *Al-Ahram Al Duwali*, November 22, 1988, translated in Joint Publications Research Service–Nuclear Developments (JPRS-TND), December 23, 1988, p. 11.
8. In April 1989, Cairo radio reported a story carried by a Kuwaiti newspaper, which quoted diplomatic sources in Japan as stating that in 1987, Iran had clandestinely purchased "large quantities of materials in Japan needed for the production of atomic weapons." "Nuclear Weapons Program Reportedly Started," Cairo Radio (MENA), April 21, 1989, 1340 GMT, reprinted in Foreign Broadcast Information Service–Near East and South Asia (FBIS-NESA), April 21, 1989, p. 46. This two-paragraph report is the most detailed of the very few recent news items on this subject.
9. Janne Nolan and Albert Wheelon, "Ballistic Missiles in the Third World" (Appendix Three of this Report).
10. Israel may have again tested the missile version of the system in June 1989 from a base in South Africa; allegedly, Israel intends to sell Pretoria a variant of the rocket. See Bill Gertz, "South Africa on Brink of Ballistic Missile Test," *Washington Times*, June 20, 1989. (South Africa has acknowledged that it recently tested a "booster.") An additional test of the missile was conducted in September 1989, with the system reaching a distance of 900 miles. The test was disclosed by the Soviet press in a report that again warned Israel against deploying the system.
11. Joel Brinkley, "Israel Fears That Peace Plan in the Persian Gulf Will Unleash Bitter Foe," *New York Times*, July 24, 1988.
12. "Testimony of Deputy Assistant Secretary of State Robert A. Peck," *Hearings on the Export of Nuclear Materials*, before the Subcommittee on Asian and Pacific Affairs of the Committee on Foreign Affairs, U.S. House of Representatives, February 18, 1988 (mimeo).
13. See note 10.
14. As part of this overall effort to use the NPT as a lever to obtain new superpower arms control, a number of non-aligned and neutral states have successfully persuaded a majority of parties to the Limited Test Ban Treaty—which prohibits nuclear testing in the atmosphere, outer space, and under water—to convene a conference aimed at amending the treaty to transform it into a comprehensive test ban. Although the United States, as a depository power, retains the right to veto any such amendment, U.S. exercise of this power would cast a long shadow on the negotiations concerning the NPT. It would place the United States in the position of rejecting a popular arms control device, even as Washington was attempting to persuade parties to NPT that it was meeting its Article VI obligations by virtue of other ongoing negotiations.
15. See Janne Nolan and Albert Wheelon, "Ballistic Missiles in the Third World" (Appendix Three of this Report).
16. For a review of recent developments with respect to negotiations on a global ban on the manufacture and stockpiling of chemical weapons, see

Kyle B. Olsen, "The Feasibility of a Chemical Weapons Control Regime," and Paul Doty, "Policy Issues in Chemical Weapons Control" (Appendices Four and Five of this Report).

17. The reverse is also true. At the Paris conference on chemical weapons last January, for example, a number of Arab states refused to condemn the spread of chemical weapon capabilities as long as Israel continued to maintain its nuclear arsenal.

18. Indeed, even in the United States, the concept of nuclear non-proliferation is being expanded to include new policies aimed at "post-proliferation restraint," such as encouraging India and Pakistan to freeze their nuclear programs at current levels or dissuading Israel from deploying a long-range missile system. So far, fortunately, the temptation is being resisted to make "regional nuclear stability" (which could call for large, diversified nuclear arsenals on the U.S. and Soviet model) the goal of non-proliferation policy. Pressures are likely to mount to adopt this focus, however.

Appendix 2

CHEMICAL WEAPONS PROLIFERATION: CURRENT CAPABILITIES AND PROSPECTS FOR CONTROL[1]

Elisa D. Harris

> Assessing the proliferation of chemical and biological weapons is one of the most difficult challenges we face in the intelligence community—now and into the next decade. It is also one of our most important tasks, for these weapons may well represent one of the most serious threats to world peace in the coming years.[2]
> *William H. Webster, Director of Central Intelligence, October 1988*

Iraq's use of chemical weapons (CW) against Iranian military forces and against its own Kurdish population and revelations concerning Libya's efforts to acquire a chemical weapons production capability have heightened concern about the spread of chemical weapons to countries outside NATO and the Warsaw Pact. This chapter examines the problem of chemical weapons proliferation in the developing world. It begins by analyzing the nature and extent of the problem, particularly which countries are believed to have chemical weapons, as well as why and how they may have acquired their capabilities. It then discusses the likely implications of the spread of chemical weapons. Finally, it examines potential solutions to the problem of CW proliferation in the developing world.

THE PROBLEM

Despite numerous press reports alleging the development, possession, or use of chemical weapons by various countries, detailed and reliable information concerning the purported chemical weapons programs of *many* of these countries is often unavailable in the public domain. This complicates efforts to explore the nature and extent of the CW proliferation problem in the developing world. Three factors contribute to the data problem on chemical weapons proliferation. First, most governments are reluctant to *identify* specific chemical weapons states. Instead, government officials speaking on the record have tended to characterize the proliferation problem in terms of the *number* of such states.

Even these numerical estimates, however, are often imprecise and contradictory, as recent statements by U.S. government officials have shown. For example, in March 1988, the Director of Naval Intelligence, Rear Admiral William O. Studeman, testified that worldwide "some *ten* countries possess a chemical warfare capability," with as many "known or thought to be actively seeking it." A few months later, Kathleen Bailey, Assistant Director of the Arms Control and Disarmament Agency (ACDA), stated that about *fifteen* countries were estimated to possess chemical weapons, with others trying to acquire them. In October 1988, the Director of Central Intelligence, William H. Webster, noted that "more than 20 countries may be developing chemical weapons." In January 1989, however, ACDA Director William F. Burns testified that although "about" twenty countries were *capable* of producing militarily significant quantities of chemical warfare agents, "no more than a handful, five or six," actually possessed stockpiles of such weapons.[3] These estimates, it should be noted, are believed to include both developing countries and members of NATO and the Warsaw Pact.

A second factor that contributes to the data problem on chemical weapons proliferation is that government officials generally do not explain how they *define* a chemical weapons state.[4] Having the capacity to produce chemical warfare agents is very different from actually possessing a stockpile of chemical weapons. Moreover, a militarily useful CW capability requires more than just the weapons themselves: it also requires training and doctrine for their use. Finally, there are important differences between countries with chemical weapons under national control and those with foreign chemical weapons deployed on their territory.

There are probably a variety of reasons why governments generally do not identify CW possessor states and are not more specific in discussing capabilities. In some cases, they may be uncertain about precisely who does in fact have what capability. After all, any country with a petrochemical, pesticide, fertilizer, or pharmaceutical industry has the potential, in terms of equipment, raw materials and technical expertise, to produce some chemical warfare agents. Moreover, without direct access to such facilities, it is probably impossible to know whether activities being undertaken are of a commercial or military nature. Equipment and chemical feedstock purchases on the international market may not reveal much either, as these could either be for commercial or for military purposes. Finally, even chemical delivery systems do not have distinctive features. An artillery shell, bomb, or missile warhead carrying a chemical warfare agent looks essentially the same as one carrying conventional high explosives.

Governments may also remain silent in order to avoid drawing attention to chemical weapons programs acquired with the assistance, wittingly or unwittingly, of their own chemical companies. In other cases, they may have political interests that preclude them from embarrassing new entrants to the chemical club. Finally, governments may fear that if they are more forthcoming with information about the chemical warfare activities of specific states, the sources of this information, and the methods by which it was acquired, might be compromised.

A third factor that contributes to the data problem on chemical weapons proliferation concerns the *credibility* of the available information. The U.S. government, it must be acknowledged, has released more information about proliferation than any other government. But the fact remains that much of what is known about chemical weapons programs in the developing world comes from press reports citing unnamed government officials and/or what are said to be classified documents.

This credibility problem is not necessarily helped by multiple press reports containing the same basic information. For example, one of the most detailed accounts of the proliferation issue, by Don Oberdorfer in a *Washington Post* story of September 1985, draws heavily from an earlier report, by the columnist Jack Anderson, said to be based on intelligence sources and classified documents.[5] Other press reports may also be derived from the same initial source or report. The possibility of erroneous information being unintentionally perpetuated must therefore not be overlooked.

It is also possible that false or exaggerated reports of CW proliferation may be propagated intentionally. Concern about CW proliferation can be used to increase support for national CW armament programs. CW possession or use charges also can be useful for discrediting a domestic or foreign adversary. Indeed, many of the more doubtful chemical weapons charges probably fall in this category.

These factors complicate, but do not preclude, an analysis of the nature and extent of the CW proliferation problem in the developing world. In the discussion which follows, the publicly available information concerning CW proliferation is organized according to specific criteria. It should be emphasized, however, that these criteria are merely a tool for organizing the available information, and that conclusions derived from them about the CW status of particular countries are based largely on this information. The criteria used in this discussion are as follows:

- *Known* CW states are those who have either declared that they possess chemical weapons or whose use of such weapons has been definitively confirmed.

- *Probable* CW states are those reported by U.S. government officials, on the record, as developing, producing, or possessing chemical weapons.

- *Possible* CW states are those reported by Western government officials, generally off the record, as seeking to acquire chemical weapons or a CW production capability, or as suspected of possessing chemical weapons.

• *Doubtful* CW states are those reported, generally by domestic or foreign adversaries, as seeking to possess, possessing, or using chemical weapons, with no confirmation by Western government officials.

On the basis of these criteria, Iraq is the only non-NATO/ Warsaw Pact country known to possess chemical weapons.[6] Eleven other countries, largely in the developing world, are probable CW states. They include Burma, China, Egypt, Ethiopia, Iran, Israel, Libya, North Korea, Syria, Taiwan, and Vietnam.[7] An additional eleven countries have been identified by unnamed Western government officials as seeking to acquire chemical weapons or a chemical weapons production capability, or as suspected of possessing chemical weapons. These possible CW states include Angola, Argentina, Cuba, India, Indonesia, Laos, Pakistan, Somalia, South Africa, South Korea, and Thailand.[8] Finally, at least eleven other countries have been accused of seeking to possess, possessing, or using chemical weapons, but there has been no confirmation of these claims, either on or off the record, by Western government officials. These doubtful chemical weapons states include Afghanistan, Chad, Chile, El Salvador, Guatemala, Jordan, Mozambique, Nicaragua, Peru, the Philippines, and the Sudan.[9]

It is difficult to know with any certainty why Iraq and the eleven probable CW states might have decided to acquire chemical weapons. Some tentative conclusions can, however, be drawn about the role of political and military incentives in those decisions.

It would appear that none of these countries acquired chemical weapons for reasons of political prestige. In order for chemical weapons to have *political* value as the "poor man's weapon of mass destruction," possessor status would have to be known *and* acknowledged by the country concerned. Yet even Iraq did not openly acknowledge its CW activities until July 1988.[10] Indeed, many developing countries have emphasized just the

Table 1   Chemical Weapons Status of Developing Countries

CW Status

Known	Probable	Possible	Doubtful
Iraq	Burma	Angola	Afghanistan
	China	Argentina	Chad
	Egypt	Cuba	Chile
	Ethiopia	India	El Salvador
	Iran	Indonesia	Guatemala
	Israel	Laos	Jordan
	Libya	Pakistan	Mozambique
	N. Korea	Somalia	Nicaragua
	Syria	S. Africa	Peru
	Taiwan	S. Korea	Philippines
	Vietnam	Thailand	Sudan

Sources: See accompanying text.

contrary—that they do not possess chemical weapons. Among the probable CW states that have denied possession are Burma, China, Egypt, Ethiopia, Israel, Libya, and Vietnam. Possible and doubtful CW states that have denied possession include Afghanistan, Argentina, Chile, India, Indonesia, Jordan, Nicaragua, Pakistan, Peru, the Philippines, South Africa, South Korea, and Thailand. This suggests that chemical weapons do not have the same sort of prestige value as nuclear weapons, and that decisions in the developing world to acquire chemical weapons are based largely on military rather than political considerations.

Developing countries may have a variety of military incentives for acquiring chemical weapons. For example, in at least five countries, chemical weapons may have been acquired for use in counter-insurgency operations in their own or neighboring states. Iraq's initial decision to obtain chemical weapons may have been related to its long history of problems with its Kurdish population. Burma is said to have sought chemical weapons for use against domestic insurgents.[11] Egypt is believed to have used chemical weapons during its intervention in the civil war in Yemen in the 1960s.[12] Ethiopia has had a longstanding problem with Eritrean secessionists. Finally, Vietnam has been accused by the United States of using the so-called yellow rain mycotoxins and other unidentified chemical agents against the Hmong in neighboring Laos and against resistance forces in Cambodia.[13]

Developing countries facing significant conventional forces may also have a powerful incentive for acquiring chemical weapons. Iraq's more recent chemical weapons program was clearly a response to the Iranian human wave attacks in the Gulf war. The Egyptian and Syrian CW efforts may be related to Israel's conventional superiority, particularly its highly effective air force. Ethiopia may value chemical weapons for use in its longstanding conflict with Somalia over the Ogaden. Libya is reported to have acquired and used chemical weapons in its war with neighboring Chad.[14] North Korea may have obtained chemical weapons for use against South Korean and U.S. conventional forces. Taiwan's chemical weapons are reportedly designed to thwart an invasion from mainland China. Finally, Vietnam is reported to have used chemical weapons in 1979 against Chinese intervention forces.[15]

At least three countries in the developing world may have acquired chemical weapons in order to deter enemy chemical use through the threat of retaliation in kind. Reports that China suffered chemical attacks during border skirmishes with the Soviet Union in 1969 and during its intervention in Vietnam in 1979 suggest a strong motive for a Chinese CW program. Israel is reported to have obtained chemical weapons in the 1970s in response to the CW threat from Egypt.[16] Iran almost certainly has acquired chemical weapons in response to Iraqi CW use in the Gulf war.

Finally, at least some developing countries may have acquired chemical weapons in order to counter an adversary's nuclear capability. Israel's alleged nuclear program, for example, may have stimulated the CW efforts of a number of Arab countries, including Iraq, Egypt, and Syria.[17]

Iraq and the eleven probable CW states thus may have had a variety of military incentives for acquiring chemical weapons. These military incentives probably outweighed existing moral and legal constraints on chemical warfare which, as evidenced in the Gulf war, clearly have weakened in recent years. CW armament programs in the developing world probably have been helped even more by the erosion of political and technological barriers to CW acquisition.

Developing countries interested in acquiring chemical weapons either can bypass the technological problems altogether by procuring such weapons from other CW states, or can seek to develop their own chemical weapons production capability by purchasing the necessary equipment and chemicals on the international market. U.S. officials have emphasized the former route to proliferation, identifying Soviet training, technical assistance, and chemical weapons transfers to allies in the developing world as key factors in the proliferation problem. In 1984, for example, columnist Jack Anderson reported that the CIA had concluded that "Soviet military assistance has been a common source and major stimulus" to the momentum of chemical weapons proliferation in the Third World.[18] General Secretary Mikhail Gorbachev has denied the U.S. charges, stating that the Soviet Union has not transferred chemical weapons to anyone, has not deployed them in the territory of other states, and "has always strictly abided by those principles in its practical policies."[19]

Gorbachev's denial notwithstanding, some developing countries apparently have benefitted from Soviet assistance, but the Soviet role almost certainly has been overstated. Six developing countries previously may have received chemical weapons and related assistance directly from the Soviet Union. These include Egypt, Ethiopia, Libya, North Korea, Syria and Vietnam.[20] Chemical weapons and technical assistance may also, however, have been provided by one developing country to another. For example, in the early 1970s, Egypt is believed to have supplied a small amount of chemical weapons to Syria.[21] More recently, Syria is reported to have helped the Iranian CW effort,[22] while Iran is said to have supplied chemical weapons to Libya in return for Soviet-made mines.[23] Israel is reported to have provided chemical agents to Taiwan, and advice on CW matters to the Chinese.[24]

U.S. officials have also acknowledged the role of commercial firms in the CW programs of developing countries.[25] A majority of these countries are now believed to possess indigenous chemical weapons production capabilities, often developed with equipment and chemicals purchased from Western companies. These include Iraq, Burma, China, Iran, Israel, Libya, North Korea, Syria, Taiwan, and Vietnam.[26] Egypt has recently acquired equipment that could be used in a chemical weapons production program, but Egyptian officials, including President Hosni Mubarak, deny that Egypt has facilities for producing, or intends to produce, chemical weapons.[27] Companies in developing countries are also beginning to play a role in these indigenous CW production programs, as evidenced by the recent involvement of Indian firms in the sale of chemicals to various countries in the Middle East.[28]

A number of conclusions emerge from this discussion. First, Iraq is the only known CW state, although eleven other countries are probable CW states. The CW status of 22 other countries is unclear. Second, the countries that appear to have acquired chemical weapons are concentrated in two regions: Asia and the Middle East. The CW proliferation problem, at least at present, is thus regional rather than global in nature. Third, developing countries that have acquired chemical weapons probably have done so for military rather than political reasons. Finally, a majority of the countries that are reported to have acquired chemical weapons appear to have done so through indigenous production programs based largely on equipment and chemicals purchased from Western companies. The Soviet role in the Third World proliferation problem has thus almost surely been overstated.

IMPLICATIONS

The spread of chemical weapons outside NATO and the Warsaw Pact is likely to have profound implications for international peace and security. If chemical weapons become more fashionable, various subnational groups, including terrorists organizations, may become more interested in acquiring a CW capability.[29] With a basic knowledge of chemistry and a small amount of money, such groups can easily produce enough chemical agent to threaten an average-size city. Research quantities of ready made agents such as mustard gas can also be purchased directly from some chemical manufacturers.[30] Opportunities to steal chemical weapons may also increase as more and more countries acquire such weapons. Finally, sub-national groups might also obtain chemical weapons directly from states such as Libya and Iran who are sympathetic to their political aspirations.

At the national level, the spread of chemical weapons may lead to further proliferation in three ways. First, non-CW states may move to acquire chemical weapons in response to the CW threat posed by neighboring states. In addition, chemical weapons may increasingly be seen as a legitimate means of countering conventional military threats, either domestic or foreign. Finally, proliferation may lead to chemical weapons being transferred more freely between states, and hence to further proliferation.

CW proliferation could also make conflict itself more likely, particularly in unstable regions. Following confirmation of Iraq's use of chemical weapons in the Gulf war, there were reports that the United States had examined the feasibility of military action against Iraqi CW sites.[31] More recently, Israel was reported to be considering a pre-emptive strike against a Syrian installation said to be developing nerve agent warheads for SS-21 and *SCUD* missiles, and President Ronald Reagan hinted at the possibility of U.S. military action against the Libyan chemical weapons plant at Rabta.[32] Any of these actions could have led to a military confrontation between the countries involved.

CW proliferation could also make conflict more destructive, particularly in areas such as the Middle East and Asia, where ballistic missiles are also proliferating. During the Gulf war, Iraq and Iran used conventionally armed missiles to attack each other's cities.[33] In the final months of the war, however, Iraq reportedly threatened to launch chemical strikes against large Iranian cities. At least seven other probable CW states—China, Egypt, Israel, Libya, North Korea, Syria, and Taiwan—also possess ballistic missiles which could be modified to carry chemical warheads.[34] The use of chemically armed ballistic missiles by any of these countries would lead to unpre-cedented destruction. Moreover, if chemically armed ballistic missiles were used against Israel, it could even trigger a nuclear response.

The proliferation of chemical weapons, and of sophisticated delivery means like ballistic missiles, also has implications for the superpowers themselves. With this type of military power in the hands of developing countries, both the United States and the Soviet Union are likely to find it increasingly difficult to pursue their regional interests. More importantly, the use of chemically armed ballistic missiles in a region like the Middle East could draw the superpowers in on the side of their respective allies, culminating in conflict between East and West, as well.[35]

POSSIBLE SOLUTIONS

Various proposals have been put forward in recent years to deal with the problem of chemical weapons proliferation. One idea that has been pursued since 1984, when it became clear that Iraq's chemical weapons had been produced with chemicals and equipment purchased from Western chemical companies, has been that of export controls on the precursor chemicals needed to make chemical warfare agents. The United States was the first to ban the sale to Iraq and Iran of specific chemicals that could be used to manufacture chemical warfare agents. The United States currently prohibits the export of forty precursor chemicals to Iraq, Iran, Syria, and Libya. Eleven of these chemicals are also controlled for all other countries, because of concerns about the wider proliferation problem.[36] Other governments, including those of Australia, Canada, Denmark, Finland, Israel, Japan, the Netherlands, Pakistan, the Republic of Ireland, the United Kingdom, and the Federal Republic of Germany, have also imposed export controls on a variety of different chemicals since 1984.[37] Bonn also placed controls on a wide range of equipment that could be used to produce chemical weapons, following reports linking a West German–made pesticide plant to Iraqi efforts to produce nerve agents. West German export controls are currently being strengthened in the aftermath of the recent controversy over the role of German firms in the construction of the Libyan chemical plant at Rabta.[38] Chemical export controls were also approved by the European Community in 1984 and again in early 1989, and the Community is currently considering ways to coordinate controls on other material, such as equipment, that could be used in the production of chemical weapons.[39] The Soviet Union has also imposed export controls on certain chemical precursors, as have other members of the Warsaw Pact.[40]

One glaring weakness in the early national non-proliferation efforts was that countries tended to include different chemicals in their export control lists. To help remedy this problem, Australia, in 1985, hosted the first in a series of coordinating meetings of Western industrialized states. The original participants in the so-called Australian Group were the then ten member states of the European Community, plus Australia, Canada, Japan, New Zealand, and the United States.[41] By September 1987, its membership had grown to twenty, the newcomers being Portugal, Spain, Norway, Switzerland, and the European Commission itself. Perhaps more importantly, the Group had succeeded in developing a uniform list of chemicals to be controlled by all member states. Nine chemicals currently are on the Group's "core list," and an additional forty-one chemicals are on a "warning list" that has been circulated to private chemical companies in the hope that they will cooperate with government agencies in controlling their sale.[42]

A second idea for halting the spread of chemical weapons was proposed by General Secretary Gorbachev in November 1985. Shortly before the Geneva Summit with President Reagan, Gorbachev advanced the "thought" that the two sides could develop a treaty to curb the spread of chemical weapons, just as they had concluded a treaty to halt the spread of nuclear weapons.[43] A few months later, in a major foreign policy address, Gorbachev suggested pursuing a chemical non-proliferation treaty, as an interim step, until all chemical weapons were eliminated under a global ban.[44] The United States rejected the Soviet proposal, arguing that the most effective means of halting CW proliferation was by concluding an agreement for the elimination of such weapons. As the U.S. State Department spokesman, Bernard Kalb, explained, "We believe that an effective and verifiable global ban on all chemical weapons is the way to solve the triple problems of existing chemical weapons capabilities, their use, and their further spread."[45]

Neither the chemical export controls promoted largely by Western industrialized states nor the chemical non-proliferation treaty suggested by the Soviet Union will solve the CW proliferation problem. Export control policies will not prevent countries that already possess civil chemical industries from developing at least some chemical warfare agents. Moreover, it is impossible to control all of the chemicals that could be used to produce chemical warfare agents, as many have legitimate commercial uses. Finally, a determined state may be able to evade export controls entirely, either by setting up front companies, or by dealing with unscrupulous chemical traders or manufacturers.[46] Chemical export controls will not, therefore, prevent a country that really wants chemical weapons from acquiring them. At best, export controls will make it more difficult and costly for the potential proliferator to acquire chemical weapons, and may provide supplier countries with early warning of such proliferation. As a U.S. government official acknowledged in 1984, chemical export controls "can achieve valuable objectives, such as the disruption of a given state's plans to produce CW quickly for immediate use in battle and the imposition of higher economic costs on such a state. But no export control policy can erect an insurmountable barrier against acquisition or at-home production of CW."[47]

Political obstacles rule out a chemical non-proliferation treaty as a solution to the problem of CW proliferation. Developing countries oppose the creation of another discriminatory, Nuclear Non-Proliferation Treaty (NPT) type of arrangement, which would allow existing members of the chemical club to retain their chemical weapons, but would prohibit the "have-nots" from acquiring them. Western countries view efforts to conclude such an agreement as a distraction from the negotiations in Geneva aimed at banning chemical weapons. As the U.S. ambassador to the Geneva negotiations, Donald Lowitz, explained in 1986: "the focus of our efforts is and must remain a comprehensive agreement that eliminates forever the scourge of these terrible weapons."[48]

A treaty banning the development, production, possession, transfer and use of chemical weapons remains the best potential solution to the problem of chemical weapons proliferation. Moreover, even if all existing members of the chemical club are not parties to such a treaty, it will still provide a number of invaluable non-proliferation benefits.[49] First, a binding international agreement banning chemical weapons will delegitimize chemical weapons. It will thus reverse the perception, arising largely out of the widespread use of poison gas in the Gulf War, that chemical weapons are acceptable instruments of military power.

Second, a chemical weapons ban will enhance ongoing efforts to prevent developing countries from acquiring the precursor chemicals and related technical assistance necessary to produce chemical weapons. As was noted earlier, nearly all of the probable CW states are believed to have indigenous production programs based largely on chemicals and equipment purchased from Western companies. A number of countries have *voluntarily* imposed export controls on various chemicals, but in many cases, as the Libyan plant at Rabta has shown, these controls have been insufficient or poorly implemented and enforced. Under the chemical weapons convention being negotiated in Geneva, countries will commit themselves not to assist other states in acquiring a chemical weapons capability. Because states will assume a binding legal obligation not to provide such assistance, this commitment is much more likely to be implemented and enforced.

Third, a chemical weapons convention will provide a legal basis for action against countries that produce chemical weapons. Under existing international law, the cornerstone of which is the 1925 Geneva Protocol, the use, but not the possession, of chemical weapons is proscribed. The chemical weapons ban currently under negotiation will make both the production and possession of chemical weapons *illegal*. It will thus provide the international community with a strong legal basis for dealing with CW activities, such as those presently underway in Libya, that threaten international peace and security.

Fourth, a chemical weapons ban will enhance the prospects of action against countries that use chemical weapons. The failure of the U.S. government, along with the rest of the international community, to react forcefully to Iraq's repeated and wide-spread use of chemical weapons against Iranian military forces and its own Kurdish population was one of the many tragedies of the Gulf war. Under a chemical weapons convention, the international norm prohibiting the use of chemical weapons will be strengthened dramatically, thus making economic and military sanctions against countries that violate this norm more defensible and probable.

Fifth, a chemical weapons convention will prevent the many countries that are capable of producing chemical weapons, but have not yet done so, from taking this step. As was noted earlier, the chemical weapons proliferation problem is currently limited to two regions: Asia and the Middle East. Even if certain countries in these regions choose to remain outside the treaty regime, much will have been gained by preventing chemical weapons from spreading to other countries and other regions. The Nuclear Non-Proliferation Treaty may be a useful analogy. Certain key states, it will be recalled, refused to sign the NPT in 1968. There is little doubt, however, but that the NPT regime has strengthened the international norm against the spread of nuclear weapons. Clearly, it has not prevented a handful of countries from continuing to pursue their nuclear ambitions. Yet without the NPT, John F. Kennedy's fear of 15 or 20 nuclear powers by 1975 may well have been realized. Similarly, without a chemical weapons convention, the world may face a situation a decade or so from now in which many more countries possess chemical weapons.

In the final analysis, policy-makers in the United States must address one question: Should a handful of Asian or Middle East states who choose to retain their chemical weapons be allowed to deny this country, and the rest of the world, the obvious benefits that would flow from a chemical weapons convention? The answer to this question undoubtedly should be based on the answer to a related question, *viz.*, whether U.S. chemical weapons deter chemical warfare activities in developing countries. On this point, it seems clear, there can be little debate. Recent experience has shown that U.S. chemical weapons do not deter developing countries from *acquiring* chemical weapons. Recent experience, primarily the Gulf war, has also shown that U.S. chemical weapons do not deter developing countries from *using* chemical weapons against one another. Finally, U.S. chemical weapons are not necessary for deterring developing countries from using chemical weapons against the United States. The wide array of highly advanced conventional weapons in the U.S. arsenal can be used to deter, and if necessary respond to, any chemical threats by a developing country against the United States. The U.S., therefore, has little to lose, and much to gain, from the conclusion of a convention banning all chemical weapons.

NOTES

1. This paper was written while the author was an SSRC-MacArthur Foundation Fellow in International Peace and Security Studies and a Guest Scholar at the Brookings Institution. It builds upon research begun in the summer of 1988 at the Royal United Services Institute (RUSI) for Defence Studies and subsequently published in the *1989 RUSI/Brassey's Defence Yearbook*. The author is grateful to Ivo H. Daalder for his helpful comments on an earlier draft.
2. "Remarks by William H. Webster, Director of Central Intelligence, at the World Affairs Council of Washington, D.C.," October 25, 1988, p. 23 (hereafter cited as Webster Remarks).
3. Emphases added. "Statement of Rear Admiral William O. Studeman, U.S. Navy, Director of Naval Intelligence, before the Seapower and Strategic and Critical Materials Subcommittee of the House Armed Services Committee, on Intelligence Issues," March 1, 1988, p. 48 (hereafter cited as Studeman Statement); United States Information Service, "Chemical Weapons Proliferation Poses Threat to Stability (Text: Bailey Address to Dallas Rotary Club)," July 12, 1988, p. 2; Webster Remarks, p. 20; and R. Jeffrey Smith, "Lawmakers Plan Chemical Weapons Curb," *Washington Post*, January 25, 1989.
4. One notable exception may be found in a 1986 interview with Kenneth Adelman, the Director of the U.S. Arms Control and Disarmament Agency. Adelman said that stockpile size is "sufficient so that it could give a military utility to the possessing country, and sufficient to cause a great deal of damage to the other side. We are not talking about experimental possession, research possession." He also said that in the main, Third World countries have purchased rather than produced chemical weapons, and that the most widely possessed agent was mustard gas, although nerve gas and incapacitants were also stockpiled. See, Lois Ember, "Worldwide Spread of Chemical Arms Receiving Increased Attention," *Chemical and Engineering News*, April 14, 1986, p. 13.

5. Don Oberdorfer, "Chemical Arms Curbs Are Sought," *Washington Post*, September 9, 1985; and Jack Anderson, "The Growing Chemical Club," *Washington Post*, August 26, 1984.

6. Robert J. McCartney, "Iraqi Official Acknowledges Chemical-Arms Use in War," *International Herald Tribune*, July 2–3, 1988; and "U.S. Says Iraq Uses Chemical Weapons in War with Iran," *International Herald Tribune*, March 6, 1984.

7. "Statement of Rear Admiral Thomas A. Brooks, U.S. Navy, Director of Naval Intelligence, before the Seapower, Strategic, and Critical Materials Subcommittee of the House Armed Services Committee, on Intelligence Issues," February 22, 1989, pp. 38–39 (hereafter cited as Brooks Statement); and Studeman Statement, p. 48. For additional information on Iran, Libya, and Syria, see "Statement of the Honorable William H. Webster, Director, Central Intelligence Agency, before the Committee on Governmental Affairs, Hearings on Global Spread of Chemical and Biological Weapons, Assessing Challenges and Responses," February 9, 1989, pp. 9–12 (hereafter cited as Webster Statement); on Israel, see Testimony of Lt. Gen. E.H. Almquist, U.S. Army, Assistant Chief of Staff for Force Development, in U.S. Senate, Subcommittee on Tactical Air Power of the Committee on Armed Services, *Hearings on Fiscal Year 1975 Authorization for Military Procurement, Research and Development, and Active Duty, Selected Reserve and Civilian Personnel Strengths*, 93rd Cong., 2nd Sess., (Washington, D.C.: U.S. Government Printing Office, 1974), Part 9, p. 4931; on North Korea, see Testimony of General John A. Wickham, U.S. Army, Chief of Staff, in U.S. House of Representatives, Subcommittee on Defense of the Committee on Appropriations, *Hearings on Department of Defense Appropriations for 1987*, 99th Cong., 2nd Sess., (Washington, D.C.: U.S. Government Printing Office, 1986), Part 1, p. 138 (hereafter cited as Wickham Statement); and on Vietnam, see U.S. Department of State, "Chemical Warfare in Southeast Asia and Afghanistan," Report to the Congress from Secretary of State Alexander M. Haig, Jr., March 22, 1982, Special Report No. 98 (hereafter cited as *The Haig Report*), and U.S. Department of State, "Chemical Warfare in Southeast Asia and Afghanistan: An Update," Report from Secretary of State George P. Shultz, November 1982, Special Report No 104 (hereafter cited as *The Shultz Report*).

8. Thom Shanker, "Lack of candor blocks chemical arms treaty," *Chicago Tribune*, April 4, 1989; and Gary Thatcher, "The paradox of proliferation," *Christian Science Monitor*, December 13, 1988, p. B9. For additional information on Angola and Cuba, see Bill Gertz, "Angola said to stockpile Cuban chemical agents," *Washington Times*, January 2, 1989; on Argentina and South Africa, see Martin Walker, "'Queues grow' for chemical weapons," *Guardian*, January 6, 1989, and Robert Toth, "Iraqi Use of Gas Spurred U.S. Action on Issue," *Los Angeles Times*, January 5, 1989; on India and Pakistan, see Michael R. Gordon with Stephen Engelberg, "Poison Gas Fears Lead U.S. To Plan New Export Curbs," *New York Times*, March 26, 1989, Brooks Statement, p. 38, and Stephen Engelberg, "Chemical Arms: Third World Trend," *New York Times*, January 7, 1989; on Indonesia and Thailand, see Engelberg, "Chemical Arms: Third World Trend"; on Laos, see *The Haig Report*, and *The Shultz Report*; on South Korea and Thailand, see Ember,

"Worldwide Spread of Chemical Arms Receiving Increased Attention"; and on Somalia, see James Dorsey, "Somalia refrains from using Libyan-delivered nerve gas," *Washington Times,* January 30, 1989.

9. On Afghanistan, see Secretary of State Haig's reference to "*some* evidence that Afghan Government forces *may* have used Soviet supplied chemical weapons against the *mujahidin* even before the Soviet invasion," *The Haig Report*, p. 6, emphases added; on Chad, see TASS, April 21, 1986, as reported in Foreign Broadcast Information Service–Soviet Union (FBIS-SU), April 25, 1986, cited in *Arms Control Reporter, 1986,* p. 704.B.172; on Chile, see David Shribman, "FBI learns Chilean plot to kill Letelier in '76 involved nerve gas," *New York Times,* December 14, 1981, and Hugh O'Shaughnessy, "Chile Link in Deadly Gas Chain," *Sunday Observer,* April 23, 1989; on El Salvador, see "Rights Group Charges Massacre by El Salvador," *New York Times,* August 13, 1981; on Guatemala, see Havana international radio, July 6, 1982, cited in Stockholm International Peace Research Institute (SIPRI), *World Armaments and Disarmament, SIPRI Yearbook, 1987* (London: Taylor and Francis, 1987), p. 111 and note 36 (hereafter cited as *SIPRI Yearbook*, with appropriate year); on Jordan, see "Jordan Seeking Chem. Warfare Delivery Systems," *Defense and Foreign Affairs Weekly,* January 23–29, 1989; on Mozambique, see James Morrison, "Mozambique accused of chemical warfare," *Washington Times,* December 31, 1986; on Nicaragua, see "Chemical Arms Used on Contras, Leader Says," *Los Angeles Times,* June 9, 1985; on Peru, see Hans Guenter Brauch, "Chemical Weapons: Arsenals and Recent Developments," paper presented at the Conference on Non-Nuclear War in Europe, Groningen, 28 Nov–1 Dec 1984, p. 3; on the Philippines, see *Ang Pahayagang Malaya,* September 27, 1984, as reported in Foreign Broadcast Information Service–Asia and Pacific (FBIS-AP), October 25, 1984; and on the Sudan, see Robert Pear, "Sudan Rebels Say They are Victims of Poison Gas," *New York Times,* January 10, 1989.

10. McCartney, "Iraqi Official Acknowledges Chemical-Arms Use in War." Two months earlier, the Iraqi Foreign Minister had warned publicly that Iraq had to repel aggression by "all means, including the use of chemical weapons, against those who seek to occupy its territory." Patrick Tyler, "Iraq Seems to Abandon Diplomacy for Missiles," *International Herald Tribune,* May 12, 1988.

11. Oberdorfer, "Chemical Arms Curbs Are Sought."

12. M. Meselson and D.E. Viney, "The Yemen," in Stephen Rose, ed., *CBW: Chemical and Biological Warfare* (Boston: Beacon Press, 1969), pp. 99–102; and "China and Israel," Foreign Report, July 12, 1984.

13. *The Haig Report*; and *The Shultz Report* . These charges, it should be noted, remain highly controversial. See, for example, Elisa D. Harris, "Sverdlovsk and Yellow Rain: Two Cases of Soviet Noncompliance?" *International Security*, Vol. 11, No. 4, 1987. Interestingly, an Army intelligence officer recently characterized the charges as "allegations" in a statement prepared for a Congressional hearing. See, "Statement of Mr. David Goldberg, Foreign Science and Technology Center, U.S. Army Intelligence Agency, before the Senate Governmental Affairs Committee and the Senate Permanent Subcommittee on Investigations," February 9, 1989, Chart 5.

14. Elaine Sciolino, "U.S. Sends 2,000 Gas Masks to the Chadians," *New York Times*, September 25, 1987; and Michael Gordon, "U.S. Thinks Libya May Plan to Make Chemical Weapons," *New York Times*, December 24, 1987.
15. "China and Israel"; and Anderson, "The Growing Chemical Club."
16. "China and Israel"; and Anderson, "The Growing Chemical Club."
17. The potential linkage between chemical and nuclear weapons in the Middle East was a major theme at the Paris Conference on chemical weapons. See Edward Cody, "Talks Show Growing Arab Consensus That Chemical Arms Balance Nuclear," *Washington Post*, January 13, 1989. See also the comments by the former head of the Egyptian chemical warfare program in "Arabs 'need chemical weapons,'" *Independent*, July 28, 1988.
18. Anderson, "The Growing Chemical Club."
19. Soviet Embassy, Information Department, Press release, "Statement by Mikhail Gorbachev," Washington, January 16, 1986, p. 7.
20. Oberdorfer, "Chemical Arms Curbs Are Sought"; and Anderson, "The Growing Chemical Club." For information on Libya, see Simon O'Dwyer-Russell, "Gaddafi arms Syria with gas warheads," *Sunday Telegraph*, November 23, 1986; on North Korea, see "U.S. Rejects Tour of Libyan Plant," *Washington Post*, December 31, 1988; and on Vietnam, see *The Haig Report*, and *The Shultz Report*.
21. Michael R. Gordon and Stephen Engelberg, "Egypt Accused of Big Advance in Gas for War," *New York Times*, March 10, 1989.
22. William Beecher, "U.S. seeking action to halt chemical arms spread," *Boston Globe*, February 4, 1986.
23. Sciolino, "U.S. Sends 2,000 Gas Masks to the Chadians."
24. "China and Israel."
25. Webster Statement; and Tom Diaz, "Chemical weapons proliferation spurred by business, panel says," *Washington Times*, May 10, 1985.
26. Brooks Statement; Studeman Statement; Webster Statement. For additional information on Iraq and Israel, see Robert Harris, "The poor man's atom bomb," *The Listener*, October 30, 1986; on Burma and Taiwan, see Oberdorfer, "Chemical Arms Curbs Are Sought"; on China, see Anderson, "The Growing Chemical Club"; on Iran, see Harvey Morris, "Iran military wants to use chemical arms," *Independent*, December 27, 1987; on Libya, see Gordon, "U.S. Thinks Libya May Plan to Make Chemical Weapons"; on North Korea, see Wickham Statement; and on Syria, see Gaylord Shaw, "Syria Reported to Be Making Chemical Arms," *Los Angeles Times*, March 26, 1986.
27. Patrick Tyler, "Mubarak Seeks Easing Doubts on Poison Gas, Aid During U.S. Visit," *Washington Post*, April 1, 1989.
28. Stephen Engelberg with Michael R. Gordon, "India Seen as Key on Chemical Arms," *New York Times*, July 10, 1989.
29. Some past reports on subnational proliferation problems may be found in *SIPRI Yearbook 1983*, p. 407; and U.S. House of Representatives, Subcommittee on International Security and Scientific Affairs of the Committee on Foreign Affairs, *Report on Binary Weapons : Implications of the U.S. Chemical Stockpile Modernization Program for Chemical Weapons Proliferation*, 98th Cong., 2nd Sess., (Washington, D.C.: U.S. Government Printing Office, 1984), pp. 69–71.

30. Gary Yerkey, "Experts study threat of chemical weapons in terrorists' hands," *Christian Science Monitor*, August 29, 1986.
31. Seymour Hersh, "U.S. Aides Say Iraqis Made Use of a Nerve Gas," *New York Times*, March 30, 1984; and Don Oberdorfer, "U.S. Curbs Chemicals to Iran, Iraq," *Washington Post*, March 31, 1984.
32. Marie Colvin and John Witherow, "Syrian nerve gas warheads alarm Israel," *Sunday Times*, January 10, 1988; and Lou Cannon and David B. Ottaway, "New Attack on Libya Discussed," *Washington Post*, December 22, 1988.
33. "Iraq, Saying it Hit Tankers, Threatens Chemical Strikes," *International Herald Tribune*, March 30, 1988.
34. International Institute for Strategic Studies, *Strategic Survey, 1988–89* (London: Brassey's, 1989), pp. 14–25.
35. These concerns are clearly articulated in Francois Heisbourg, "Missiles: Steps That Might Check Proliferation," *International Herald Tribune*, March 30, 1988.
36. The Australian Group countries are exempted from these controls. "Statement of Ambassador Reginald Bartholomew, Under Secretary of State for Security Assistance, Science and Technology, U.S. Department of State, before the Subcommittee on International Finance and Monetary Policy of the Senate Committee on Banking, Housing and Urban Affairs, on Chemical and Biological Weapons Policy," June 22, 1989, pp. 3–4 (hereafter cited as Bartholomew Statement); U.S. Department of Commerce News, "U.S. Imposes Export Controls on Chemical and Biological Agents," February 23, 1989; and U.S. Department of Commerce, Bureau of Export Administration, Office of Technology and Policy Analysis, *1989 Annual Foreign Policy Report to the Congress*, pp. 31–32.
37. *SIPRI Yearbook, 1985*, pp. 174–175; *SIPRI Yearbook, 1988*, p. 104; and UN General Assembly, *Doc. No. A/S-15/PV.11*, June 10, 1988, p. 81.
38. John Tagliabue, "Bonn Limits Export of Chemical-Arms Materials," *New York Times*, August 8, 1984; and Serge Schmemann, "Bonn Will Tighten Curb on Export of Deadly Goods," *New York Times*, January 11, 1989.
39. *SIPRI Yearbook 1985*, pp. 174–175; David Buchan, "EC backs controls on chemicals for weapons," *Financial Times*, February 21, 1989; and Bartholomew Statement, p. 8.
40. *International Affairs* (Moscow), April 1986, pp. 151–152; and "Statement of H. Allen Holmes, Assistant Secretary for Politico-Military Affairs, Department of State, before the Senate Governmental Affairs Committee and Permanent Subcommittee, on Investigations on CBW Proliferation and Related Issues," February 10, 1989, p. 9.
41. Ember, "Worldwide Spread of Chemical Arms Receiving Increased Attention," p. 11.
42. *SIPRI Yearbook, 1988*, p. 104; and Bartholomew Statement, p. 6.
43. Leslie H. Gelb, "U.S.–Soviet Pact on Chemical Arms Said to Be Near," *New York Times*, November 12, 1985.
44. Soviet Embassy, "Statement by Mikhail Gorbachev," p. 7.
45. "U.S. rejects chemical weapons plan," *Boston Globe*, February 11, 1986. See also, Thomas W. Netter, "U.S. Rebuffs Soviet on Chemical Arms," *New York Times*, February 12, 1986.

46. Iraq reportedly has used both these tactics. See, "A plague of 'hellish poison,'" *US News and World Report*, October 26, 1987; and Steven Dickman, "Nerve gas cloud hangs over West German firms," *Nature*, April 14, 1988, p. 573.
47. U.S. Senate, Committee on Foreign Relations and Subcommittee on Energy, Nuclear Proliferation and Government Processes of the Committee on Governmental Affairs, *Joint Hearing on Chemical Warfare : Arms Control and Nonproliferation*, 98th Cong., 2nd Sess., (Washington, DC: U.S. Government Printing Office, 1984), p. 17.
48. Netter, "U.S. Rebuffs Soviet on Chemical Arms."
49. For a thoughtful analysis of the pros and cons of a chemical weapons ban, see Lewis A. Dunn, "Chemical Weapons Arms Control: Hard Choices for the Bush Administration," *Survival*, May/June 1989, pp. 209–224.

Appendix 3

BALLISTIC MISSILES IN THE THIRD WORLD

Janne Nolan and Albert Wheelon

BACKGROUND

Long-range ballistic missiles have been the coin of the realm in the strategic contest between the United States and Soviet Union for three decades. The two countries began to develop intercontinental ballistic missiles (ICBMs) in 1953 when the lithium deuteride route to thermonuclear weapons design provided an approach to build lightweight weapons with significant yields: i.e., one megaton in 1,000 lbs. Since a ballistic missile's total weight scales with its warhead, the advent of lightweight weapons meant that long-range missiles of reasonable size and construction could be built. Both countries launched their first ICBM in 1957 and went on to deploy modest numbers[1] of the first generation liquid fueled missiles. Significant deployments of American ICBMs were delayed until the solid propellant, inertially-guided Minuteman became available in the 1960s.

A family of American intermediate-range ballistic missiles (IRBMs) was developed concurrently with ICBMs. With ranges of approximately 1,500 nm, *Thor* and *Jupiter* IRBMs were deployed in England, Italy and Turkey between 1958 and 1963, but were withdrawn following the resolution of the Cuban Missile Crisis.

Solid propellant, inertially-guided missiles were also built by the Navy for deployment on nuclear submarines. The first generation *Polaris* was an IRBM that could be launched to Soviet targets from offshore positions. In subsequent versions, the range was progressively extended and allowed the submarines to target from ever greater distances. The most recent version (*Trident* D-5) has intercontinental range and can be launched from U.S. coastal waters if necessary.

The Soviets developed a greater variety of long-range missiles and made extensive deployments in the 1970s. They also developed several types of theater ballistic missiles for carrying conventional, chemical, and nuclear warheads. They have provided short-range missiles to a large number of client states. The United States developed a small number of short-range missiles, and preferred to maintain a relative monopoly on ballistic missile delivery capabilities in the West.

The French rebelled against this U.S. export restraint policy and built two generations of ballistic missiles that could carry nuclear warheads from France to targets in the Soviet Union. In doing so, they mastered the technologies of guidance, propulsion and re-entry needed for additional types of ballistic missiles.

The British followed a different course, and purchased both nuclear submarines and sea-launched ballistic missiles from the United States. To these, they added British nuclear warheads in order to establish an independent strategic nuclear force.

Following their rupture with the Soviet Union in 1959, the Chinese went on to establish their own nuclear and ballistic missile capabilities. They now have a variety of short- and long-range ballistic missiles which they have begun to export.

In addition to these strategic rocket programs, a European space consortium developed the *Ariane* space launcher for commercial and scientific missions. Although the liquid fueled *Ariane* is not a suitable strategic weapon, its development helped to provide rocket technologies to a half dozen European countries. This technology has since diffused to other countries through commercial channels.

This paper is about the transfer of ballistic missile technology and missile systems to countries other than the Big Four producers: USSR, USA, France, and China. We explore the specific ways in which the transfers have taken place, the ways in which exported systems have been modified and enhanced by local efforts, and how countries other than the Big Four have developed and produced ballistic missiles indigenously. We shall try to establish a current picture of the inventories in the eighteen countries that now have ballistic missiles. These inventories will be correlated with existing or anticipated nuclear weapon production capabilities, and with chemical weapon capacity. Next, we examine the likely military effectiveness and probable targets pertinent to the eighteen countries' missile capabilities, taking into account range, accuracy, and warhead options. These topics comprise the first half of the paper.

The second half of the paper is devoted to political and policy issues raised by emerging missile capabilities. We examine the political objectives sought by countries in acquiring such forces and review the agreements, regimes, and policies which have been used to impede the diffusion of ballistic missiles. Finally, we consider the challenges posed by the potential diffusion of futuristic technologies, such as stealth and satellite technology. This paper stops short of advocating a specific policy for managing the dissemination of critical military technology. However, it demonstrates what can happen when one has no coherent policy. The linkages between industrial policy and military technology transfer (or their lack) are explored, keeping in mind that the United States and Soviet Union no longer enjoy an exclusive control on high technology and are beginning to develop a common cause on a wide range of important issues.

THE SUPPLIERS

Not surprisingly, the primary developers of ballistic missile technology also have been the primary suppliers of missile systems. China, France, the United States and the Soviet Union have pursued rather different policies. Moreover, their policies have changed with time.

The United States has been a restrained supplier of missile systems.[2] *Honest John* missiles, with a range of 20 miles, were transferred to Greece, Turkey and South Korea in the 1950s. The United States supplied the *Nike-Hercules* anti-aircraft missile

system to a number of countries. Israel appealed to the United
States in the early 1970s to provide the *Pershing* IA missile, but
this request was finally rejected in 1975 for fear the Israelis would
use it to deliver nuclear weapons. The United States did supply
Israel with 200 *Lance* missiles in 1972, a dual capable (i.e., nuclear
and conventional warhead) system which has a relatively short
range (70 miles) and a payload of 1,000 lbs.

France has declined to export its long-range missile systems to
other countries. However, the French firm Dassault provided at
least fourteen *Jericho* I missiles to Israel during the 1960s. This
mobile system has a range of 300 to 400 miles, and a payload of
approximately 1,200 lbs. The total number of *Jericho* I rockets
available is not known because the total number of missiles
actually delivered from France is uncertain, and because it is
suspected that the Israelis have built copies indigenously.
However, the number of missiles probably has been regulated
by the availability of Israeli nuclear warheads.

In March 1988, China agreed to supply Saudi Arabia with an
undisclosed number of its CSS-2 intermediate-range ballistic
missiles. The significance of this sale is the long range of CSS-2,
which places many Middle Eastern countries potentially within
its reach. The original Chinese CSS-2 can carry a one to three
megaton nuclear warhead 2,200 miles, with an accuracy of about
a mile. The version sold to the Saudis, however, is reported to
carry a 4,500 lb. conventional warhead to a range of only 1,500
miles. To allay U.S. and regional concerns, the Saudis have given
assurances that the missiles will remain non-nuclear and have
agreed to sign the Nuclear Non-Proliferation Treaty.

The USSR has provided a continuing supply of various ballistic missiles. Five different types of short-range missiles have
been given or sold to Soviet client states, primarily in the Middle
East. A large number of states in a very unstable part of the world
now possess ballistic missiles, albeit mostly of short-range. The
most significant missile exported is the *Scud* B, which was used
extensively in the Iran-Iraq war. It is a single-stage, liquid
propellant missile that carries an 1,100 lb. warhead to a range of
180 miles. It is reported to have an accuracy of about 1,000 yards
at this range. Soviet missile transfers are summarized in Table 1.

Table 1   Soviet Exports of Ballistic Missiles

Name/Type	Range	Model Year	Exported To
Frog-4/5	30 mi.	1957	Algeria, Egypt, North Korea
Frog-7	40 mi.	1965	Algeria, Egypt, India, Iraq, Kuwait, Libya, North Korea, Yemen, Yugoslavia
SS-21	70 mi.	1978	North Yemen, Syria, South Yemen
Scud-B	180 mi.	1965	Egypt, Iraq, Libya, Syria, South Yemen, Iran, North Korea
SS-12	570 mi.	1984	Iraq[3]

THE MODIFIERS

The path to ballistic missile acquisition discussed most frequently is the relatively simple conversion of space launch vehicles acquired for peaceful purposes. However, some emerging missile programs are the result of direct imports. Once missile systems are in the hands of sovereign nations, they can be modified if there is an incentive to do so. Such a need arose during the Iran-Iraq war. The Iranian *Scud*-B missiles could easily reach Baghdad because of the proximity of the Iran-Iraq border. By contrast, Tehran was out of range of Iraq's 190 mile *Scud*-B missiles. Iraq set out to lighten the *Scud*-B warhead and extend its range. In doing so, they undoubtedly received help from West European and possibly East German technicians. It does not matter just how they went about it: the fact is that such technical assistance is available, and the range of the Iraqi *Scud*-Bs was extended from 190 to probably 380 miles.

The South Koreans own and operate anti-aircraft *Nike-Hercules* missile with conventional warheads. Confronted with North Korean acquisition of *Scud*-B missiles,[4] the South Koreans undertook an expensive program to convert their two stage *Nikes* into surface-to-surface missiles. In this mode, the NH-K missile has a range of 110 to 160 miles, and provides both a military and political counter to North Korea.

The South Korean and Iraqi programs demonstrate that missile system characteristics can be changed rather dramatically if there is a need and will to do so. There is apparently ample opportunity to convert, modify, and enhance well-defined and controlled systems.

THE DEVELOPERS

A number of nations have chosen to develop their own ballistic missile systems. Some have done so because they could not buy missiles from the Big Four. Others have done so because such development is a significant indication of national prestige and technological "arrival." A third group appears to be doing so as a commercial venture to supply a rising worldwide demand. In the process, these countries strengthen their high technology and weapons production base. Interesting collaborations between nations that want missiles and/or wish to develop the capability to build them, are emerging on a worldwide basis (discussed below).

A remarkable amount of ballistic missile technology is available on the open market. An MIT study conducted in 1981 for the Arms Control and Disarmament Agency (ACDA)[5] identified ten solid rocket motors that were then commercially available on the world market.[6] If used for a single stage ballistic missile, these rockets could propel a thousand pound payload 600 miles or more if a suitable guidance system can be found. If these motors are combined to form two stage missiles, much larger payload and range performance is possible.

Even though advanced guidance systems for ballistic missiles are generally not available for export, sophisticated inertial systems are not required for short-range missiles. To be specific, a velocity cutoff error of one foot per second produces a miss of one mile at 5,000 mile range. At a range of 500 miles, the same miss can be achieved with a guidance system that controls the cutoff error to only 10 feet per second, allowing a much cruder guidance technology to be used.

The basic components for a short-range guidance system are employed in fifteen inertial navigation systems built for commercial and military aircraft.[7] To be sure, their combination and flight computer functions would be quite different. Aircraft navigation is essentially a two dimensional problem, whereas the powered flight of a ballistic missile is necessarily a three dimensional problem. It is likely that Third World guidance systems built from such components would be "strap-down" systems rather than actual IMU systems because they are simpler to develop and adequate for short ranges. On balance, however, one should assume that commercial inertial navigation systems can provide the instrument technology for guiding short-range ballistic missiles.

There are other paths to develop or acquire ballistic missiles. The simplest is to adapt space launch vehicles, which are very much like missiles in their propulsion and guidance requirements. The United States, France and the Soviet Union have provided space launch technology to Japan, India, Brazil and Argentina. It should be no surprise that three of these four recipients are now developing ballistic missiles.[8]

Another avenue to missile development is to acquire technical assistance from companies which are already involved in producing missile subsystems for the advanced countries. This assistance can be acquired clandestinely (i.e., Egypt, Pakistan) or by direct subcontract. A growing number of engineers and organizations have demonstrated their willingness to support such developments in return for handsome payments. An advanced technology base established for reasons of national security or space research can be eroded by exports driven purely by commercial gain. The international technology control system has proven very porous. Morevoer, sovereign governments are reluctant to acknowledge the problem—as evidenced in the recent transfer of poison gas materials and technology by West European companies to several Third World states.

In 1987, the United States, England, France, Germany, Canada, Italy and Japan agreed to try to control the diffusion of such technology by multilateral agreement to restrict missile-related exports. The Missile Technology Control Regime (MTCR) is intended to limit export of technology for ballistic missiles capable of delivering at least 500 kg payload to a range of 182 miles. It is an important first step but considerable diffusion of missile tech-nology already had occurred before it was implemented. The net result of the thirty years of missile proliferation is described below.

Israel

Outside the Big Four, the Israeli ballistic missile program is the most advanced. The *Jericho* I missile initially was developed with French help and deployed in 1973. It had a range of 280 to 350 miles, with a payload of 450 to 680 lbs. This would have allowed it to hit targets in Egypt and Syria, but not targets in Iraq, Iran, Libya or Saudi Arabia.

When the United States refused to provide Israel with the *Pershing* IA missile in 1975, Israel apparently set out to develop its own long-range missile—possibly with continuing help from abroad. The *Jericho* II is a two stage, solid propellant missile that was first tested in May 1987. There is considerable uncertainty about the range payload capability of the *Jericho* II. It has recently been tested to a range of 800 miles.[9] It is likely that the same rocket was used with a third stage to launch the first Israeli satellite in September 1988. Technical analysis of this launch suggests that the *Jericho* II may be able to propel a 1,000 kg warhead to a range as great as 1,500 miles; with a payload of 500 kg, it could have a range capacity of up to 2,200 miles.[10]

There is little doubt that the *Jericho* II is nuclear armed, as the first generation presumably was. It represents an intimidating deterrent to other states who have not yet attained Israel's level of nuclear or missile capability. There are indications that Israel has collaborated with Iran, Taiwan, South Africa and China in missile development, although it is unlikely that Israel much needs their help at this point.

India

India startled the world in May 1989 by successfully launching its *Agni* ballistic missile to a range of 1,500 miles. The two stage *Agni* was derived from space launch technology provided by France and the Soviet Union. Ironically, the United States was preparing to provide additional space technology on the eve of this first flight test and may still be planning to do so. India's recent achievement is the result of a program that began in 1967, with a succession of progressively more capable missile and space launch systems leading up to the successful test of the *Agni*. The *Agni* is not the only ballistic missile in India's arsenal. India also has developed a 150 mile mobile system (the *Prithvi*) which can carry a 2,200 lb. warhead and can hit most targets in Pakistan. India has a broadly based technical program to develop a variety of guidance systems, and is building numerous missile test sites. In addition, India has acquired the capability to cast solid propellant rocket motors indigenously. We should expect that India will eventually develop an even longer-range missile than the *Agni*, if it feels a military or political need to do so.

South Africa

South Africa has a large, indigenous arms industry that supplies its own defense needs, and has the capacity to export arms. The government has recently revealed the existence of a classified missile development program. Very little information about it is available in the open literature. It is reported that a facility for assessing missile tests has been established on Marion Island, 1,200 miles southeast of Cape Town, and a missile launch site in the Kalahari Desert. Israel has assisted the program with technology, possibly in exchange for enriched uranium. With an aging bomber fleet, a South African capability for missile delivery would have substantial appeal if they chose to develop nuclear weapons.

Taiwan

Taiwan builds a wide variety of missiles for its own use. Working through the Chungshan Institute of Science and Technology, Taiwan developed a short range (60 miles) ballistic missile in the 1970s (*Queen Bee*). It is believed that this program was based on *Lance* missile technology provided by Israel. Chungshan is reportedly now developing a 600 mile missile (*Sky Horse*), but little more is known about it.

North Korea

North Korea is now producing and exporting a version of the *Scud*-B missile, which it apparently acquired from the PRC. Press accounts state that North Korea is helping Egypt and possibly Iran to establish facilities to manufacture *Scud*-Bs.

Afghanistan

The Soviet Union reportedly transferred an undisclosed number of *Scud*-Bs to Afghanistan in September 1988, but there is no evidence of any indigenous efforts to produce or modify these.

Pakistan

Pakistan claims to have launched its own ballistic missile (*King Hawk*) in April 1988. Press reports indicate that it carries an 1,100 lb. warhead to a range of 180 miles. If this is correct, the missile was surely developed with considerable foreign assistance, probably from the Chinese. Earlier this year, Pakistan revealed two new missiles, the *Haft* I and II, with ranges of 50 and 62 miles respectively, and payload capacities of 1,200 lbs.

Egypt

Egypt is establishing a large and sophisticated arms industry. It seems clear that Egypt is bent on developing and producing missiles. Egypt is now producing a 50 mile rocket and may be getting ready to build the *Scud*-B indigenously. The United States has recently filed criminal charges against five individuals, including two Egyptian army colonels, for attempting to acquire missile technology for Egypt. Egypt was previously involved with Iraq and Argentina in a joint program to produce a solid-fueled, inertially-guided ballistic missile based on the *Condor* II with a range of 500 to 600 miles. Egypt reportedly terminated its participation in this program in September 1989.[11]

Iran

Iran launched a considerable number of short-range ballistic missiles against Iraq. Many of these were apparently *Scud* Bs purchased from China or North Korea. There are reports that Iran is trying to establish its own capability to build short-range (25 and 80 mile) missiles and a longer range system (200 miles) with Chinese and possibly North Korean assistance. Israel apparently continues to support Iran with technology and weapons.

Iraq

Iraq recently has acquired a diverse missile development capability, based largely on modifications of the Soviet *Scud*-B. Its operational system, the *Al-Husayn*, extended the range of the *Scud*-B to 380 miles. The follow-on missile, the *Al-Abbas*, which is still under development, is to have a range of 550 miles. The Iraqis have established a large infrastructure for missile development, focused in a research and development complex called Sa'ad 16. Among the systems which Iraq hopes to bring into production are the *Fahd* (170 mile range), another missile of twice that range, and cluster munitions. Iraq relies on Western European, Egyptian, and Eastern Bloc assistance. In addition, it recently signed an agreement with Brazil to train Iraqi missile engineers.

Libya

There are unconfirmed reports that Libya is developing a 300 mile missile indigenously. Libya is working with Brazil on a large arms deal and it appears that this involves ballistic missiles of up to 500 mile range. It also sought to purchase the Chinese CSS-2 last year, apparently without success.

Argentina

Like Brazil and India, Argentina began a space program three decades ago. Argentina developed a single stage rocket with limited range (60 miles) and has pursued a sounding rocket program assisted by Europe. Argentina has been developing a two stage ballistic missile since 1982. Financial assistance reportedly is provided by Egypt and Iraq. Technical assistance was provided by firms in Western Europe, but this may have slowed as a result of the MTCR. Argentina's major program, the *Condor* II solid propellant rocket, was to carry a 1,000 lb. warhead to a range of 500 or 600 miles, and employ a modern French inertial guidance system. Due to high costs—estimated at $3.2 billion for 400 missiles—and impeded access to components due to MTCR restrictions, the *Condor* program appears to have stopped for now. If this missile were provided to Egypt, Iraq, or other Middle East countries, it could provide an important step up from the

Scud-B forces they now possess. The international impact of this missile program is thus likely to be felt as a result of Argentina's role as a missile supplier.

Brazil

Brazil has established a vigorous arms industry, and exports its products without restrictions on use or re-transfer. Since 1960, they have pursued a space program with four generations of sounding rockets developed indigenously with European, Canadian and American assistance. They are now receiving help from China, possibly in the area of guidance. The most recent in this series (*Sonda* IV) can lift 1,100 lbs. to an altitude of 400 miles. These solid propellant sounding rockets provide the basis for a family of ballistic missiles being developed by two firms.

An inertially guided tactical missile (MB/EE 150) is being developed by Orbita to carry 1,100 lbs. to a range of 90 miles. Avibras is developing a 185 mile missile (SS-300) that uses a Brazilian guidance system, solid propellants, and can carry various warheads with its 2,200 lb. payload capacity. Press reports indicate that both Libya and Iraq have expressed interest in buying the 185 mile missile. Avibras also is reported to be developing a longer-range version (SS-1000) that could fly to 740 miles.

The purpose of these missile developments seems to be primarily commercial. Brazil is developing its industrial and technology base by building and selling weapons systems around the world. With an unconstrained export policy, they are succeeding fairly rapidly. The availability of domestically produced missiles also serves to counter Argentine capabilities on the South American stage.

THIRD WORLD INVENTORY

The foregoing discussions indicate how ballistic missiles are imported, modified and developed. It is useful to summarize the current missile arsenals in Third World countries as a basis for subsequent discussions. Reliable data on inventory quantities are not available in the open literature, but there is general agreement on the types of systems possessed by each of the

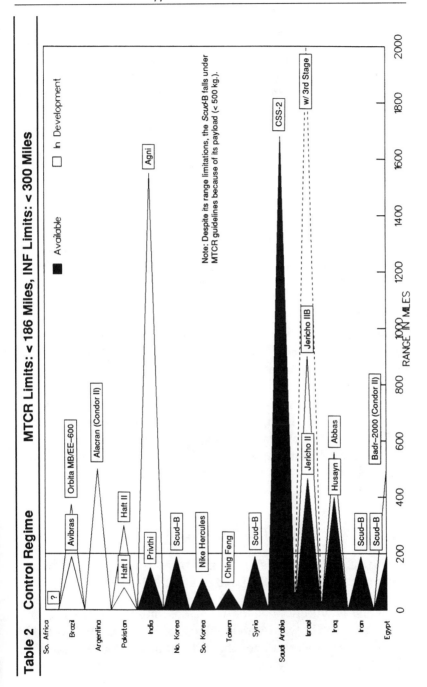

Table 2   Control Regime   MTCR Limits: < 186 Miles, INF Limits: < 300 Miles

Note: Despite its range limitations, the *Scud-B* falls under MTCR guidelines because of its payload (< 500 kg.).

seventeen countries. The reach of the longest range missile possessed by each country is a useful measure of its potential political and military significance. In Table 2, we show the longest range systems available to each country that are presumed to be operational as well as those under development. We have indicated that Egypt and Iraq may acquire a 500 mile capability by way of their participation in the transnational *Condor* program.

The lower range limit of the Missile Technology Control Regime is shown as a vertical line at 180 miles. If one focuses only on missiles with ranges longer than *Scud*-B, a good deal of Table 2 is removed from the discussion of export controls based on range limitations. However, this exclusion does not remove those missiles from military and political concern in areas of the world where countries are small and closely clustered. The most significant of these short-range systems, the *Scud*-B, would actually be subject to MTCR restrictions as a result of its payload capacity, which is in excess of 500 kg.

Table 2 indicates the dramatic change which occurs as a result of Israeli, Indian, and Saudi missile efforts. Another significant trend revealed in the data presented in Table 2 is the emergence of a new family, missiles with a range of 500 miles or more. If these proliferate, they will tend to move the present boundary at 180 miles well to the right, as countries vie with one another to acquire comparable capabilities. We would thus arrive at a second threshold of missile proliferation, qualitatively different from the first threshold which was established by the USSR's proliferation of *Scud*-Bs.

NUCLEAR CAPABILITIES

It is useful to compare the ballistic missile inventory shown in Table 2 with the capability to develop nuclear weapons.[12]

* Israel is widely believed to possess nuclear warheads and refuses to allow international inspection of its nuclear facilities. One must presume that the *Jericho* I and II rockets were designed to carry nuclear warheads.

- India has an active nuclear program and exploded a nuclear device in 1974. India also refuses international inspection of its nuclear reprocessing plant. Official statements deny the existence of a program to develop a nuclear force. The testing of the *Agni* missile undercuts the credibility of those assertions.

- South Africa refuses international controls on its nuclear enrichments plant, and has stated that it can build nuclear weapons whenever it wishes to do so.

- Pakistan has long been in the political spotlight, denying an interest in developing nuclear weapons while trying to acquire the technology through espionage and outright purchase. Its nuclear enrichment plan is outside the international inspection system.

- Brazil and Argentina are not signatories to the Non-Proliferation Treaty, and therefore have no controls on their nuclear capabilities. It is a common judgment that they could build nuclear weapons by the turn of the century if they decide to do so.

- Taiwan and South Korea have pledged not to build nuclear weapons and have signed the Non-Proliferation Treaty. This is certainly welcome, given their rapidly growing nuclear programs.

When one cross correlates these capabilities with the missile data on Table 2, it reinforces concern about the long-range missile capabilities of Israel, India, and South Africa. A decade from now, we may be equally concerned about Brazil and Argentina—and their customers.

CHEMICAL WEAPON CAPABILITIES

The Iran-Iraq conflict put chemical warfare back on the world's agenda. Subsequent efforts by Libya to acquire a chemical production capability, and German and Indian exports of chemical weapon materials to the Third World, have only heightened sensitivities. The *Scud*-B missile was designed by the USSR to carry chemical, as well as nuclear and high explosive warheads. Given the number of countries that have *Scud*-B missiles, the threat of chemical agents delivered by ballistic missiles has become a genuine problem.[13]

It is known that the following countries can now produce chemical weapons: Iran, Iraq, Libya, Syria, China, the Koreas, Taiwan and probably Israel. Egypt may also be developing a production capability. The first four producers have particular incentives to add a chemical capability to their *Scud*-B forces, given Israel's nuclear arsenal. It is reported that Syria has already done so. This has caused alarm in Israel, which is within range of Syrian rockets.

The correlation of missile inventories and chemical weapon capability is profoundly disturbing. It compels us to think of ballistic missiles in a wider context than simply as nuclear weapon delivery systems. We examine the military and political impact of this development below.

MILITARY EFFECTIVENESS

From the first days of the Second World War, ballistic missiles have held great allure for military planners. Missiles provide a prompt way to deliver warheads to distant targets. Their delivery cannot be frustrated by air defense systems. To be sure, most strategic thinking has been focused on prompt delivery of *nuclear* weapons by ballistic missiles. But that is how it began, not how it has evolved. If the missile's range and accuracy are adequate for non-nuclear warheads, the same qualities of surprise and assured penetration become appealing for conventional operations.

The question then arises: How much payload and accuracy are required to make non-nuclear warheads threatening? The numbers are somewhat surprising. A *Scud*-B can carry 1,200 lbs. of VX agent to a distance of 180 miles. If this chemical agent is released at 4,000 feet, it will produce 50% casualties over a strip 0.3 miles by 2.5 miles oriented along the wind direction.[14] This capability could be effective against an airfield.

A one thousand pound high explosive warhead can destroy buildings 150 feet away and kill personnel within 300 to 400 feet of the point of impact. The 4,500 lb. warhead planned for the Saudi missiles would double this lethal range. Cluster bombs further enhance these effects by detonating a large number of submunitions over a large area, thereby providing a blanket rather than point explosion.[15]

Let us compare these requirements with the impact accuracies that are likely to be achieved in emerging missile programs. A first approximation is obtained by using the velocity accuracy of inertial instruments employed in aircraft navigation systems.[16] A velocity error of 2 to 4 feet per second after a long flight is typical of such systems. At a range of 200 miles, a ballistic missile using instruments of the same accuracy would yield a CEP of 800 to 1,600 ft. For a ballistic missile traveling to 500 miles, the CEP would vary from 1,200 to 2,500 ft. However, these estimates are probably unduly conservative.[17]

Twenty years ago, American inertial guidance systems could control velocity cutoff error to 0.6 feet per second or better. It is likely that this technology has diffused to much of the Third World by now. At a range of 500 miles, such an instrument quality would give a miss of 400 or less feet. At 200 miles, it would be about 300 feet. Such estimates provide sufficient assurance to make high explosive warheads effective against point targets. With cluster bombs or chemical weapons, this degree of accuracy is adequate against troops or populations.

Without overselling the capability, we can say that short-range missiles with guidance systems available to developing countries can provide militarily significant delivery for non-nuclear warheads. The traditional preoccupation of policy officials with nuclear proliferation has tended to obscure this result.

All of the missiles shown in Table 2 have payloads of 1,000 to 2,000 lbs. This is adequate for most nuclear warheads that are likely to be available to the Third World.[18] Moreover, these systems can carry conventional warheads which are militarily significant. The other variables—range and geography—are analyzed below.

1. *Egypt* – With its *Scud*-B missiles, Egypt can reach most targets in Israel and Jordan. If it acquires a 500-mile missile it will be able to attack targets in Syria and U.S. bases in Greece and Turkey.

2. *Iran* – Iran launched several hundred attacks against Baghdad with its *Scud*-B missiles. The same missile can reach Kuwait, Bahrain, Qatar and Turkey, but few interesting targets in Pakistan or Afghanistan.

3. *Iraq* – Iraq reached Tehran by extending the range of its *Scud*-B missiles. This capability now could threaten Syria, Israel, Jordan, Egypt, Turkey and the Gulf States.

4. *Israel* – If the *Jericho* II has a range of 900 miles, it is able to reach all of Egypt, Syria, Jordan, Iraq, Tehran, Turkey and the Gulf States, and a few targets in the Southern part of the USSR.

5. *Libya* – The current inventory of *Scud*-Bs threaten only Southern Tunisia and Western Egypt—areas that are lightly populated. Libya would seem to be a strong customer for longer range missiles. If it acquires a 500-mile missile, it could hit targets in Italy, Egypt and parts of Israel.

6. *Saudi Arabia* – With their new long-range Chinese missiles, the Saudis can project their missile forces over a wide area: From Tripoli in the west; to Israel; to Kenya in the South; and Iran, Iraq, Pakistan, and Afghanistan and a few cities in India to the east. U.S bases in Greece and Turkey are within its reach, as are targets in the southern part of the USSR.

7. *Syria* – Their *Scud*-Bs cover all of Israel, Lebanon and important targets in Jordan, but very little of Iraq.

8. *North Yemen* covers *South Yemen* and vice versa.

9. *South Africa* – If South African test missiles launched from the Kalahari are designed to land near the facility in Marion Island, this would suggest a range of at least 1,000 miles, which would put much of southern Africa within range of a missile force.

10. *India* – With its 1,500-mile missile, India can cover the western half of China, Iran, Pakistan, the Gulf States, Southeast Asia, U.S. bases in the Indian Ocean and targets in the southern USSR.

11. **Pakistan** – Will be able to reach targets in New Delhi and Ahmadabad in India if it fields a 200-mile missile.
12. **Taiwan** – Can reach Shanghai and Canton if it develops a 500-mile missile.
13. **South Korea** and **North Korea** cover each other's territories with their ballistic missiles.
14. **Afghanistan** – Can reach targets in the West of Pakistan with *Scud*-Bs deployed in Kabul.
15. **Argentina** – Can reach the Falkland Islands with a 500-mile missile, all of Chile, Uruguay, and Paraguay but very little of Brazil.
16. **Brazil** – Can reach most of its neighbors in South America from some point in Brazil with the 500-mile missile it is trying to develop, but Buenos Aires seems just out of this range.

There is another dimension to military effectiveness. It is psychological rather than technical. It is the effect that ballistic missiles have upon civilian populations and their will to continue to support a war. History records two wars that used ballistic missiles in large numbers, each with telling psychological effect. Germany launched almost 1,000 V-2 ballistic rockets against England in World War II. They were not very accurate, but they carried a 2,000 lb. warhead and had a significant effect on civilian morale as an instrument of terror. An equivalent number of missiles were launched with similar effect in the "War of the Cities" during the Iran-Iraq war with similar effects. Despite the terrible slaughter which already had occurred at the front, the sudden arrival of ballistic missiles at Tehran and Baghdad is thought to have played a significant role in accelerating the peace process.

POLITICAL EFFECTIVENESS
AND POLICY IMPLICATIONS

The transition of new states into the missile age will have political repercussions well before these countries' programs achieve commensurate military significance. Ballistic missile production programs provide a tangible example of the dedicated efforts by developing countries to acquire the means to prosecute national ambitions immune from the dictates of the great powers. With several developing states already providing technical assistance to other Third World producers, missile proliferation may become increasingly a matter of intra-Third World diplomacy. This could circumscribe the ability of the industrial powers to impose meaningful trade controls or exert decisive influence over clients' military policies.

Many developing countries apparently do not share our concerns about missile non-proliferation. Expression of such concerns often incur jaundiced accusations of hypocrisy from states whose arsenals are dwarfed by those of the advanced countries. Even as the superpowers are embarking on more ambitious ways to reach accommodations at the strategic level and in Europe, the proliferation of ballistic missiles indicates that the prospects for conflict among heavily armed states in Third World regions may be on the rise. This is especially so in areas where the interests of the superpowers intersect, including the Middle East, the Persian Gulf, and South and East Asia. The decline of great power leverage over clients' force structures may impinge on efforts to reach political accommodations in other areas, including attempts to resolve regional tensions, to stem nuclear and chemical weapon proliferation, and to avoid direct involvement in conflicts which are beyond their control.

In the following section, we discuss the political objectives which countries seek from missile development, the range of policy instruments available to the supplying countries to try to contain the adverse consequences of missile proliferation, and the lessons one could draw for managing the challenges of advanced technology diffusion in the future.

Political Effectiveness

In an international system in which military prowess has always been a leading determinant of national status, it was predictable that Third World nations would try to acquire the most advanced military products available on the international market. In both developed and developing countries, ballistic missiles long have been perceived as providing states with enhanced military power. Despite operational limitations on current models, the attraction of missiles compared to aircraft and naval platforms is their ability to penetrate defenses, their relatively lower demands on infrastructure compared to other advanced weapons (such as aircraft), their utility for non-conventional operations, and the speed with which they can be delivered.

Understanding the implications of the spread of ballistic missiles is complicated by the divergences among missile producing countries. Although states with long-standing enmities account for much of the recent missile acquisitions, the incentives for investing in missile programs do not correlate directly with military threats or reveal much about military intentions. The consequences of missile proliferation will depend on regional and local realities.

Contrary to more dire predictions, the achievement of a fully indigenous capacity to develop advanced ballistic missiles may elude most developing states for many years. Internal and external constraints on Third World programs are forcing frequent interruptions in technological ventures, including slowed or abandoned programs and outright failures. These constraints range from a scarcity of technological resources, domestic political upheavals or international realignments, changing military threats and priorities, chronic fiscal shortages, and external interference by the great powers.

In most instances, Third World development of ballistic missiles is not consonant with traditional criteria of military or economic efficiency. The instabilities associated with deployment of vulnerable missile forces, may actually reduce security, giving enemies incentives to try to attack missiles pre-emptively before they become fully operational. The high cost of missile programs also may divert resources from more critical defense requirements, and actually reduce preparedness and relevant combat capabilities.

The technical difficulties involved in trying to develop components vital to missile development, such as guidance systems, may be compounded by the reduced reliability of systems which are produced indigenously. As such, some states have found themselves condemned to expending scarce resources not only to reinvent the wheel, but with less effectiveness and at a higher cost.

As was the case in the advanced countries in prior decades, however, the capability to produce modern weapons has become the *sine qua non* of modern statehood in the Third World. The principal rationale for producing weapons is the perception of national sovereignty. Despite immense technical and political impediments, the perseverance of key states to achieve missile production capabilities demonstrates that this is neither a transitory nor easily reversible impulse.

In states such as Israel, South Korea, Taiwan, Brazil, Argentina, and India, the defense industrial sector is accorded unique symbolic importance as an indicator of modernization. It exerts a dominant influence on overall scientific and technical priorities. The ability to produce weapons is thought to contribute positively to technical advancement in a number of ways, from providing exposure to modern production and management techniques, to providing experience in the use of such advanced technologies as computers and electronics. Investment in satellites and other space technologies has been valued for its potential contribution to economic development activities, such as communications, weather forecasting, and agricultural exploitation, as well as military applications. Even rudimentary weapon systems or components which are produced indigenously can be a source of export revenues and serve as means of forging new diplomatic relationships.

The shift in developing countries' dependency for imported military goods from weapon systems to components over the last three decades has hastened the pace of technology diffusion. The increasing competitiveness of the international defense technology market, along with the maturation of emerging defense industrial sectors, has given purchasing states latitude to acquire technologies from multiple sources, and to mitigate the effects of supplier restrictions. Even in cases where countries have been denied access to advanced technologies, efforts to develop weapons have proceeded with the assistance provided through an expanding international system of private entrepreneurs and the commercial availability of dual-use components and systems.

In some cases, initiating a missile production program has accorded developing states greater access to weapon imports and co-production agreements from advanced countries in return for slowing or abandoning the project. As is the case for countries with nuclear programs, the preferred (or perhaps only) instrument of dissuasion against missile producers is to provide advanced conventional technologies that are considered less destabilizing. U.S. efforts to halt South Korea's development of a long-range surface-to-surface missile in the 1970s, for instance, were accompanied by compensatory transfers of military equipment and agreements to allow Korean participation in the production of weapons, such as the F-5 fighter. The equipment, infrastructure, and expertise gained from transactions of this kind unavoidably add to a country's latent capabilities to resume missile programs at a later time.

As emerging defense production bases mature, intra-Third World defense cooperation is likely to become a more important variable in international politics. Spurred by an interest in circumventing interference from industrialized nations, Third World countries have formed partnerships for missile and space launch vehicle development, such as the consortium to develop the *Condor* II ballistic missile. Israel's assistance to Taiwan in developing the *Ching Feng* surface-to-surface missile, and the PRC's offer to develop missile prototypes for Middle East countries willing to underwrite the costs of development are further examples. Although these ventures are marriages of convenience for now, cooperative defense arrangements which involve states hostile to the West, such as the reported Chinese-Iranian missile development agreement, may alter international political alignments in adverse ways over time.

The continued spread of missile technology in the Third World poses a number of dilemmas for the United States, not the least of which is the likely impact on the future conduct of U.S. military operations. The growing sophistication of missile arsenals in countries which may be willing to incur the risk of attacking U.S. forces could complicate decisions about whether and when to intervene in regional conflicts. And it could force the United States to take additional steps to protect forces and overseas military installations.

Over time, this trend may exert influence over the composition and organization of forces to address changing regional threats. The authors of the 1988 report, *Discriminate Deterrence*, for example, argue that military developments in the Third World will require a reorientation of U.S. strategy to de-emphasize traditional alliance obligations in favor of a greater focus on regional crises. Third World missiles also have prompted interest in defensive technologies, including anti-tactical ballistic missiles, equipment for troops operating in proximity to chemical weapons, and even a national anti-ballistic missile system to protect the United States against a non-Soviet missile threat.

Restraints on Missile Proliferation: Policy Options

The export of military equipment to the Third World throughout the post-war period has been guided by the common assumption that industrial states would retain sufficient technological superiority to stay ahead of, and to counter potential threats posed by, the growing military capabilities of developing nations. The idea that the international system would remain technologically stratified served as the underpinning of an implicit concept of stability. The provision of conventional armaments traditionally has been the principal means of dissuading states from pursuing nuclear ambitions, and as such, was itself an instrument to ensure a continued military hierarchy between nuclear and non-nuclear states.

Structural changes in the international technology market may be testing the pertinence of traditional definitions of leverage deriving from technological stratification. The international trade in arms has evolved from the provision of obsolescent weapons transferred to close allies in the 1950s to the widespread transfer of state-of-the art military equipment to clients who increasingly demand a share in the production process as an essential *quid pro quo*. Leaving aside the prospect that the acquisition of advanced long-range systems could give states the capability to attack Western military forces with increasing lethality, the use of advanced weapons by combatants in the Falkland conflict and in the Persian Gulf underscored that it is not only the most sophisticated technologies that can pose military risks to the great powers.

In contrast to the relative clarity of objectives which have guided the nuclear non-proliferation regime—simply, to try to prevent new nations from acquiring the means to build and test nuclear weapons—efforts to limit conventional weapons have been plagued by an inability to develop even a modest consensus among the industrialized nations about the degree to which restraint efforts should be allowed to compete with other domestic or foreign policy objectives. The United States and its allies have used a variety of formal and tacit arrangements since World War II to restrict the diffusion of advanced technologies to countries whose objectives are perceived to be inimical. A preoccupation with East-West technology diffusion, however, has tended to overshadow problems posed by the parallel problem of diffusion to newly-industrialized and industrializing countries.

Still, missiles have been singled out for more stringent export controls than is applied to other weapon systems. In part this is because of the linkage between nuclear proliferation and advanced missile delivery capabilities. Surface-to-surface missiles were discussed as possible systems for restraint in the U.S.–Soviet Conventional Arms Transfer negotiations during the Carter Administration. Both the United States and the Soviet Union observed tacit restraint in transferring long-range missiles to allies in Korea and the Middle East throughout the 1960s and 1970s.

President Reagan signed National Security Decision Directive (NSDD-70) in November 1982, calling for the investigation of ways to control missile proliferation. This led to the agreement among seven industrial countries to establish consensual restraint guidelines for missile-related exports, formalized as the Missile Technology Control Regime (MTCR) in April 1987. Both the Reagan and Bush Administrations discussed the problem of missile proliferation in several demarches to the Soviet Union, and have raised the issue with regional security partners as well. Over time, missile restraint has become a more routine part of a broader diplomatic agenda, including the international nuclear non-proliferation regime, efforts to control chemical weapons, and discussions with key states about ways to contain regional military tensions.

Although the MTCR is a significant achievement, the consensual supplier cartel among seven partners is not likely to curtail the global trade in missile technologies over the long run. Unlike institutional arrangements which have evolved for nuclear non-proliferation, such as the International Atomic Energy Agency (IAEA), the MTCR has no international agency to monitor compliance, and no enforcement mechanisms. A more ambitious restraint regime would require a far more ambitious diplomatic infrastructure, and the cooperation of other important suppliers and recipients.

Given the central importance of foreign technology to Third World missile programs, the first issue for the MTCR will be the degree to which signatories actually forego cooperation with new missile producers. Most of the technology needed for guidance, fusing, heat shielding, and other aspects of missile programs continue to come from Western Europe. Though clearly more stringent in its adherence to the MTCR, the United States also contributed, although perhaps unwittingly, to the development of the Iraqi *Sa'ad* 16 missile research and development center, and is about to provide India with technology useful for missile testing.

A recent dispute between the French division of the European aerospace consortium Arianespace and McDonnell-Douglas over a pending contract for rocket technology with Brazil presages the kind of inter-allied commercial competition which may impede coordinated efforts to stem proliferation. Barred from meeting Brazilian requirements by a strict U.S. government interpretation of the MTCR, McDonnell-Douglas has had to cede pending space contracts with Brazil to the Europeans, who apparently accord greater importance to the commercial viability of their own space sector than to concerns about missile proliferation.

Aside from inducing signatories to adhere more strictly to its guidelines, an even greater challenge for the MTCR will be to elicit additional countries to join in, particularly the Soviet Union and China. The Soviets have significant financial and political stakes in missile-related exports, and are not likely to participate in a Western initiative in which they have had no say. At the same time, the Soviet government reportedly has not dismissed the idea of adopting restraint guidelines unilaterally, pending some form of compensation which could include, *inter alia*, U.S. permission for the Soviets to provide space launch services to U.S. companies.

The PRC appears to have modified its policy of permissive missile exports following U.S. objections to the sale of CSS-2 IRBMs to Saudi Arabia. Cosmetic or not, assurances were given to the United States in March 1989 that the PRC would cease exporting ballistic missiles. The PRC's adherence to this stric-ture is in conflict with severe structural pressures to promote exports to finance its own modernization. There is continued evidence of covert Chinese marketing of missiles, including participation in missile ventures in Iran and Pakistan. In the current political climate, any predictions about PRC policy are entirely conjectural.

However desirable in the short-term, controls on missile exports on the part of a few countries have to be understood as exercises in delay. They represent efforts to assert great power prerogatives in a world in which the foundations for such prerogatives are eroding. It is axiomatic that policies which appear to developing countries as discriminatory eventually will be circumvented. Indeed, the global proliferation of ballistic missiles is probably already sufficiently advanced that it cannot be reversed or eliminated, even if some of its most troublesome aspects can be contained.

Any effort to encourage international restraint in the development and use of ballistic missiles will require both carrots and sticks, reducing demand not only by raising the costs to countries engaged in missile programs (the goal of export controls and trade sanctions), but by increasing the perceptions of benefits associated with consent to limitations. Restraint measures ultimately must appeal to states' self-interest, and cannot be seen solely as a crusade among a few countries aimed at preserving their position of privilege.

The focus of U.S. policy has been to prevent technology from proliferating, not on what to do once prevention has failed. In the long-term, efforts to restrain missile programs are likely to be more effective if pursued as part of initiatives to end or contain regional conflicts, identified as one of several policy instruments intended to manage the transition to a world of genuine pluralism, and more codified means of resolving disputes peacefully.

As a first step, the United States and its allies could focus on instruments aimed at containing the adverse consequences of missile programs already underway, to try to develop the foundations for encouraging broader restraint in the future. Confidence and security building measures (CSBMs), including information and intelligence exchanges, reciprocal on-site visits of defense production and space launch facilities, prior notification of missile tests, and other mechanisms to promote consultations among regional rivals could help ease unwarranted suspicions about missile production efforts, limit their political and military consequences, and, perhaps, reduce some of the incentives now propelling the expansion of these programs.

CSBMs can reduce tensions by mitigating the mystery surrounding rivals' military activities, providing channels for routine interaction, and demonstrating adversaries' interests in reassuring other states about their military objectives. Although these instruments are only valuable as indicators of political will and can be violated at any time, they can serve as the beginnings of the diplomatic infrastructure needed for broader accommodations. Examples of existing regional CSBMs include a recent agreement between India and Pakistan not to attack one another's nuclear facilities; the process of on-site visits to nuclear facilities and exchanges of information being pursued by Argentina and Brazil; and informal discussions between the United States and Middle Eastern countries about ways to limit the acquisition and use of missile systems in the region.

More ambitious CSBMs that could be considered include the application of international safeguards and on-site inspections of space launch facilities to ensure they are not being used to develop military systems; the development of an international space launch facility to give countries access to space in return for not developing their own space-launch vehicles; regional export controls, such as an agreement by Brazil and Argentina not to sell missiles to particular countries; and routine military exchanges between rival states to discuss common security concerns.

The United States can play an important role in encouraging regional powers to pursue restraint, although the choice of initiatives ultimately must come from the states themselves and reflect local realities. As was the case in the NPT, the United States is a source of leadership and operational expertise about such mechanisms which are often genuinely unfamiliar to Third World officials. Even U.S. assistance in such prosaic areas as customs enforcement, technical means of assessing force balances, and mechanisms to monitor compliance with restraint agreements can be useful.

The consideration of more ambitious regimes, such as an international missile non-proliferation regime patterned after the NPT, must take into account the extent to which missile programs are already deeply rooted in international politics. The limited number of examples of conscious military restraint among developing countries, like the 1976 Treaty for the Prohibition of Nuclear Weapons in Latin America, does not inspire great optimism for more comprehensive initiatives. No system of international controls has ever been fully articulated, or been deemed a sufficient international priority to elicit enduring support.

Realism need not be a pretext for fatalism. The proliferation of ballistic missiles cannot be reversed or eliminated, but some of its most troublesome aspects probably can be mitigated. As has been demonstrated in the nuclear non-proliferation area and the use of trade controls to protect advanced Western technologies, even an imperfect regime is preferable to one in which the trade in dangerous technologies is left to market forces.

Technology Diffusion in the 21st Century

Ballistic missile proliferation is symptomatic of the diffusion of industrial and military capacity in an international system no longer dominated by a few great powers. The proliferation of ballistic missiles can be seen as a harbinger of more profound alterations in international power alignments in the future, and the declining utility of traditional policy instruments available to the advanced countries to influence international developments.

The underlying question posed by the proliferation of ballistic missiles is how the United States and its allies will balance the imperatives for broader international military and industrial cooperation against the enduring requirement to protect the technological edge on which Western security traditionally has relied. This is a conundrum that has been part of alliance policy throughout the post-war period, the *leitmotif* of the chronic controversies over how best to implement trade controls against military adversaries without unduly penalizing Western economic and political interests.

Devising ways to regulate ballistic missile proliferation could be an important first step toward integrating the problems of North-South technology diffusion into the routine conduct of force planning, long-term threat assessments, and overall trade and industrial policy. Aside from controlling missiles, the real challenge may be to develop durable policy instruments for anticipating the kinds of technological diffusion which could undercut industrial and military interests more severely, and to develop a policy infrastructure which has the flexibility to manage the consequences of such diffusion in constructive ways. If it is too late to reverse the spread of ballistic missiles, perhaps it is still possible to consider ways to temper the pace of proliferation of future generations of military technology, such as stealth, reconnaissance, electronic countermeasures, biotechnology, or directed energy weapons.

The challenges of missile proliferation suggest that significant alterations in the existing policy apparatus may be required to identify which technologies warrant control. As has occurred in the nuclear proliferation area, the focus of conventional weapons proliferation policy is moving towards earlier and earlier stages of the production cycle: from aircraft and missiles, for instance, to guidance and propulsion technology. Over time, the progression will continue to move towards more intangible elements of the manufacturing process, including subcomponents, technical data packages, and expertise.

The complexity of defining pertinent technology and technological processes is accompanied by a progressive attenuation of traditional levers of supplier control. End-use assurances have little relevance to complicated manufacturing processes such as integrated circuitry, where the distribution of the products cannot be monitored. The growing international commercialization of high technology industries may further blunt the ability of governments to exert leverage over patterns of trade. And no one has ever devised effective barriers to the proliferation of scientific and technical knowledge, which recognizes no national borders.

Emerging defense technologies also could increase the difficulty of determining which exports should be subject to regulation. New technologies which are at the cutting edge of Western military modernization, including, *inter alia*, advanced information processing, composite materials, biotechnologies, and space systems, are to varying degrees equally vital to civilian modernization. Advances in biotechnology for pathogens usable in biological warfare, for example, also could be used to develop more efficient agricultural techniques and medicines. Although biotechnologies could be highly destabilizing in a military sense, they could have extremely positive effects on stability in countries where poverty and disease are important determinants of social unrest.

Advanced satellite imaging and electronic intercept capabilities also are likely to be in increasingly high demand in the Third World, not just for targeting and other aspects of military operations, but for enhancing military and political stability, to say nothing of their civilian application. Real time, accurate intelligence made possible by satellites could be vital for countries to get assurance that they are not under attack by adversaries' missile forces, or to get warning of impending attack. Without such capabilities, developing countries may be left subject to the kinds of unstable military conditions which are prompting concern today.

The specific effects of technology dissemination for U.S. and international security will depend on the technology and its destination. Calibrating the competing goals sought from military and dual-use exports against the requirement to protect highly sensitive technologies undoubtedly will be a more complex undertaking in the future. East-West trade controls at least had the benefit of a coherent geographic and political framework, as well as relatively straightforward objectives. In the North-South context, efforts to manage military trade are impeded by the geopolitical diversity of the regions, and by the absence of any common agreement about the desirability and effectiveness of alternative diplomatic instruments. The relatively modest prohibitions covered by the MTCR already have sparked protracted inter-agency and inter-allied frictions over their interpretation.

For all of its limitations, the MTCR should be seen as a constructive first step in the arduous process of developing a bureaucratic and international infrastructure for understanding and managing the challenges of technology diffusion outside the Soviet bloc. Since missile proliferation cuts across traditional boundaries of economic, diplomatic, and military policy, frictions are inevitable. Even in the early days of the Cold War, U.S. efforts to restrict exports to communist nations were opposed by the European countries and Japan, whose commercial interests were cosmetically disguised as principled opposition to a policy of economic warfare against the East. The implementation of COCOM guidelines in the United States, moreover, has been plagued since its inception by protracted interagency disputes over conflicting interpretations of U.S. goals.

The MTCR is only one of several instruments which will have to be brought to bear on the broader problem of technological and military diffusion. In addition to efforts to encourage accommodations among combatant states and to contain the incidence and scope of regional conflicts, managing the transition to a more complex international system will require better coordination of industrial countries' policies towards the Third World, especially to develop a consensus about which technologies are sufficiently critical to Western security to warrant protection from commercial pressures. It must be recognized that the various apparatus guiding security and economic assistance, international space cooperation, and trade and industrial policy cannot continue to operate as if they were separate entities. The global diffusion of advanced technology impinges on all of these areas. It cuts at the heart of military preparedness, economic capacity, technological innovation, and diplomatic stature.

Military developments in the Third World have never been considered as vital as other elements of U.S. containment strategy, coming well after strategic forces and the defense of Europe in order of priority. Indeed, one can still find this subject called simply "other issues" in official analyses of U.S. defense priorities.

In the current international system, the perception of the developing world as a collection of compliant client states is dangerously atavistic. It is time to recognize that there may no longer be any validity to the concept of a "Third World". If it ever existed, it has been replaced by a system of competing regional powers with distinct ambitions and a growing capacity to fulfill those ambitions with or without the sanction of the industrialized nations. As a practical matter, the military challenges posed by developing countries, especially nuclear, chemical, and missile proliferation, have to be considered as part of U.S. military planning, and less exclusively as an arms control issue.

Efforts to work with governments in cooperative ventures to promote stabilizing doctrines and force deployments often has been impeded by the competing notion that this could be construed as legitimation of unwarranted military ambitions. But in the emerging environment, assuming that developing countries' military objectives will continue to be subject to change simply through external coercion could prove far more self-defeating than accepting that these are limitations on U.S. influence and that using that influence judiciously is as vital as it is difficult. The ability to exert influence over developing countries may have been progressively attenuated, but the stakes in-

volved in containing adverse international developments have
never been more urgent.

NOTES

1. A postulated missile gap alleging Soviet deployment superiority was a
    major issue in the 1960 presidential campaign, but was later disproved by
    satellite reconnaissance.
2. With the possible exception of the transfer of *Polaris* and *Trident* subma-
    rines and rockets to the British.
3. There is considerable question as to whether the longer range SS-12, which
    is equivalent to the *Pershing* IA, has actually been provided to Iraq; and
    under what conditions.
4. Imported from the USSR or Egypt and subsequently produced in-country.
5. M. Balaschak, J. Ruina, G. Steinberg and A. Yaron, "Assessing the Compa-
    rability of Dual-Use Technologies for Ballistic Missile Development." MIT
    Center for International Studies, A.C.D.A. Contract # ACOWC 113, 1982.
6. Solid rocket motors are manufactured in the U.S., USSR, U.K., France, Italy,
    Japan, Brazil, Israel, Pakistan, India, Argentina, and perhaps others, in-
    cluding North Korea.
7. Complete INS systems are manufactured in most of the industrial coun-
    tries, and are under development in several Third World states, including
    India.
8. Japan agreed not to convert or transfer the *Delta* it acquired from the United
    States.
9. David B. Ottoway, "Israel Reported to Test Controversial Missile," *Wash-
    ington Post*, September 16, 1989, p. A17.
10. One of the crucial performance characteristics of ballistic missiles is their
    impact accuracy. The strategic contest between the United States and the
    Soviet Union has been dominated by long-range missiles. The ballistic
    missiles that are in the hands of some eighteen smaller countries are of
    short range. In their original form, these missiles did not have great
    accuracy. However, there is abundant evidence of missile modification,
    upgrades and conversions. An important question thus arises:
    "What accuracy can be achieved by the proliferated short-range missiles
    if their guidance systems are progressively improved?"
    The answer to this question determines whether such missiles can
    deliver chemical and high explosive warheads with sufficient accuracy to
    make them militarily effective. Put another way, one can ask if these
    missiles are only effective if they are coupled with nuclear warheads.
    The impact accuracy of ballistic missiles is determined primarily by the
    precision with which the burnout velocity is controlled. If the burnout
    speed is denoted by $_o$, we are interested in the precision with which $_o$ and
    its inclination are controlled. We are also concerned about any normal
    component u of the total velocity that may point out of the trajectory plane
    that connects the launch site and target, since such an error will create cross
    range errors at impact. The velocity vector is usually elevated so as to

achieve maximum range. For short-range missiles, this elevation is 45° with respect to the local vertical. Firing at the maximum range elevation also means that the downrange impact error is insensitive to small variations in this angle, which is a second powerful reason for choosing this setting. The down range impact is thus influenced only by errors in the speed ∂_o and the cross range impact only by velocity components ∂u out of the desired trajectory plane. At short range, one can express these impact errors in terms of the errors in velocity components as follows:

$$\text{Down range Error} = 2 \left\lceil \frac{|R|}{g} \right\rceil^{\frac{1}{2}} \partial_o$$
(1)

$$\text{Cross range Error} = 1.4 \left\lceil \frac{|R|}{g} \right\rceil^{\frac{1}{2}} \partial u$$
(2)

Where g=32 ft/sec² is the acceleration of gravity and R is the actual range of the missile. The factors in front of the velocity errors are called "Error Coefficients" and give the trajectory sensitivity of a ballistic missile impact to its guidance system errors. We tabulate these error coefficients in Table 3 for three different ranges.

Table 3		
R	$\dfrac{\partial R}{\partial_o OO}$	∂O
200 nm	0.064 nm/fps	0.045 nm/fps
500	0.101	0.071
1,000	0.143	0.02

We can apply these error coefficients to estimate the impact accuracy that could be achieved with gyroscopes and accelerometers that are used in commercially available aircraft inertial navigation systems. The MIT study made in 1981 indicates that velocity can be measured to approximately 2 feet per second, with such instruments over a long flight.

$$\partial_o = \partial u = 2 \text{ fps}$$

Multiplying these values by the error coefficients in Table 3.

R 200 nm
∂R	=	0.128 nm
∂CR	=	0.090
CEP	=	0.131
	=	800 ft.

R=500 nm	∂R	=	0.202 nm
	∂CR	=	0.142
	CEP	=	0.206
		=	1,240 ft.

R=1,000 nm	∂R	=	0.286 nm
	∂CR	=	0.204
	CEP	=	0.294
		=	1,800 ft.

In these estimates, we have computed the circular probably error (CEP) using the formula

$$CEP = 0.6[\partial R + \partial CR],$$

which is valid so long as ∂R and ∂CR are about the same.

These estimates are unduly pessimistic, because the instrument accuracy needed for aircraft inertial navigation systems is not great and there is no incentive to do better. Long-range ballistic missiles do have such a need, since their trajectories are extraordinarily sensitive to burnout errors. This requirement has driven the technology for building precision gyroscopes and accelerometers to extraordinary limits, much of which is highly classified. However, the MIT Draper Laboratory prepared an unclassified assessment (David Hoag, "Ballistic Missile Guidance," June 1970) of inertial navigation system accuracy in 1970 for the Department of Defense to use in arms talks with the Soviet Union. This report suggests that the burnout speed errors can be controlled to the following levels or better:

$$\partial_o = 0.6 \text{ fps}$$
$$\partial u = 0.9 \text{ fps}$$

If we combine these estimates with the error coefficients in Table 3, we come to the following impact accuracies:

R = 200 nm	∂R	=	0.038 nm
	∂CR	=	0.041
	CEP	=	0.047
		=	280 ft

R = 500 nm	∂R	=	0.061 nm
	∂CR	=	0.063
	CEP	=	0.074
		=	440 ft

R = 1000 nm	∂R	=	0.086 nm
	$\partial CR=$		0.090
	CEP=		0.106
		=	640 ft

One should be cautioned that the burnout velocity precision estimates on which these impact errors are twenty years old, and there has been enormous technical progress in the last two decades. Moreover, one must recognize that the MIT Report was intentionally conservative so as not to reveal the ultimate capabilities of American inertial technology at the time. The combined result is that the above impact errors must be considered as conservative upper bounds on what can be achieved by short-range ballistic missiles.

11. David B. Ottoway, "Egypt Drops Out of Missile Project," *Washington Post,* September 21, 1989.
12. For additional discussion, see Leonard S. Spector, "Nuclear Proliferation in the 1990s: The Storm After the Lull" (Appendix One of this report).
13. For further discussion of chemical weapon capabilities, see Elisa D. Harris, "Chemical Weapons Proliferation: Current Capabilities and Prospects for Control" (Appendix Two of this report).
14. "Soviet Chemical Weapons Threat," DIA Report, DSI-1620F-051-85 (1985), p. 8.
15. Israel and Brazil both manufacture cluster bombs.
16. Such systems must operate for much longer times than missile units (i.e., 5 to 10 hours vs. 5 minutes) which amplifies accelerometer drift (g) error. On the other hand, a missile experiences much greater acceleration loads than an airplane and this amplifies accelerometer imbalances (g2) errors. It is impossible to sort the two efforts out if the instrument details are not available.
17. Israel launched a satellite into low earth orbit for the first time on September 19, 1988. Given the limited resources for such activities, it is likely that they employed their *Jericho* II ballistic missile to provide the first two stages of the normal three stage space launcher. Steven Gray has analyzed this event in several Livermore studies. Although his analytical technique is different from our own, we now arrive at substantially the same results for the range-payload capability of the two stage *Jericho* II missile.

    The satellite was launched due west from Israel (32° north) with an inclination of 148° measured from the normal satellite launching direction to the east, which takes maximum advantage of the earth's rotation. It was placed in an orbit 250 km by 1,150 km. Gray has studied the available photographs and statements. He concludes that the scientific payload plus a reasonable guidance system weighed 200 kg, and we concur.

    We assume that a solid propellant third stage was added to the *Jericho* II missile. We have estimated the velocity increment that this stage supplied under a range of reasonable assumptions. When we subtract this third stage velocity increase from the known orbital velocity, we obtain the burnout speed of the second stage. This second stage burnout velocity plus the modeled weight of the third stage provides the range payload capability of the two stage *Jericho* II.

    One needs one equation to perform this analysis. It is the velocity increment provided by the third stage operating in vacuum.

    $$v3 = I_{sp}g \log_e \left\lceil \frac{M_o}{M_f} \right\rceil$$

I_{sp} is the specific impulse of the propellants used in the rocket motor, and g is the acceleration of gravity (32 ft/sec2). Mo denotes the initial mass of the third stage and includes the structure, the guidance system, the scientific payload and the solid propellants used in the motor. M_f is the final mass of the third stage and is just M_o less the weight of propellents expended. We judge that the structural weight is no more than ten percent of the stage weight. We assume that the solid propellents expelled into a vacuum provide a specific impulse.

$$I_{sp} = 290 \text{ seconds}$$
(2)

Substituting these values into Equation (1) provides numerical estimates for the velocity provided by the third stage that depend only on the third stage mass M_3.

$$v_3 = 9280 \text{ fps } \log_e \left[\frac{M_3 + 200}{0.1M_3 + 200} \right]$$
(3)

The values of v_3 corresponding to various M_3 values are given in Table 4.

Table 4 Relation of Third Stage Mass and Velocity Impulse	
M_3	v_3
700 kg	10,100 FPS
800	11,800
900	12,400
1,000	12,900
1,100	13,350
1,200	13,800

The next step is to subtract these third stage velocity increments from the known orbital speed that was actually achieved. This provides the burnout speed of the second stage as it might have carried the various third stage assumed in Table 3.

$$v_2 = 27,300 - v_3$$
(4)

The crucial step is to observe that had the two stage missile carried a warhead weighing the same as the third stage, it would have accelerated it to this velocity. Another way to look at this is to note that the third stage would have gone this far if it had not ignited. One can relate burnout speed to range using standard formulas, which produce the range payload performance figures shown in Table 5.

Table 5	Estimated Range-Payload of *Jericho* II Missile	
Throw Weight	**Burnout Speed**	**Range**
900 kg	17,200 fps	1,980 nm
1,000	15,500	1,520
1,100	14,900	1,360
1,200	14,400	1,270
1,300	13,900	1,170
1,400	13,500	1,100

18. U.S. and USSR nuclear warheads are comparatively much lighter. China helped Iran to manufacture three short-range (under 40 miles) ballistic missiles (*Oghab*, *Nazeat*, and *Shahin*-2). Commission on Integrated Long-term Strategy, Regional Conflict Working Group, *Commitment to Freedom: Security Assistance as a U.S. Policy Instrument in the Third World, May 1988.*

Appendix 4

FEASIBILITY OF A CHEMICAL WEAPONS CONTROL REGIME

Kyle B. Olson

The American chemical industry has worked extensively to help the U.S. government complete negotiations on a treaty to ban chemical weapons. The unprecedented industry/government relationship has permitted access by the diplomatic community to technical expertise critical to an understanding and resolution of the outstanding treaty issues.

The proposed convention to eliminate chemical weapons, currently under discussion by a 40-nation conference in Geneva, is remarkable in many respects. The prospect of eliminating an entire weapons type, rather than a subgroup or class (as in the intermediate range missile treaty), the multilateral scope of the treaty, and the complicating aspect of the weapons' recent use in the Middle East; all of these elements make the chemical weapons negotiations unique. Perhaps the most singular dimension of the proposed treaty, however, is the provision calling for an ongoing, permanent system of verification. The rolling text draft of the treaty envisions the creation of a permanent international agency which would police the treaty through a system of reports and inspections of both government and commercial chemical manufacturing and consuming facilities.

While there have been similar efforts on a smaller scale, e.g., the controls on nuclear materials though the International Atomic Energy Agency and the on-site inspections under the

INF, the sheer scope of the chemical industry and the complexity of chemical weapons (CW) verification poses problems of an entirely higher order of magnitude. By some estimates there are as many as 50,000 chemical manufacturing and consuming locations in the United States alone. And the United States represents only about 1/3 of the world's chemical production and consumption.

In order to fully appreciate the complexity of the problem, consider: the difficulty of discerning by observation the differences between a chemical weapons production plant and a peaceful, commercial manufacturing facility; the need to protect legitimate national security information and commercial intellectual property; and the daunting logistics associated with monitoring global implementation of the treaty. Even in a world without limits of time or money, the question of feasibility would demand an answer.

The U.S. chemical industry, through its principal trade association, the Chemical Manufacturers Association (CMA),[1] has been wrestling with the implications of the chemical weapons ban for over a decade. CMA's Board of Directors has taken a strong stand in support of a global, comprehensive treaty that will outlaw the manufacture, possession and use of CW. While supporting such a ban, it has acknowledged on several occasions its concerns over some of the technical issues surrounding verification. Another major issue is the potential cost, both direct and indirect, for industry under the proposed CW regime. These costs include the disruption of production, additional paperwork burdens and, most significantly, the potential loss of intellectual property. Over the last several years, CMA has interacted regularly with its counterparts from Europe, Japan, Canada, and Australia concerning the proposed convention.

This paper has been developed on the basis of original research, discussions with government officials both here and abroad, and the industry's practical experience with domestic and international regulatory enforcement. The paper will address the questions surrounding verification by examining the various groups or "schedules" of chemicals covered by the "rolling text" of the proposed convention, beginning with the least strictly controlled and working to those substances to be virtually banned. The paper will then address more generic technical and logistic issues associated with assuring compliance.[2]

TECHNICAL FEASIBILITY

From a technical point of view, treaty compliance poses a thoroughly fascinating problem. The rolling text essentially sets out three different verification problems. These are:

- Monitor production of Schedule 3 materials (commercial chemicals with chemical weapon potential which are produced on a large scale);

- Verify production of Schedule 2 materials (key chemical weapon precursors) for purposes consistent with the treaty; and

- Verify nonproduction of weapons agents (Schedule 1).[3]

Each of these three tasks is difficult, though for significantly different reasons. It may be that in studying these problems and the implications they pose for verification that a greater understanding of the feasibility question can be gained.

SCHEDULE 3

Schedule 3 verification will primarily be accomplished through the review of data provided to the Technical Secretariat of the international agency by signatory states. This data will, in all likelihood, be reported in an aggregate format. What this means is that rather than identifying individual companies producing Schedule 3 materials or identifying the specific customers receiving that material, the state parties will present a report of national totals produced, consumed, exported, and imported. These numbers will, in turn, be used to produce a world wide "mass balance," i.e. a sort of accountants balance sheet, with each nation being debited and credited in each category. The primary utility of such a mass balance would be to identify unusually large production, consumption, or perhaps most ominously, losses of certain materials in international trade.

To illustrate , assume Country A is a signatory to the convention. Three companies within Country A's borders produce phosgene in an aggregate quantity of 1 million tons. Ten other companies within Country A consume 500,000 tons of phosgene. Country A's companies export 600,000 tons while other companies import 100,000 tons. As a result, Country A will report the following information to the international agency enforcing the treaty:

- phosgene produced – 1 million tons

- phosgene consumed – 500,000 tons

- phosgene exported – 600,000 tons*

- phosgene imported – 100,000 tons

*Aggregate exports will, presumably, be broken down by nation of destination. For example, Country B – 20,000 tons. Country C – 40,000 tons, Country D – 40,000 tons. It is also assumed that imports would be accounted for in the same manner.

Schedule 3 essentially exists as an acknowledgement by the negotiators in Geneva that certain materials are produced in such large quantities and used so widely that attempts to aggressively monitor them would have little chance of success while being terribly resource intensive. It has also been noted that these materials, while perhaps having the potential to be used as chemical weapons agents, are substantially less effective in this application than the nerve agents and mustards found on Schedule 1. The combination of limited military utility and widespread use have resulted in a political decision regarding the degree of control felt necessary for these materials.

As a result, the Schedule 3 regime would be extremely hard pressed to detect a low level, long-term program to build up a stockpile for possible military use. On the other hand, gross deviations from established trading patterns could show up. In addition, apparently aberrant orders could be verified through consultation with the affected state parties who will have more detailed information at their disposal. As will be noted below, definitions of feasibility are very fluid. Nonetheless, the international reporting and monitoring scheme proposed for Schedule 3 seems not only feasible, but inexpensive in implementation. Given the costs of the other treaty provisions, being able to adequately verify this production "on the cheap" is a major attribute.

Critics of the system of verification, reporting, and monitoring for Schedule 3 have noted that a nation determined to cheat could easily falsify its declarations of production and consumption, particularly as they apply to transactions which are wholly domestic in nature. While this might be true, and could be rather easily done in a closed, non-market economy state, there is generally a variety of independent sources of data, both public and private, which can be used to cross check the information being provided to the international authority. Again, given the relative inefficiency of Schedule 3 materials, it is unlikely that a state would choose to place its emphasis on developing weapons in this category.

SCHEDULE 2

In many ways, verification of nonproduction of Schedule 2 materials for weapons purposes is the thorniest of the problems associated with the proposed convention. On the one hand, the key precursors identified in that list also have significant commercial applications. Depending on the definitions used (more on this later), Schedule 2 materials are produced at perhaps hundreds of locations around the world and utilized by hundreds more. Each signatory state will be required to identify and declare all such facilities as part of its compliance with the convention. Such declarations will include not only information on the location of the facility, but also data on the quantities of Schedule 2 chemicals produced and/or consumed at that location. These declarations will subsequently be verified by inspection teams from the technical secretariat.[4] These teams will attempt to prove both a positive and a negative:

- That the plant is producing the materials and the quantities stated in its declaration, and

- That the plant is not exceeding its declared quantities nor producing prohibited materials (Schedule 1).

Both exercises pose problems. Verification of production will call primarily for the skills of an experienced accountant, in that inspectors will be forced to rely upon the documents and records in the plant concerning raw materials, production, work schedules, and shipments of finished product as the most important instruments available to them. No matter how expert he or she may be, a chemical engineer cannot simply look at a reactor vessel and gauge how much material has or has not been generated during the preceding year—perhaps top end capability, but not actual production, which is a function of many other factors. This is time consuming and specialized work requiring the talents of an auditor, a chemical engineer, and perhaps a forensic pathologist thrown in for good measure.

An obvious concern is that a country or a facility intent on violating the treaty could convincingly falsify the records and thus camouflage illegal production. While undoubtedly the case, one might question whether any state would choose to use a declared facility for illicit weapons manufacture in the first place. The very fact that on-site inspections will take place is a significant deterrent. In fact, the use of undeclared facilities to circumvent the treaty is a far more substantial source of concern. Nonetheless, the paper audit will be far more valuable and far better focused in western facilities than will the various sampling and measuring activities in the production facility itself.

The distinction between western countries and those in the Third World or Eastern Bloc is made because of the vast amount of corroborative evidence available to a paper auditor. Among these bits of evidence are the numerous environmental and safety and health driven reporting requirements mandated by U.S., European, Japanese and other national government regulations. The situation may be different in the South and East, where documentation and corroborative evidence may be more difficult to come by. In particular, the less sophisticated reporting and record keeping standards of some industrial Third World industries and, conversely, the Soviet penchant for making all the numbers come out right will make the problem more difficult.

The inspection of actual production facilities and the taking of samples from various points in that facility will produce information that, at best, may suggest violations and which will, more often, serve only as a demonstration of the Technical Secretariat's authority to enter and examine the workings of declared facilities. Much has been made of the need to secure transport and analyze the samples taken as part of an on-sight inspection. This is primarily a question of logistics with the majority of the remaining questions centering on means of assuring adequate protection of the data from a confidentiality standpoint. This issue should not be minimized. The chemical industry has important and legitimate concerns over the collection of data regarding its intellectual property and the handling of same.

To address the other facet of this compliance problem, the proving of the negative, the inspection team will be forced to rely heavily on in-plant examinations. Given that some records will be off limits to the verification team in the interests of preserving confidentiality, the paperwork could be essentially useless for this purpose. It is here that sampling and equipment inspections could pay dividends, though again the likelihood of a nation utilizing a declared Schedule 2 facility as a weapons production plant seems remote. (That, of course, is precisely because the facility is declared and subject to routine inspections in the first place.)

The analytical work associated with verification, including the taking, sealing and transportation of samples, and the actual scientific appraisal is relatively straight forward, at least in terms of detecting constituent chemicals. Modern gas chromatographs routinely identify materials at levels approaching parts per trillion. (This is the equivalent of standing out in space and picking out one inch segments of a line 15,000,000 miles long!) The problem will lie in interpreting the results of analysis. For example, if an analysis of waste streams samples taken from a consuming plant resulted in an anomaly at levels of 1 or 2 parts per billion or even trillion, how would the inspectorate and the treaty signatories react? Our increasingly sophisticated analytical capabilities raise the prospect of false positives to the level of near certainty. While it represents a political question, the resolution of such matters will have significant impacts on the procedures observed by the personnel of the technical secretariat.

SCHEDULE 1

Finally, there is the technical issue associated with verification of the controls placed on production of Schedule 1 materials. Given the tightly controlled nature of the facilities which will be allowed to participate in such production, this activity should present very few technical problems. Again, in terms of verifying the presence or absence of Schedule 1 materials which might be produced illicitly at a declared facility or other facility inspected under the treaty (see the discussion of ad hoc inspections below), the analytical methods are there. Schedule 1 materials, in particular, have the verification virtue of being extremely nasty and therefore relatively easy to discern from other materials.

RESOURCES

If we acknowledge that the technology probably exists to verify a chemical weapons ban, it is still necessary to come to grips with the question of how best to equip the international agency to be created by the treaty. In the last year or so, a growing appreciation for the magnitude of the problem, and the levels of funding and manpower necessary to adequately verify treaty compliance, has pushed the annual operating estimates for the international authority into the 200–300 million dollar range. These numbers assume a verification regime which attempts to visit all declared production and consumption facilities (Schedule 2) on a regular and perhaps annual basis.

The international agency will also monitor the destruction of existing CW stocks, the operation of the few government Schedule 1 facilities producing such materials for research, and challenge inspections.

Finally, the agency's Technical Secretariat will also have to staff and maintain chemical analysis laboratories; many industry experts believe a 1:1 ratio of lab support to inspectors will be necessary.

None of these activities, however, are as potentially demanding of resources as the proposed extension of verification to non-declared facilities, both military and commercial. Negotiators in Geneva are currently looking for a mechanism that would send inspectors into such locations in order to guard against clandestine production. Proposals for an "ad hoc" regime have been offered by the Federal Republic of Germany and the United Kingdom, which, while differing in detail, are similar in that they both vastly expand the number of sites subject to inspection. It is very likely that the treaty will encompass an "ad hoc" system of some kind, though the regime is still subject to considerable development. Such inspections will probably need to be more narrowly drawn than routine or challenge inspections. Inspectors will not have site-specific agreements to work from or detailed declarations of production to verify. It is likely that the goal of ad hoc inspections will simply be to demonstrate the absence of Schedule 1 or 2 chemicals at a distinct facility within a larger site. This should be a task which can be accomplished with minimum intrusion and disruption. More detailed follow-ups would probably require an escalation of the inspection to the far more accusatory challenge level.

In industry's analysis, ad hoc inspections will have a curious effect on the allocation of manpower within the agency. First, inspections of declared facilities will become less and less "rewarding" through repetition in the years following implementation. This means the inspectorate will be tempted to place more and more emphasis on other targets.

Second, if the current proposal for "quotas" for nations interested in calling for such inspections is realized, past experience suggests some nations (including the USA and USSR) will make a point of calling for the maximum number of such visits. This will be done to reinforce their right to call for ad hoc inspections in the future.

Given the zero-sum nature of the equation, each ad hoc inspection means one less routine Schedule 2 inspection. With a system of quotas and the larger number of western nations, this also means more ad hoc inspections could be targeted at the Soviet Union and its allies than towards the U.S. and Europe. This is significant because the current structure of the worldwide chemical industry assures a large majority of "routine" Schedule 2 inspections will be targeted at the West—where the plants are.

Returning to the question of feasibility, it has been suggested that automated monitoring systems could not only better police treaty compliance but also reduce demands on the Inspectorate's manpower. The Soviet Union has been particularly enthusiastic on this point in its comments in Geneva.

There are problems with this thinking. After years of experience with remote sensors and recorders in industry, the overwhelming consensus of industry experts is that things break. Any monitor would need to be maintained, presumably by representatives of the international agency. Since many Schedule 2 facilities are "batch" plants, which change their products on a regular basis, any monitor would need to be recalibrated regularly as well.

Although a smart, robust monitor system is certainly not beyond our technology today, pulling that hardware together will require research and development. This will pose an additional drain on the international agency's bank account.

A final factor, which also impacts technical feasibility, concerns the number of chemicals to be monitored. While the schedules in the rolling text of the draft convention are fairly brief, the use of classes or families of chemicals, such as organo-phosphorous compounds with ethyl or methyl bonds, expands the list to potentially thousands of materials. While most have not even been synthesized, the extension of the schedules in this manner can profoundly complicate verification, from the targeting of inspections to the analysis of samples. An additional factor is the cloud placed over legitimate research into the commercial uses of schedule materials.

One approach to the problem might be to limit the lists to specific materials but retain a flexible system for case-by-case expansion. The treaty is designed to outlaw intent, anyway; the schedules primarily exist as an administrative tool.

In any event, the range of facilities and materials actively addressed by the convention will define the resources needed.

POLITICAL

The final area in which feasibility must be questioned is the political. Given all the foregoing and admittedly optimistic assertions regarding the technology of verification, and assuming financial support adequate to do the job right, the following point will always be true:

Verification is not and cannot be foolproof.

A state which is determined to obtain CW can and will do. It may be difficult and it could be somewhat more expensive, but it can be done. This is a function of the relatively low-technology needed to produce simple weapons and the availability of basic materials.

Politically, then, is a treaty feasible? It has been argued that the moral force of a treaty is important enough in its own right to justify the convention politically. While this may be correct, the fact is that what may be acceptable to the United States or Soviet Union may not work for Israel or Chad.

Given the minor role CW plays in their arsenals and the sophistication of their defenses against attack, the superpowers might be satisfied with a confidence level of, for instance, 75%. That is, a verification regime that has a 25% chance of missing a violation. Attacks against their forces, which are already unlikely, become even more remote improbabilities.

A smaller state confronted by an aggressive neighbor is going to need stronger assurances. This problem remains to be addressed and delves into the question of how to punish nations which violate the treaty. Ironclad guarantees will be wanted by small nations with CW stockpiles before they will be willing to renounce them.

This final question, then, is the one which begs an answer and for which none is yet forthcoming. The greater the degree of assurance required, the greater the need for an ever more intrusive regime. The more intrusive the regime, the greater the resources needed. The greater the resources needed, the greater the expectations of assurance. And the greater the dissatisfaction with the regime that is imperfect.

CONCLUSIONS

A chemical weapons ban is feasible if certain limitations are recognized as inevitable. The questions of resources and political acceptability are more problematic than are the technical; even there, however, considerable work remains to be done.

A comprehensive chemical weapons ban should be pursued, but even a ten year phase-in, as called for in the rolling text, may represent an optimistic timetable.

NOTES

1. CMA is a non-profit trade association whose members represent more than 90% of the basic chemical production in the United States. CMA has been involved in efforts to control chemical weapons for over a decade. Early efforts primarily consisted of industry comments on proposed treaty concepts and language, with the focus on the technical feasibility of certain approaches to control and verification.
    Over the last several years, CMA efforts have broadened to include other issues of importance to the treaty, including the development of on-site inspection procedures and the creation of a "resource group" of senior corporate analytical chemists. This latter group has considered the problem of sample analysis and the possibility of developing remote monitoring equipment.
    A key industry concern is the protection of confidential information which will be turned over to the international agency to be created by the convention. Information on a company's production plans, capacities, customers, process design and other operating parameters could be extremely valuable to a competitor. International patent law is still, at times, an uncertain shield, with many companies choosing to leave certain trade secrets unpatented in order to better protect them. The diplomatic community in Geneva has, after years of discussion, taken steps to address this issue. Provisions on confidentiality which move the treaty in a helpful direction were added to the Rolling Text of the Treaty in August of this year.

The sense of many observers is that the negotiators appreciated the multi-million dollar price tag attached to potential trade secret losses. Another factor was the growing awareness that the same language could protect *state* secrets just as well as those of corporations. Also see P. Doty's "Policy Issues in Chemical Weapons Control" (Appendix Five of this report). An additional group of materials, known as super-toxic lethal chemicals, has been discussed for consideration as a Schedule 4. While not useful for CW purposes, the equipment used in their production could be converted to weapons production. This approach has very little support in Geneva, having been eclipsed by interest in ad hoc inspections. For a look at how an inspection might be conducted, see the attached report on the National Trial Inspection conducted by the United States at a chemical plant in West Virginia in early 1989.

2. Also see P. Doty's "Policy Issues in Chemical Weapons Control."
3. An additional group of materials, know as super-toxic lethal chemicals, has been discussed for consideration as a Schedule 4. While not useful for CW purposes, the equipment used in their production could be converted to weapons production. This approach has very little support in Geneva, having been eclipsed by interest in ad hoc inspections.
4. For a look at how an inspection might be conducted, see the report on the National Trial Inspection conducted by the United States at a chemical plant in West Virginia in early 1989, Conference on Disarmament Report CD/922, 22 June 1989.

Appendix 5

POLICY ISSUES IN
CHEMICAL WEAPONS CONTROL

Paul Doty

After nearly a decade of formal discussions and negotiations a Convention on Chemical Weapons is nearing completion in Geneva. Its goal is a complete ban on the development, production, acquisition, possession, transfer, or use of chemical weapons. It is being negotiated by the delegations of 40 nations and may be ready for signature in one to two years. The Convention's main outline and most of its detailed procedures are now agreed upon. Following completion of the draft Convention, several years may be required to obtain the requisite signa- tures and subsequent ratifications. During this time the organization for implementing the treaty would be formed and trained. This organization will be required to carry out many and complex verification procedures required by the Convention. Upon ratification and coming into force, a ten year period is prescribed in which all chemical weapons, chemical weapons production facilities and all but a small quantity of chemical agents will be destroyed. Through inspections, surveillance and verification procedures, this state of affairs is to continue on a permanent basis.

This Convention would set in motion a worldwide or near worldwide commitment to control chemical weapons that is more extensive and more intrusive than that attempted by any other treaty heretofore. It will involve the formation of the largest administrating and implementing organization in arms control. Its success would insure the removal of a potentially major weapon of war from the world's arsenals and with this the elimination of an important path of conflict escalation.

It is therefore timely and prudent that the system of control that is being negotiated become widely understood, the remaining issues examined and informed judgments made.

This paper will note some of the basic facts on chemical weapons and their deployment, summarize briefly the negotiating history of the Convention, identify the major features agreed upon, indicate the remaining issues in the negotiation, relate the recent U.S.–USSR agreements, and comment on the overall security issues.

This menu omits two very important aspects of chemical weapons control that are being treated in separate papers: (1) that of the capabilities of countries who have recently acquired chemical weapons capability and that of proliferation of chemical weapons to countries not now possessing them (treated by Elisa Harris in Appendix Two); and (2) the increased feasibility of a chemical weapons ban due to progress made in controlling or banning the production and trade in chemicals that are weapons-capable, or serve as precursors to the manufacture of such chemicals (treated by Kyle Olson in Appendix Four).

To provide further background, reference should be made to two current reviews,[1] the sections on chemical weapons from the last three Strategic Surveys of the International Institute for Strategic Studies (IISS),[2] and three recent Op Ed pieces covering differing views.[3]

CHEMICAL WEAPONS BACKGROUND

The chemical agents used in chemical weapons fall into differing categories according to their physiological impact: nerve, skin (blister), lungs (choking), blood, irritant/emetic, and hallucinogens. Such agents exist as liquids or vapors that can be dispersed from artillery shells, bombs, missile warheads, or sprayed from low-flying aircraft. Their effectiveness depends not only on their intrinsic lethality or incapacitating ability, but very strongly on the effectiveness of dispersal following release from the munition and meteorological conditions such as wind and rain.

An earlier Report of the Aspen Strategy Group and the European Strategy Group[4] summarized their military usefulness as follows:

"As battlefield weapons, the military value of chemical weapons lies less in their leathality than in their ability to disrupt or delay an adversary's combat operations. Chemical weapons could be used by the attacking side to produce panic and prompt casualties among unprotected troops; to force the other side into a cumbersome protective posture that reduces force effectiveness; or to deny access to, or easy use of, key facilities such as airfields, ports, supply depots, or command centers. . . .

"Chemicals are not without their drawbacks, however. Chemical attacks are inherently sensitive to the topological characteristics of the target area and to local weather conditions—barometric pressure, wind patterns, precipitation—that are beyond the control of local commanders. For these reasons, the effectiveness of chemical attacks will always be hard to predict. Another problem is downwind drift. Depending on the size of an attack and the wind velocity, military planners must prudently assume a downwind hazard—not only to civilians and enemy troops, but also to friendly forces—of potentially tens of kilometers in range. Finally there is the issue of defensive responses to chemical weapons. The toxic effect of all known chemical agents can be greatly reduced or defeated for periods of time with the expeditious use of chemical weapons protective measures. Beyond a rate of fire that forces the other side to 'suit up' with defense gear, additional chemical weapons munitions are less effective than the lethal effect of a corresponding inventory of high explosive munitions."

To appreciate the scale involved in military use of chemical weapons, we quote from Meselson's review (see footnote 1):

"Under common meteorological conditions, approximately one ton of nerve agent or approximately 10 tons of blister agent is sufficient to cause heavy casualties to unprotected personnel within a square kilometer, and additional casualties down wind. The delivery of one ton of nerve agent by 155 mm artillery, for example, would require firing some 300 projectiles. This makes nerve agents competitive with or superior to conventional high explosive munitions for the attack of troops lacking anti-chemical protection. The situation is reversed, however, if the target personnel are wearing gas masks and protective clothing. . . ."

A valuable review of chemical weapons is to be found in the *Military Balance 1988–89* of IISS.[5]

Among the industrialized countries only the Soviet Union and the United States maintain chemical weapons arsenals and these are very large. Recent disclosures set the Soviet stockpile at 50,000 agent tons and that of the Unites States at about 30,000. Much of this is not in the form of munitions, but stored in bulk. The U.S. stocks were produced in the 1950s and 1960s. A part of this is becoming unoperational and destruction has begun; other parts remain usable indefinitely. Destruction turns out to be very expensive, being estimated at more than one billion dollars per 10,000 tons. Soviet production continued until recently; their plans to begin destruction have encountered substantial delays.

The United States has maintained a deterrent chemical weapons stockpile in the Federal Republic of Germany (FRG) for a long time. The size is classified but various public estimates put it at about 500 agent tons. This would provide for several days use according to training doctrine. The Soviet Union claims that none of their chemical weapons is deployed in Eastern Europe but it could be brought forward rather easily.

Because of the rise of public opposition to chemical weapons in the FRG, President Reagan promised Chancellor Kohl to remove the chemical weapons by 1992 or possibly sooner. As a result we would not have any chemical weap-ons deterrent in Europe. It could be returned, in principle, if the FRG chancellor requested it in a crisis. But in a crisis it is unlikely that it would have high enough priority to be transported.

Since the U.S. production of chemical weapons ceased in 1968 and it was known that the existing chemical weapons arsenal would deteriorate in time, new munitions were planned. A new binary form in which two chemicals are mixed to form the chemical weapons agent during flight of the munition finally won congressional support after a decade of delay. Production of artillery shells of this type has begun, but the development of a bomb for air delivery is encountering great difficulties. Continued funding for both munitions is uncertain.

NEGOTIATING THE CONVENTION

Although discussions of controlling chemical weapons has a long history, the present course began with exploratory discussion in 1968 at the Committee on Disarmament in Geneva. Negotiations began in earnest in 1984 partly in response to a detailed U.S. draft treaty being tabled by then Vice-President Bush who had taken a strong personal interest in this matter.

The negotiations accelerated in 1987 for several reasons: The Soviets admitted, for the first time, that they possessed chemical weapons and claimed to have just ceased production; U.S., Soviet, and British delegations exchanged visits to each other's chemical weapons facilities; the Soviets accepted the principle of challenge inspection: and they provided their own figure on the amount of chemical agents in their stockpile. These developments together with the rapidly growing concern of actual use of chemical weapons in the Iraq-Iran War, beginning in 1983, and the growing proliferation of chemical weapons in the Third World have stimulated a quickened interest in concluding the Convention.

It should be noted that the negotiations in Geneva are by a 40-member Ad Hoc Committee representing the Conference on Disarmament. But since so many problems involve only the United States and the USSR, these two countries carry out parallel bi-lateral discussions and make recommendations when they agree to the Ad Hoc Committee.

Since 1987 more developments have contributed to an upsurge of interest in completing this negotiation. A listing of some of these gives a sense of how much movement is taking place.

• Further use and presumed improvement of chemical weapons by Iraq in 1987 and early 1988 and growing concern over the inadequacy of the protests.

• The failure to stem the export of chemical weapon precursors and production facilities as illustrated by the large plant built in Libya with international aid.

• The estimate of CIA Director Webster that as many as 20 countries may be developing chemical weapons.

• Numerous trial inspections of chemical plants in various countries (now 16) help illuminate the requirements for effective on-site inspections.

• Meetings of chemical manufacturers from most industrialized nations to help in defining what inspection of declared facilities require, and what chemicals should be subject to inspection.

• An Australian initiative has brought together 19 industrialized countries in a chemical suppliers' group that agrees not to sell a limited list of chemicals and equipment related to chemical weapons.

• The shift in the position of the French government from insisting on retention of a minimal amount of chemical weapons to agreement with a total ban.

• President Reagan's focus on chemical weapons control in his final appearance before the United Nations.

• The Paris Conference on Chemical Weapons convened by Mitterrand (January 1989) which brought together representatives of 149 countries in a consciousness-raising appeal for a speedy conclusion of the Chemical Weapons Convention.

- The assumption of the presidency of the United States by Bush, who had long championed a chemical weapons convention and who has frequently reaffirmed the very high priority he gives it.

- The U.S. destruction facility began operation in May 1988. The completion of the Soviet destruction facility is expected by the end of 1989.

- In mid-1989, 75 senators (including a majority of both parties) sent Mr. Bush a letter urging the conclusion of of the Convention. And more recently the House voted a nonbinding resolution to this effect, 441 to 4.

- Remarkable progress in mid-1989 in reducing the differences between the Soviet Union and the United States in the draft treaty.

The present state of negotiations is represented by a "rolling text" of a draft Convention approaching 200 pages containing roughly 85% of agreed text and 15% of alternate phrasing or blank spacing. The narrowing of differences between the United States and the USSR is essential but not sufficient for completing the Convention. Now that a Convention seems a real possibility, many Third World countries are becoming keenly interested in seeing what the Convention will mean to them and their current plans.

Clearly there are diverse interests among the many participating delegations and some time will be required to resolve these quite apart from remaining U.S.–Soviet differences. For example, a number of the Middle East nations have voiced reluctance to ban chemicals without addressing the regional nuclear problem. Other Third World countries imply that since they are not involved in such weaponry, they should not share in the cost of implementing a treaty, or should receive some compensation for going along. Most industrialized countries want assurances that inspection of chemical plants will not divulge proprietary information. The United States and some other nations want certain classified areas to be excluded from search.

WHAT HAS BEEN AGREED

Any attempt to extract from the incomplete "rolling text"[6] the main agreements is subject to some uncertainty due to the extreme condensation and subjective judgments required in making a brief list. With this caveat, the Convention binds each party as follows.

- Not to develop, produce, otherwise acquire, stockpile, or retain chemical weapons; not to assist others in producing chemical weapons; not to use chemical weapons; to destroy chemical weapons in its possession; and to destroy production facilities.

- To adopt a definition of chemical weapons that includes in addition to super-toxic lethal chemicals, certain other lethal chemicals and precursors as well as munitions and related devices, but allowing certain exceptions that do not violate the intent of the Convention.

- To declare whether it has under its jurisdiction or control chemical weapons, chemical weapons production facilities, chemical weapons R&D sites, or whether it has transferred chemical weapons to anyone since a given date and to specify the location and inventory of any chemical weapons and plans for its destruction.

- To permit systematic international on-site inspection to verify declarations of chemical weapons and related production facilities.

- To undertake the destruction of all chemical weapons beginning within 12 months and ending within 10 years.

- To close all chemical weapons production facilities within 3 months and to destroy them within 10 years.

- To permit systematic on-site inspection and continuous technical monitoring with instruments of declared chemical weapons stocks, closed production facilities, and the verification of their destruction.

- To permit systematic on-site inspection and technical monitoring of chemical industry facilities producing and using key chemical weapons precursors in legitimate activities.

- To accept an international "Organization for the Prohibition of Chemical Weapons," with an international inspectorate to carry out the Convention's inspection and monitoring provisions.

- To accept the procedures in the Convention for consultation, cooperation, fact-finding, and judgment to be applied to suspected violations.

Such is an outline of the main agreements as of September 1988. Shortly thereafter, a widening interest in the Convention was shown by Libya, Syria, Bangladesh, Malaysia, North Korea and South Korea, requesting observer status at the Ad Hoc Committee. Early in 1989 some progress was made on outstanding issues: how to maintain confidentiality during verification of non-production of chemical weapons in the chemical industry; and how challenge inspections were to be conducted. But judged by the interest and momentum displayed at the Paris Conference in January 1989, the accomplishments in Geneva in the first half of 1989 were modest due in part to the U.S. National Strategic Review that had to be completed before any U.S. positions could change. Nevertheless several delegations began urging that the end of 1990 be set as the deadline for completing the draft Convention.

REMAINING MAJOR ISSUES TO BE NEGOTIATED

By late spring of 1989 there seemed to be agreement that the remaining major issues were:

1. *The order of destruction of existing chemical weapons stocks and chemical weapons production facilities.* Although the majority of problems here concern the United States and the USSR, other countries are concerned. For example, if a coun-

try has only one production facility, when should it be destroyed in the ten year period if the condition of undiminished security during the transition period is to be met?

2. *The nature of challenge inspections.* Although there was wide agreement (but with major exceptions) on the need for mandatory challenge inspections there were wide differences on the details such as how they would be initiated, the specificity of the request, who should do the inspecting, the time lapse before access to the facility is guaranteed, and who does the reporting and the assessing.

3. *What data (on locations and inventories of chemical weapons stocks and production facilities) is to be exchanged and should this data be verified prior to concluding the Convention or afterwards.* U.S. Senate ratification may depend on confidence in knowing the size and location of Soviet stocks.

4. *The effective monitoring of non-production.* This is particularly challenging when many thousands of chemical facilities will require monitoring and the production, use and transport of dozens of chemicals will need to be controlled. Should overflights, air and water sampling be included in the control techniques to be applied?

5. *The nature of the organization to implement the Convention.* It is envisaged that a Preparatory Commission would begin developing the required capabilities upon completion of the draft Convention or even earlier. The overall responsibility will rest with a General Conference composed of delegates from each adhering nation: it is agreed there will not be a right of veto. The Executive Council shall be the executive organ of the General Conference and will be aided by a Technical Secretariat. The membership of the Executive Council is not yet determined and will be crucial since it must be broadly representative, including representative of countries having major chemical plants, and yet be small enough to get business done. In addition agreement is needed on the procedures to be used to insure the effectiveness of investi-

gations of suspected violations and maintaining high competence in the required monitoring and inspections.

6. *Financing the Convention.* Although the high costs of destruction are to be borne by the countries possessing chemical weapons stocks and production facilities, the financing of the normal operation of the monitoring, verification, and other functions of the organizations implementing the Convention is likely to be of the order of 50–300 million dollars annually. Difficult decisions on trade-offs between additional activities and budget limitations can easily be foreseen. These essential arrangements remain to be settled.

7. *The completion of the lists (schedules) of the three groups of chemicals to be controlled.* The procedures for revising these lists also needs to be settled.

8. *Assistance in case of chemical weapons attack or threat of attack.* To what extent shall the Parties to the Convention react in event of violations, attacks, or threats of attack remains to be determined.

9. *Maximizing adherence to the Convention.* What steps shall be taken to secure universal adherence? How many signatories will be required to bring the Convention into force? Should sanctions and other measures be imposed on countries who do not adhere? In the event of significant and prolonged non-adherence, should allowance be made for minimal chemical weapons stocks to be retained for deterrent purposes? Beyond these questions lies a more important issue: the willingness of the leading industrialized countries to be understanding and sensitive to the concerns and interests of the less developed countries. The developing countries will want to guard against restrictions that they see as unnecessarily binding in the future. Indeed, at issue is the ability of the developed countries to lead in the formation of a worldwide coalition in which all are seen to gain. The failure to do so may risk denying the benefits of the Convention to all.

These nine major issues are imposing and indicate the extensive work required before concluding the Convention. And there remain many lessor issues that will also have to be dealt with. At the present rate of work concluding the Convention by the end of 1990 may well be optimistic. However, as has been the case with other treaties, as the end of negotiations nears, greater resources are put to work, greater political emergencies and deadlines are met.

RECENT U.S.–USSR AGREEMENTS

Progress toward concluding the Convention was very considerably advanced in June and July 1989 by agreement on the first three of the above points being reached by the United States and the USSR. The recommendations that they will make to the Ad Hoc Committee may need revisions before acceptance, but it is widely agreed that a major hurdle has been crossed.

These agreements came in two parts. The first in late June[7] dealt with agreement on a comprehensive exchange of data on chemical weapons, including sites for their storage and production. Further agreement was reached on the order of destruction of these weapons and production facilities over the ten-year period. Finally, the two parties agreed to a very complete, detailed proposal for the conduct of surprise inspections at sites where one country suspects the other of cheating, that is, the challenge inspections.

In the second part of the bilateral agreements[8] the Soviet Union accepted the U.S. demand for detailed inventories and the beginning of on-site inspections to verify the data exchange before the draft Convention is concluded and initialed. The on-site inspections would continue thereafter and would presumably settle the dispute over the size of the Soviet chemical weapons stockpile which is suspected by some to be several times larger than the 50,000 agent tons announced. The Soviet Union indicates that by going this far they want to insure the conclusion of a treaty. Hence they have said it should be possible to proceed to the signing within four months of completing the exchange of information and beginning the on-site inspections.

This is a very short time to carry out the inspections and to reach agreement with other delegations who may find the procedures adopted by the Soviet Union and the United States too intrusive. Indeed, the United States may have a problem in accommodating the search procedures with the Fourth Amendment which prohibits "unreasonable searches and seizures." Thus, the four month period may need to be longer, but this bilateral agreement seems to place a tight schedule on the United States and USSR reaching a readiness to initial the draft Convention. However this plays out, these two bilateral accords represent a long step toward concluding the Convention.

OVERALL SECURITY ISSUES

With a chemical weapons ban becoming a real possibility, the United States will have to assess again whether its fundamental security interests are served by the Convention that is taking shape. Without the active support of the United States, there can be no treaty. Therefore the United States has the choice between ultimately preventing a chemical weapons ban from coming about, or of having a good chance that it will come to pass with active U.S. support.

One might assess the negative side by noting how difficult the maintenance of a chemical weapons ban regime will be. As the IISS notes (see footnote 5):

"The sheer complexity of the task, the opposition of commercial interests to the proposals for intrusive (but essential) verification procedures and the problem of preventing further proliferation, all combine to make the task of completing the Chemical Weapons Convention very difficult."

But the completing of the Convention will be only the beginning of a most demanding period of doing all that will be necessary to make it work. Not the least demanding will be getting all actual and potential proliferators to adhere to the Convention initially and in the long future. This will require continuous attention, the willingness to go beyond the requirements of the

Convention to make sure the organization works and to invest diplomatic capital and to risk the threat or use of sanctions to insure its continuing survival. Surely the easier path would be to avoid this commitment, but to do so would probably mean foregoing the slowly evolving sense of obligation that leading nations have to promoting long term world order.

The direct benefit that the United States and Europe would derive from a functional Convention would be the elimination of the very large chemical weapons arsenals of the Soviet Union at a time when NATO's deterrent chemical weapons are being removed from Europe. This is a remarkably asymmetric benefit to the West. The situation has arisen because President Reagan, perhaps motivated for other reasons, responded to Chancellor Kohl's request for the removal of the chemical weapons that the United States had deployed in the FRG. This request was due in large part to rising public opposition to chemical weap-ons in Germany. It was agreed that this would be accomplished by 1992 and that if a crisis or war occurred, the chancellor of the FRG could request the re-introduction of chemical weapons from the continental United States. However, if such crises did develop, it is most unlikely that chemical weap-ons would be given such high priority in the tight transport situation. Therefore NATO faces a future unlike the past in which it is by its own actions denied an effective chemical weapons deterrent in place in Europe. It is difficult to imagine a more attractive bargain than this: to eliminate the far larger stockpile that could be used against NATO for a non-existent deterrent.

A working Convention would diminish or even eliminate the use of chemical weapons elsewhere, and thereby help to lower the likelihood of wars and the possibility of escalation that would involve the United States or other leading nations in ways that could escalate to large scale war. A further consideration is that in the short term most actual or potential chemical weapons capable states require outside help to become so. But with time, many Third World countries will become increasingly capable in chemical manufacture and will eventually be able to manufac-ture chemical weapons on their own. The virtue of creating this Convention in the near future is that it would greatly diminish the temptation to proliferate when the restraints of the treaty (not to produce and not to transfer either weapons or equipment to produce them) would be most effective.

With a Convention in place, monitoring of chemical weapons activities even in non-adhering countries would be greatly facilitated in contrast to the increasing difficulties now being encountered. More importantly, within the framework of a Convention a mechanism would exist to exert political pressure on non-adherents that would be missing without a Convention.

Finally such a working Convention would create a strong international legal, political, and moral norm prohibiting the production and use of chemical weapons. And the cooperation required to make the Convention work would provide an experience that would most likely encourage cooperation in other areas and a growing respect for international agreements and the benefits they can bring to an increasingly crowded and interdependent Earth.

The opposition to proceeding with the creation of a Chemical Weapons Convention and joining it is set forth rather starkly in recent essays (see the first and third reference in footnote 3). The basic arguments are: (1) past treaties have not worked: neither will this one; (2) verification is unable to insure non-production and non-storage; (3) the West will give up its only deterrent to chemical weapons first-use and the ability to retaliate in kind; (4) Western countries will likely abandon their own investment in defensive gear against chemical weapons and thereby become more vulnerable to surprise attack; (5) no treaty can eliminate chemical weapons proliferation.

Such wisdom as these claims contain is clearly in conflict with the views and policies of nearly all governments, especially those who have devoted so many years of labor to the negotiations. While these claims can be rebutted in detail, it is more relevant to recognize that the underlying conflict and source of opposition arises in two different ways that people look at the future. One is the conflict between seeing our security tied to being self-dependent; denying ourselves no resource that might help in future conflict; to trusting ourselves and not others; in short, to favor isolation over interdependence. The position one takes on this issue is determined much more by one's mindset than by rational argument.

The other way is the willingness to accept or reject the possibility of success in a vast international undertaking in which the rules of agreed behavior will be very complex, the demands on the implementing organization very high, and the implementation likely to be less than perfect. Unlike the relatively simple treaties dealing with nuclear weapons, a chemical weapons treaty will involve so many requirements of varying relevance that the parties will find themselves immersed in a legal structure analogous to complex domestic legal codes. Laws dealing with taxes, regulation, or crime are complex because they must deal with such a variety of violations. Since violations can cover the whole spectrum from serious to trivial, compliance is not expected to be perfect, but to be kept at a tolerable level by the extent of enforcement that the community is willing to afford. The analogy with complex arms control treaties is limited, but some aspects of domestic legal codes will hold. If hundreds of chemical plants are to be monitored on a permanent basis, some violations can be expected, and, when discovered, should be punished. But the very high level of compliance common to nuclear treaties will not be possible. Instead, the working of the Convention should expect and treat varying violations arising either by design or default, and deal with them in ways that will prevent any successive violations from becoming militarily significant or a threat to any party.

Thus the test of whether a Convention can be concluded and made to work is a test of the state of maturity of nations and their governments, of their readiness to envisage the extension of legal systems from the national scene to the international scene, with the short-comings but overall benefit that well-ordered countries enjoy.

ADDENDUM

In the two months that have elapsed since this paper was written in August 1989 the United States and the Soviet Union have taken important initiatives toward chemical weapons control. On September 24, 1989 Secretary of State Baker and Foreign Minister Shevardnadze signed a Memorandum of Understanding that committed the two nations to a detailed exchange of data on chemical stockpiles and mutual inspection to check such data. The first of two phases is to be completed in about one year; the second, four months before the Convention on Chemical Weapons is to be initialed. This agreement should resolve the dispute over the declared size of the Soviet stockpile, provide useful experience in on-site verification, and facilitate the completion of the negotiations in Geneva. In addition, the two nations agreed to cooperate in the technology of destruction of chemical agents, agreed on some procedures for conducting challenge inspections, and on the order of destruction of chemical weapons and chemical weapons production plants. All in all, these agreements represented real, but measured, progress toward reducing the enormous stockpiles of the superpowers and in accelerating the Geneva negotiations.

On the following day, President Bush, in a major address at the United Nations, announced three steps that the United States is ready to take to help the negotiation of the Convention. These were: (1) that the United States would in the first 8 years of the treaty destroy 98% of its stockpile provided that the Soviet Union will do likewise; (2) would in the first 10 years of the treaty destroy all of its chemical stockpile if all nations capable of making chemical weapons accept the total ban; and (3) would begin soon—before the treaty is completed—to destroy 80% of its stockpile if the Soviet Union agreed to do the same. These steps deserve separate comment.

The first step proposes a useful schedule of destruction for the superpowers to follow in the first 8 years of the treaty. If agreed upon it would relieve other nations of the fear that either of the superpowers would retain large stockpiles as long as possible.

The third step proposes that the the Soviet Union join in an immediate program of substantial destruction while the negotiations continue. Since the U.S. Congress has already mandated a comparable schedule of reduction of existing U.S. chemical agents, this step merely proposes that the Soviet Union join. Although this makes a virtue of necessity, it would be an important accomplishment much in spirit with the agreement reached in Wyoming. And it should go far in convincing the other negotiating nations of the superpowers' intent.

The second step is perhaps more complex than it appears. It proposes that 2% of present U.S. stockpile would be withheld until all relevant nations had signed and ratified the treaty. Failing this, it indicates that it would retain a small deterrent stockpile as long as any other nation was suspect. The new United States' position has a certain logic and would create pressure on reluctant states to adhere to the treaty. But it raises the problem of defining chemical weapons making states, the problem of which states would have similar rights and the question of whether one or a few holdouts, even if not intending to make chemical weapons, could prevent the treaty from reaching the stage of a comprehensive ban. Moreover, it might encourage some non-chemical weapons states to attain that capability before signing on to the treaty so that they would have comparable rights of retention of residual stocks. Hence it could encourage the very proliferation that the treaty aims to prevent.

A further complication has arisen in this connection by the report[9] that the United States will seek a revision of the agreed part of the Convention which now bans chemical weapons production when the treaty goes into effect and requires the closing of all chemical weapons production plants three months thereafter. The United States' proposal is that production be permitted to continue if the weapons being produced are replacements for those that could be retained while the proscribed destruction is underway. The motive behind this curious exception appears to be that the United States wishes to carry out its program for the production of binary chemical weapons, and to see that it is these kind of weapons that fill its allowed quota during the destruction period and subsequently if there is a hold at 8 years as described in the first step. Thus the binary weapons program, which has had such a long and divisive domestic history,[10] threatens to play a similar role internationally since the revisions that this proposal would entail on what has been agreed upon will hardly be welcome by most of the negotiating nations.

To complete this update of unusual recent activity, it should be noted that Mr. Shevardnadze, in his United Nations speech of September 27, welcomed Mr. Bush's suggestion on joint Soviet–United States reduction prior to the signing of the treaty, but went further to propose that the bilateral destruction proceed faster and further and that all further production be banned. Despite some real differences, the U.S. administration judged this to be a "constructive response" indicating that "we are on the same wavelength." Thus there is every reason to await the next session of the Geneva negotiations with much more interest than heretofore. On balance, the recent Soviet-American dialogue has advanced the likelihood of reaching a treaty but the prediction of its being completed in a year remains optimistic.

NOTES

1. Lewis A. Dunn, "Chemical Weapons Arms Control," *Survival*, May/June 1989, pp. 209–224; and Matthew Meselson, "Prospects for a Chemical Weapons Disarmament Treaty," *Challenges of the 1990s for Arms Control and National Security*, National Academy of Sciences (forthcoming, 1989).
2. *Strategic Survey 1986–87, 1987–88*, and *1988–89*, International Institute for Strategic Studies (IISS), London, 1987, 1988, 1989.
3. Amoretta M. Hoeber and Douglas J. Feith, "Poison Gas, Poisoned Treaties," *New York Times*, Dec. 6, 1988; Elisa Harris, "Make violations too great a risk," *San Diego Union*, Feb. 5, 1989; and Frank J. Gaffney, Jr., "Too many ways to hide cheating," ibid.
4. *Chemical Weapons and Western Security Policy*, The Aspen Strategy Group and University Press of America, 1987.
5. *The Military Balance 1988–1989*, IISS, London, 1988, pp. 242–249.
6. *Report of the Ad Hoc Committee on Chemical Weapons to the Conference on Disarmament*, CD/952, August 18, 1989.
7. The *New York Times*, "U.S. and Moscow settle key issues on chemical arms," July 18, 1989.
8. The *New York Times*, "Kremlin Accepts Early Inspection on Chemical Arms," August 3, 1989.
9. The *Washington Post*, October 9, 1989, p. 1, "U.S. to Keep Producing Poison Gas."
10. Since some but by no means all U.S. chemical weapons are so old as to become subject to leakage, how they should be replaced has been argued for more than a decade. The option to produce binary weapons, in which two less toxic components are mixed during delivery to form the active agent, eventually became U.S. policy, and artillery shells of this type are

now being produced despite some doubts about their performance. Bombs and other weapons are delayed because of inherent difficulties with insuring that the chemical reaction proceeds to completion under the variety of conditions of temperature and pressure experienced in combat use. Thus, there is some difference of opinion as to the wisdom of proceeding in this direction since the simpler unitary weapons have not exhibited any risk in storage or transport within their proper lifetimes, and, moreover, have been exhaustively tested, a requirement that cannot be met by the binary weapons.

Appendix 6

SOLVING PROLIFERATION PROBLEMS IN A REGIONAL CONTEXT: SOUTH ASIA

Stephen Philip Cohen

I. THE REGIONAL APPROACH

This essay suggests ways in which the United States can prevent, limit, or contain the proliferation of nuclear weapons in South Asia. While concerned about the immediate future it will also review past policies (part II), regional realities (part III), before proposing a comprehensive short and long term American regional non-proliferation policy (part IV) and explaining how such a policy should be implemented (part V).

The exact nuclear status of India and Pakistan is a matter of conjecture. It is our understanding that neither state has a working nuclear weapon but that both could quickly convert existing stocks of fissile material into a deliverable device. Given time, both could produce sufficient nuclear weapons to deploy a small first strike nuclear force. Certainly, India (with its large stocks of plutonium) has the capacity for a much larger force. Both states also possess adequate means for delivery in the form of advanced fighter-bombers. Both have recently tested short-range missiles, and on May 21, 1989, India launched the *Agni*, a medium range missile—offering no pretense that it was engaged in purely peaceful research or testing.[1]

First India and then Pakistan moved close to acquiring a nuclear weapon. The overall Indian nuclear program is mature and well-developed. Indian nuclear research began in the 1940s, a bomb program was widely discussed and studied in the 1960s, and a so-called PNE—peaceful nuclear explosion—was tested in 1974. Despite this history of nuclear research—and predictions of imminent weaponization—the Indian leadership has crept very slowly along the nuclear path. This was not the perception of some Pakistani leaders. Misjudging Indian intentions, they pressed for a Pakistani program as early as 1964.

Thus there are two states in South Asia unconstrained by strong outside alliances, beset by a range of internal and external security problems, engaged in a long-term political struggle with each other, and close to two other nuclear powers. They now possess the means to acquire military nuclear systems. That they have not done so is no less significant, and provides American policy-makers with both an insight into Indian and Pakistani nuclear politics and an entry point into their nuclear decisions.

This essay takes a frankly regional perspective. Few in the larger non-proliferation community have a firm grasp of the political calculations that have driven India and Pakistan towards weaponization. Since 1964 regional proliferation dynamics have often been misunderstood when they have not been ignored. While America's *regional* specialists sometimes line up uncritically behind the Indians or the Pakistanis, a different angle of vision—even a little "clientitis"—might be useful in the debate over coping with regional proliferation. While we must be concerned with the impact of South Asian nuclear events upon proliferation elsewhere, with the importance of preserving the Non-Proliferation Treaty (NPT) and with the virtue of policy consistency, South Asia now constitutes so much of the proliferation problem and the regional outcomes are so uncertain, that a strong case can be made for taking the narrow view. A comprehensive and consistent American non-proliferation policy that works only where there is no danger of proliferation and which has no impact or even accelerates the weaponization process in South Asia does not strike me as much of an accomplishment.

South Asia will demand close and constant attention in the next few years. We should not be optimistic just because India and Pakistan have not yet plunged into overt nuclear programs. Both states are not only driven by the logic of technology, their own interactive relationship, and other strategic and political considerations, they are running out of alternatives to weaponization. The central goal of American policy should be to see that attractive alternatives exist. Failing that, there is an even chance that the slow, measured pace that has characterized nuclear decisions in the region will become increasingly interactive and threatening.

II. PAST POLICIES

Six Strategies
America's non-proliferation policy in South Asia has always been to oppose the acquisition of nuclear weapons by regional states. Over the years the United States has successively deployed six different strategies in an attempt to advance this South Asian non-proliferation policy. These have been pursued with varying degrees of energy and success. Many of these strategies complement each other and some have overlapped. A comprehensive American policy for the 1990s will have to incorporate elements of several of these strategies.

Sublimating the Nuclear Mystique. Initially, America's non-proliferation policy in South Asia assumed that by channeling regional interest in the atom towards civilian uses the desire to acquire nuclear weapons would wane. Since the United States (or an-other responsible power) was the sole source of nuclear tech-nology and fissile material, local programs could be carefully monitored. The Atoms for Peace program eventually led to the construction of power and research reactors in India and Pakistan (including East Pakistan, now Bangladesh) and the training of thousands of regional scientists in American labs and universities.

The NPT: Potlatch or Condominium? When it became clear that spreading peaceful nuclear technology was a policy that had begun to work too well, the United States turned to a comprehensive plan that would link civilian nuclear ambitions to arms control, and link each to important concessions to be made by the major nuclear powers—the Non-Proliferation Treaty.

This treaty was to be a great exchange, a trade, between the nuclear haves and nuclear have-nots. The West and the Soviets would reduce their nuclear forces if the non-nuclear states would give up any attempt to acquire them; the reward for the latter would also include civilian nuclear technology. The NPT was offered as a kind of superpower potlatch: they would give up something substantial, destroying and trading away their most destructive systems. The non-nuclear world would become more secure and would reap a bonus in the form of power reactors.

This was a perfectly acceptable arrangement for almost all nations and the NPT has been signed and ratified by well over one hundred and thirty states. Most of these states either belonged to a superpower alliance or they had no interest in acquiring nuclear weapons. Indeed, most states who were *not* alliance members had no need—or lacked the capacity—to go nuclear. The NPT made it easy for both classes of states to avoid doing what they did not want to or could not afford to do. In several cases (South Korea, Taiwan) states were able to parlay their adherence to the NPT into enhanced commitments from a superpower.

But, for two other classes of nations the NPT was a bad deal. For states with real enemies and threats that lacked superpower guarantees, the bomb seemed quite attractive (South Africa, Pakistan). And, for states that had regional aspirations of their own the NPT was certainly restrictive (China and India fall into this category). Such states most strongly protested against the "Yalta syndrome," since any such international arrangement as the NPT places severe limits on their regional and extra-regional ambitions.[2] They will continue to hold this view as long as nuclear weapons are linked to great power status.

Technology Denial. For the states that stayed out of the NPT, particularly Pakistan, the United States turned to a policy of strict technology denial in the mid-1970s. Formalized in the

London suppliers club, elaborate covert and overt mechanisms were developed to monitor and limit the flow of nuclear technology to Pakistan, which was highly dependent upon outside suppliers. Even where an item or a technology could not be kept from such states, it was possible to make it more difficult or costly to acquire it, presumably slowing down the pace of a nuclear program. The Nuclear Non-Proliferation Act of 1978 (NNPA) placed greater restraint on American nuclear contacts with non-NPT states, banning all nuclear exports, requiring full-scope safeguards, and even banning talks on nuclear safety (the United States now has nuclear safety talks with countries such as the Soviet Union and China, but not with India and Pakistan).

Buying Influence: Aid, Trade, and Technology. In contrast, the main effort with regard to India seems to have been to use aid, trade, and technology to acquire influence in nuclear decisions (the difference between the strategies for Pakistan and India can be traced in part to the stronger evidence of a military nuclear program in Pakistan, but also because India could absorb, and had sought, a wide range of dual use technologies that—in the minds of American officials—offered some influence over nuclear decisions). If nothing else, aid and dual-use technologies put a foot in the diplomatic door. On several occasions after 1982 American officials traveling to South Asia to discuss proliferation matters were provided with a military item for Pakistan and a piece of dual-use technology for India.

Enhancing Security. By 1981 it had become clear that Pakistan's price for giving up its nuclear program was too great. Pakistan wanted NATO-like guarantees from the United States against an Indian attack as well as from a Soviet/Afghan attack. U.S. policy-makers refused to offer such guarantees. Instead, they proposed to Congress that American military aid to Pakistan would, in addition to providing Pakistan with the means to defend itself against threats from Soviet-occupied Afghanistan, enhance Pakistan's overall feeling of security, thus reducing Pakistan's desire for a nuclear weapon.

While this was the first time that military aid was positively and publicly linked to nuclear proliferation in South Asia, there were other regional examples of this policy. In South Asia the Soviet-Indian arms relationship must have been seen in Moscow (if not New Delhi) as one way of limiting India's nuclear ambitions. The Soviets have never encouraged an Indian nuclear program—besides adding another state to the nuclear ring surrounding the Soviet Union, an independent Indian nuclear program would reduce Delhi's dependence on Moscow and would probably increase the prospects of Sino–Indian normalization. Elsewhere, the U.S.–Israel and U.S.–Taiwan relationships also provide the recipient state with enhanced security and, presumably, make less important the need for nuclear weapons.

A Regional Approach. Finally, American policy has tentatively turned in the direction of *regional* approach. From about 1985 (marked by the special mission of NSC staff member Don Fortier and Undersecretary of State Michael Armacost in September) American officials came to see South Asian proliferation as an interactive problem that had to be dealt with in both regional capitals. Subsequently, it was realized that on two counts China was part of the region as far as nuclear matters were concerned: First, there was the suspicion that China had provided nuclear assistance to Pakistan, and second, some old hands remembered that the Indian program was originally triggered by the 1964 Chinese test. The Soviets were informed about this regional approach to South Asian proliferation although there is no evidence of any cooperative action.

Successes and Failures

Each of these strategies and policies met with some success, otherwise we might now be talking about a fully-proliferated South Asia. American policy did make a difference since the United States was the only state that combined excellent intelligence and technical capabilities, good ties to India and Pakistan, a legitimate interest in non-proliferation, and an array of incentives and disincentives that could be deployed to support its non-proliferation policy. However, each of these approaches also had certain shortcomings.

For example, the earliest, best-intentioned American efforts to help the nuclear programs of South Asia seem now to have been excessive, and perhaps harmful to non-proliferation interests. They transferred nuclear technology, skills, and, often, critical materials to states that might not have needed them for legitimate energy or research needs. Second, these programs provided the pretext for later military or dual-use programs: all of the suspicious Indian and Pakistani programs have been justified as "peaceful" or "civilian." Finally, these early programs expanded or created Indian and Pakistani nuclear bureaucracies which were then exposed to what was essentially a Western and American double-standard—"our programs can be military and peaceful since we are responsible people, yours must be only peaceful, since we do not know whether we can trust you with these devices."[3]

Atoms for Peace thus convinced many South Asian scientists that they could be admitted to the outer hallway, but the living room and dining room were reserved for the "great" powers. Thus was planted the equation (reinforced by a great deal of public hand-wringing over how heavy a burden it was to be a nuclear weapons state) that great power equals nuclear power.

The NPT was even worse. It rang hollow in Delhi and Islamabad where it was seen as a double betrayal. The nuclear states were not going to disarm, nor were they really serious about transferring nuclear technology at a price that poor states could afford. The NPT was likened to one of those false pledges of freedom that the British had repeatedly offered and withdrew. Promises were cheap; while no Indian or Pakistani leader of any significance wanted to go nuclear in 1964–5 (except for the very junior Zulfiqar Ali Bhutto in Pakistan, and one of India's foremost nuclear scientists, Homi Bhabha), very few Indians or Pakistanis saw the NPT as advancing their national interests. Indians and Pakistanis were in agreement on this and both were genuinely surprised when few other states joined them in opposing to the NPT.

With the collapse of the NPT as a non-proliferation strategy for South Asia, the sticks of technology denial, on the one hand, and the carrots of aid and technology, on the other, were only stop-gaps. They did buy access and time. In 1981 my own view was that the U.S. aid package to Pakistan would have a marginal impact on the Pakistani nuclear program and that the U.S. tie would defer, but not terminate, Pakistani weaponization.[4] The Soviets must have come to the same calculation in the case of India. Aid as influence had its role and its limits; we would only pay so much to be heard, and in exchange, India and Pakistan would, at best, postpone critical decisions (or slice them very thinly) while we were talking.

The shortcomings of the Reagan administration's regional approach are well known. It was at first driven by Afghan-related considerations. The United States could not continue to supply the mujahidin through Pakistan nor could it arm Pakistan if Congress were to cut off assistance because of Islamabad's nuclear program. But Pakistan itself was driven to a nuclear program in part because of its India-related fears. During this period, in an attempt to bury the idea of an "Islamic bomb" (which, indeed, was one of Zulfiqar Ali Bhutto's original objectives in beginning the program), all Pakistani officials stressed, rather disingenuously, that the threat from India lay behind their own nuclear program. Thus, New Delhi had to be brought into the American effort to save the Pakistan aid package. The Indians were perfectly aware of this but saw an opportunity to move closer to Pakistan's chief patron. They also wanted the opportunity to embarrass Pakistan, and constantly used their closer ties to Washington to point out Pakistan's errant nuclear ways.[5]

Despite important shortcomings in conception and implementation, the regional approach had (from an American perspective) a positive impact on Indian and Pakistan nuclear policies. American officials may have underestimated the impact of their efforts on Indian and Pakistani decision-makers. Thus, while there were sporadic discussions and plans for a comprehensive regional non-proliferation policy, such a policy was never fully staffed out.[6]

If nothing else, the new regional approach may have encouraged India and Pakistan (as they competed for American favor) to run up a whole series of proposals for regional nuclear and conventional arms control. Most of these were not to be taken seriously, and at the very moment Delhi and Islamabad were gushing with suggestions for mutual inspection, verification, and force reduction, the two states almost slipped into war. Nevertheless, American interest in a regional approach did influence regional officials and strategists. It caused them to *think* about regional arms control and non-proliferation, and it began to shape a common vocabulary with which to discuss and talk about such issues (one important stage in the evolution of U.S.–Soviet arms control negotiations was the emergence of such a common vocabulary, including agreement upon shared definitions of key terms and phrases).

The regional approach met with opposition from two important American groups.[7] One included those in the non-proliferation community who had advocated a consistent, global, American non-proliferation policy. They saw the regional approach as a fig-leaf for a continuing relationship with Pakistan and a sell-out of non-proliferation objectives. In their view the regional approach was aimed at persuading Congress to avert its eyes, not at persuading India and Pakistan to give up their nuclear programs. This is too harsh, especially since their own alternative of a get-tough policy would have pushed both India and Pakistan into the nuclear weapons column.

The other opponents of a regional approach were the advocates of a strong alliance with Pakistan. They saw Pakistan as the pivot of a larger Middle East strategy. Some may have privately seen a nuclear Pakistan as a more effective protector of American interests (we may yet hear more of "nuclear surrogates" and of the need to get the new nuclears "on our side"). There are good arguments for moving closer to a regional nuclear power, but there are equally persuasive ones for keeping one's distance from such states.

This review of recent American non-proliferation strategies in South Asia suggests some of the ingredients for a long-term policy:

- While a new policy will have to be built from the ground up, we can build upon many past accomplishments;

- The NPT has reached its limits as far as South Asia is concerned;

- The South Asian proliferation problem is beyond the reach of technical harassment and only with difficulty, and careful planning, amenable to a mixture of political, military, and economic inducements;

- The United States cannot provide the kind of security guarantees that Pakistan wants nor will the United States or the Soviet Union provide wide-ranging guarantees to India (certainly, if the United States or the Soviet Union were to provide such assurances to one regional state it would trigger a nuclear program in the other, quite possibly placing Washington and Moscow on opposite sides of a regional nuclear competition, with China holding the wild card);

- A South Asian non-proliferation policy must rest upon a regional approach, even if there are inconsistencies with a global strategy based on the NPT.

III. REGIONAL REALITIES, AMERICAN MISPERCEPTIONS

Before moving to a discussion of current American interests and policies it is essential to review several regional realities. Misperceptions of the region tend to cluster around three points: the motives and nature of the India-Pakistan "arms race," the internal politics of these programs, and the likely outcome of this competition.

An India-Pakistan Arms Race?

Most American officials believe that the Indian and Pakistani nuclear programs are driven by competition between the two states. It would be foolish to argue that their nuclear policies do not influence each other, but it is wrong to characterize their relationship solely—or even primarily—as an arms race. India's

PNE program was, initially, a response to the Chinese test of 1964 and Beijing's subsequent weaponization. It was also a way to demonstrate to both the United States and the USSR that India was a power to be reckoned with. Recently, China has again figured in Indian strategic and nuclear calculations, and informed Indian hawks now speculate that the Sino-Soviet summit of June 1989 means that the Soviet "umbrella" over India, epitomized in the Indo-Soviet Treaty of Peace and Friendship, has been furled.[8] The Pakistan program has been important in Indian calculations only since the late 1970s, and even then they were made in the context of the broader (if shifting) strategic picture.

While the Pakistan program *began* as a response to the Indian nuclear debate of the 1960s, and was accelerated by the 1974 Indian test, it also was conceived in larger terms.[9] First Zulfiqar Ali Bhutto, and then Zia ul-Haq (and thus the military, which was opposed to nuclearization under President Ayub Khan) saw Pakistan as a stable, advanced Islamic state; a Pakistani bomb would not only deter the conventional and nuclear threat from India, it would put Pakistan in the forefront of the Islamic world. Note also that the Pakistanis early came to an appreciation of extended deterrence; here they were following the Israeli and NATO examples, not India's.[10]

A Peoples' Bomb?

Americans have also consistently misjudged the intensity of support for nuclear weapons in India and Pakistan. This has led some to a fatalistic view of the inevitability of proliferation. But public opinion polls in India and Pakistan have consistently shown a majority against weaponization in both states. These figures were overwhelmingly anti-nuclear in the 1960s and 1970s, they are still marginally anti-nuclear. Yet, when asked whether India or Pakistan should possess a nuclear weapon if the other has it, or if their country were to be threatened by another outside power, virtually all respondents indicate strong support for a bomb. In other words, regional public opinion has reservations about nuclear weapons, but stronger reservations about being taken by surprise. This is, as one would expect, the view of most Indian and Pakistani politicians.

The armed forces in neither state have pressed for the bomb. Ayub Khan rejected Bhutto's suggestion that Pakistan go nuclear and fired him as foreign minister. Pressure for a nuclear program came from Pakistani civilians, not the armed forces. The same was true of India. None of the Indian armed services favored going nuclear until very recently—each was afraid that the nuclear program would divert resources from conventional arms purchases and each was concerned that another service might gain control over the bomb.

If the public did not favor nuclearization, and the armed forces were neutral, at best, then how did these two states move to the edge of a military nuclear capability? There are different answers to this question for India and for Pakistan.

In India's case, a coalition of hawkish scientists, bureaucrats, and strategists have kept the pressure on successive governments. All Indian leaders since Nehru's have resisted "the next step," but most have moved further down the nuclear path in the absence of a good reason to freeze or to dismantle their nuclear programs.[11] Since Lal Bahadur Shastri's term as prime minister (1964–66) this deferral of the go/no go decision, while simultaneously allowing research and development to move ahead, has acquired the label of the "option" strategy.[12] As a result, a wide range of programs have been authorized, started, and allowed to mature without a clear policy decision about their consequence.

In the 1960s the option strategy was invented in response to a perceived threat from China; in 1971 (when work on the PNE was authorized) India came under pressure from both the United States and the USSR in conjunction with the newly-minted NPT and in the context of heightened tension with Pakistan. By maintaining a nuclear option Delhi could at least assert its nuclear independence (even as its dependence on others for conventional arms was growing). By the late 1970s the option strategy was firmly embedded in Indian policy.

The news of Pakistan's nuclear program almost precipitated a weaponization decision (there was also talk of a take-out of Pakistan's enrichment facility at Kahuta), but it was decided to continue to broaden the technical base of the nuclear program and speed up missile development. Only in 1974 (and the actual decision to test the PNE) did domestic factors play a role: Indira Gandhi was in deep political trouble, and the test may have impressed some Indians. What we see now (in the shape of the missile tests, statements about uranium enrichment, and other examples of a broad-based Indian program) are the result of decisions taken many years ago. Still, there is no strong evidence that the Indian leadership has committed itself to a full-scale, deployed nuclear and/or missile program.

Pakistan has been more purposive. From the beginning Bhutto wanted a nuclear weapon. He saw the bomb as a way of balancing India's conventional superiority, neutralizing the Indian nuclear threat, and reviving Pakistan's shattered strategic reputation. This policy met with near-universal support in Pakistan, and enabled Islamabad to operate one of history's most sophisticated industrial espionage programs.

The American connection may have modified Pakistan's plans, but it did not fundamentally alter them. Pakistan, also, wants to have an option, but one with a very short fuse. It models itself after Israel—ambiguity about its own nuclear program brings it many of the benefits of nuclearization yet allows it to retain a tie with its major outside weapons supplier, the United States.

Unlike India, where support for the nuclear program has broadened over the years, it has weakened in Pakistan. When Pakistan was an isolated and threatened country, the bomb seemed very attractive. But as Pakistan has emerged from the Zia years as a respected, reasonably stable, and militarily more impressive state, different Pakistani groups have had second thoughts about the nuclear program. The military still see it as problematic, the diplomats are fully aware of the strains that it has caused in Pakistan's relations with the United States and other Western states, and no Pakistani politician today has the experience and skill of Zulfiqar Ali Bhutto. They are more like their Indian counterparts—in the absence of a clear-cut alternative, they are willing to tolerate the nuclear program. Only the scientists involved in the program are true believers, although there are reports of a peace movement among some Pakistani scientists not directly engaged in the enrichment and weapons programs.

A Stable or Unstable Region?

Finally, outside observers have had trouble judging the stability of a proliferated South Asia. They tend towards two extreme views. One is the alarmist position that India and Pakistan, driven by racial and religious hatreds, are locked into a deadly arms race that could (at worst) lead to regional and/or global nuclear war, or (at best) produce a nuclear accident, nuclear theft, or the transfer of fissile material and sensitive technology to other near-nuclears. The perception is widespread that regional governments are unstable and insecure, that they cannot be trusted with nuclear weapons.

On the other hand there is a minority view that nuclear weapons themselves generate their own logic—that of deterrence. This position holds that any pair of nuclear antagonists, such as India and Pakistan, will replicate and evolve on a small scale the peaceful deadlock that has characterized the U.S.–Soviet relationship.[13]

Perhaps the most honest conclusion we can reach about the stability of a proliferated South Asia is that we do not know what will happen. One of the unknowns about the future of proliferation is the degree of evolutionary congruence between technology and strategy. It took decades and billions of dollars for the West, the Soviet Union, and China to integrate strategy and military technology. But the new nuclear states (especially India) are likely to be born with fully mature military systems. Will their nuclear doctrine be as developed? What kind of doctrine will be adopted by non-aligned nuclear states that also have complex conventional military threats? Looking at the problem in the abstract, Intriligator and Brito note that as the number of nuclear states are increased, there are more weapons, targets, and decision-centers. Further, the chances of an irrational or crazy state appearing are also increased. This may be balanced—once again, in the abstract—by the power of deterrence logic: increasing the number of nuclear states also increases the number of partners available for deterrence.[14]

But we do have some evidence about the crisis behavior of Indian and Pakistani decision-makers. This evidence, like the theoretical analysis, is inconclusive. India and Pakistan have gone to war four times, and India fought a war with China in 1962; further, there have been a number of border crises, most recently in 1987, when India confronted both Pakistan and China. Pessimists can point to the growth of ethnic disturbances in all three states, to their propensity of such conflict to spill across borders, to the misperceptions and stereotypes held by leaders in each major state, and to the strong influence of domestic politics on the foreign policies of India and Pakistan.

Yet, South Asia's two major military powers have reached significant arms control agreements with each other. They have also managed to exclude outside states from their own bilateral relationship (formalized in the 1972 Simla agreement between Bhutto and Mrs. Gandhi), and regional leaders are increasingly aware of the impossible costs of a major war.[15]

My own speculative view is that nuclear proliferation will stabilize the Indo-Pakistan relationship about to the degree that nuclear weapons have introduced caution into U.S.–Soviet and Soviet–Chinese relations (a judgment that does not imply much enthusiasm about proliferation's beneficial side-effects). India and Pakistan have, in fact, been engaged in a kind of nuclear diplomacy for several years, and there is strong evidence that in 1987 (during the height of the crisis caused by Operation Brasstacks) both sides understood this perfectly. President Zia stated the obvious when he told visitors in July 1988 that India and Pakistan had achieved deterrence stability because of uncertainty as to whether each possessed nuclear weapons and how many they might have. More recently, nuclear and conventional arms control agreements between India and Pakistan may have been made possible by the knowledge in both states that escalation could lead to nuclear war—or at least the overt display of nuclear capabilities. For these reasons, proliferation may have a calming, even stabilizing regional effect.

On the other hand, there is the possibility of accident, misunderstanding, or misperception. We know of one missed signal: During India's Operation Brasstacks, Pakistan sent a message to India via an Indian journalist who delayed publishing his story for purely commercial reasons. We also know that neither India nor Pakistan have done much work on nuclear doctrine, and both will face formidable command and control problems. How will they move beyond the present stage of nuclear ambiguity, bluff, and gamesmanship to the world of stable, second-strike deterrence? Will such a progression be as smooth as it apparently was for the United States and the Soviets? Will the cost and complexity of a stable, mobile, and reliable deterrent be beyond their capacity (especially Pakistan's)? Will outsiders step in with technical assistance—possibly leading to a very slippery slope of the direct involvement of outsiders in regional nuclear calculations? Finally, will India and Pakistan duplicate the behavior of almost every other nuclear weapons state, and provide assistance to other states that wish to go nuclear?

These and other questions suggest how complex are the motives and processes which will determine whether or not India and Pakistan acquire nuclear weapons. They also suggest something of the difficulty we face in constructing an American policy that can cope with regional proliferation and its associated consequences.

IV. TOWARDS AN AMERICAN POLICY

American Interests

America's South Asian non-proliferation interests fall into or touch upon three different areas. First, there are purely *non-proliferation*-related interests. These include:

- Slowing down or controlling regional military nuclear programs by stemming or stopping the flow of nuclear materials and technology to India and Pakistan;

- Ensuring that India and Pakistan do not aid other states with their military programs;

- Seeing to it that the South Asian example of creeping proliferation is not emulated or admired elsewhere; and

- Protecting the NPT (due for renewal in 1995), especially since it has recently come under Indian attack.

Second, there are two American *strategic/global* interests associated with regional proliferation:

- Containment of Soviet (and, earlier, Chinese) influence in South Asia has always interacted with our regional proliferation policy—usually to the detriment of the latter. However, with the Soviet withdrawal from Afghanistan, proliferation becomes one area where further cooperation with the Soviets, and even the Chinese, makes sense, and might enhance both non-proliferation interests and the remnants of containment policy; and

- Looking ahead to a world of five great powers (Japan, the European Community—with its two independent nuclear systems, China, the Soviet Union and the United States), U.S. policy-makers will want to ensure that if regional proliferation occurs it will not destabilize what will already be a very complicated nuclear world.

Finally, there are a number of *regional* interests at stake:

- American policy has, since 1947, favored the emergence of a stable and cooperative South Asian regional system based upon Indian and Pakistani cooperation so that all regional states might better solve their pressing economic and developmental problems;

- Our bilateral relationship with Pakistan has become something of a limited partnership, since we have parallel interests with a moderate, Islamic Pakistan in the Persian Gulf and Middle East; these interests will remain important even after the Afghan crisis is resolved, and justify a limited strategic connection; and

- In the case of India we are dealing with a strategically unique state. India is emerging as more than a regional power but less than a multiregional or global power. Not only will India dominate the rest of South Asia (raising particular problems for our Pakistan connection), it could challenge China and other large powers (including the United States) in the

Indian Ocean and nearby regions if it feels its economic, ethnic and strategic interests are threatened. Since Indian strategists are divided as to what those interests are, India's behavior could be especially unpredictable.

Policy Criteria

A South Asian non-proliferation policy must meet four tests. First, it must address and balance the wide range of American interests outlined above. Second, it must be consistent. Any new policies must be linked with and evolve out of past efforts, and not involve any sharp or sudden turns. This is not a matter of policy elegance as much as bureaucratic politics: Non-proliferation touches upon so many different bureaucratic and political concerns that a successful strategy must co-opt numerous veto groups in Washington that are poised to shoot down new policies.[16] Third, the policy must be simple, flexible, and capable of implementation in a system notorious for its fragmentation. Finally, it must not require substantial new financial resources.

An Enhanced South Asian Non-Proliferation Policy

An enhanced South Asian non-proliferation policy can meet these criteria. The policy outlined below would *build upon* current policy in that it focuses upon the regional security calculations which motivate the Indian and Pakistani nuclear programs. It will also draw upon a wide range of incentives and disincentives to influence regional actions. This policy *differs* from current thinking in that it refines and differentiates the approach to Indian and Pakistani elites, draws upon new regional and extra-regional partners, and defines "region" in a broader context than presently used.

The *immediate* objective of this enhanced regional policy should be to seek a regional standstill or nuclear freeze, either tacit or explicit, ensuring that India or Pakistan will not plunge ahead into a military nuclear program by miscalculation. Simultaneously, the United States should develop a policy that looks to the future. Its approach should be to influence the assessments of influential Indians and Pakistanis concerning their nuclear programs.

In order of increasing difficulty, the objectives of a *long-term* strategy should be to: 1) constrain India and Pakistan from helping others to obtain nuclear weapons; 2) ensure that they do not damage the global NPT regime; 3) encourage Islamabad and Delhi to further stabilize their nuclear "option" posture and avert an all-out nuclear arms race, and, possibly, beyond the reach of any strategy; and 4) persuade them to give up the option altogether. Achieving these goals will require an array of incentives and disincentives and the cooperation of a number of regional and extra-regional powers.

The Short Term: Getting Through 1991

Aside from the fact that India and Pakistan have nuclear programs which could be quickly militarized, there are a number of critical events and dates which suggest that the United States and other interested governments move quickly to address the most pressing regional proliferation issues.[17]

The United States should immediately declare, as a regional non-pro-liferation goal, that it encourages a freeze or standstill in regional military nuclear programs. It should simultaneously begin the public monitoring, or verification, of such a freeze while inviting the two regional states to separate discussions over freezing or leveling off their nuclear programs. At this stage the United States should offer no incentive other than the argument that a precipitous arms race between India and Pakistan is in the interest of neither state.

Actually, the United States has for years provided a *de facto* verification service for Indian and Pakistani officials. Through our formal and informal statements to the press, Congress, and to regional leaders themselves, the United States has not only commented upon but has influenced regional nuclear decisions. Washington should formalize and expand this de facto proliferation watchdog role. Whether through official U.S. channels, through some international, binational, or multinational forum (or a private group), the United States can provide assurances to regional decision-makers that both sides have not crossed the weaponization line. Ideally these assurances will be given in cooperation with other interested states, especially the Soviet

Union. This arrangement would be publicly resented but privately welcomed in New Delhi; Pakistan would probably support it, since we now provide detailed public statements about the Pakistan program as it is. In effect, the United States (with, one hopes, other countries) would engage in intelligence sharing between two rivals, providing timely alert to either concerning events in the other state.

Such a "verification watch" would buy some time. While it would become the subject of controversy it would also strengthen the hand of groups in both countries that wanted to move slowly on weaponization since it would provide assurances that neither state has a covert supply of deliverable nuclear weapons.

Without a comprehensive follow-on policy a nuclear standstill would be a mere gimmick. Pursuing a regional freeze is clearly an effort to buy time, and in that sense does not differ significantly from many past efforts. America's long term objectives should be to use this time to help regional states and others to build a stable, non-nuclear South Asian security regime at minimal cost and risk to the United States. But such a detailed policy will take time to plan and implement. The following are the broad contours of such a policy.

Beyond 1992

An effective regional non-proliferation policy must, first and foremost, address the ambitions and concerns of potential nuclear states. In South Asia the United States should address those concerns which affect India and Pakistan together, and separately.

India and Pakistan. The core of American regional policy should be the argument that going nuclear (or even maintaining an unstable and precarious option) will decrease, rather than increase security. If India and Pakistan go down the complex path of nuclear deterrence, local conditions may create unusual risks and greater costs than they anticipated. Their systems will threaten each other, and in turn they will be threatened by other regional and global nuclear systems. Further, their example will likely cause new states to go nuclear, increasing sharply the risk to their own security. Finally, while overt nuclear programs will probably reduce the likelihood of conventional war between the two states, the example of every other nuclear power indicates that it will not reduce the need to acquire and deploy vast amounts of conventional forces.

Until very recently, it was difficult for Americans—who have built and deployed over 20,000 nuclear weapons—to make these kinds of arguments. But, with historic agreements already behind us and more to come, U.S. credibility and that of the Soviets has been greatly enhanced: The United States needs to help informed South Asians draw the correct inferences about the relative cost, risk, and gain of being nuclear weapons states. Right now, the hawks are dominant in India, but opinion remains divided in Pakistan and India about the wisdom of actually becoming a nuclear power, and there is still a strong residue of anti-nuclear feeling in both states. These moderate views can be strengthened in various ways. One would be an array of "negative" assurances offered by existing nuclear weapons states. The United States, the Soviet Union, and China could declare, or restate existing pledges, that they would not use nuclear weapons against a non-nuclear regional state. Such pledges would be largely symbolic in nature, but they could acquire more meaning if they were linked to the consideration of positive assurances to non-nuclear states threatened by nuclear states.

Besides weaponization, there are other American non-proliferation interests embedded in U.S. relations with India and Pakistan.

- Chief among these is obtaining agreement not to transfer sensitive materials and technologies to other states. This may require agreement outside the framework of the NPT, or it could be based upon a series of bilateral agreements between both states and other nuclear powers. In either case, the United States should discuss with other significant states the possibility of coordinated sanctions against a non-NPT signatory that pursued such policies. While there may be political or economic reasons for India or Pakistan to help others acquire military nuclear technology, their security will, in the long run, be adversely affected by the addition of new nuclear states in their own region. In this sense, non-proliferation is very much in Pakistan's and India's interests.

- The NPT regime itself has come under attack from India—it is conceivable that Pakistan might join the effort. We will discuss below some specific steps to organize an international effort to advance such policies, but our regional policies, and regional non-proliferation interests must both be tied to and used to enhance our support for the larger NPT regime.

- Nuclear safety should become part of an extended U.S.–South Asian dialogue. The NNPA prohibits discussions on nuclear safety with India and Pakistan, presumably as punishment for their refusal to sign the NPT and to open up all facilities to full-scope inspection. This is a self-defeating policy which blocks an important channel through which Americans can influence key South Asian nuclear officials.

To Pakistan. The United States should restore its earlier policy of proportionate incentives and disincentives in its relationship with Islamabad. This policy was implied in the 1981 decision to link the provision of conventional weapons to Pakistan to that state's overall sense of security, and thus to make nuclear weapons less attractive. As long as the Soviets were in Afghanistan American officials (including many in Congress) were reluctant to enforce their own policies with regard to Pakistan's nuclear program. The Reagan administration considered, but rejected, a policy of proportionality: cutting or limiting military aid to the degree that Pakistan's nuclear program itself was militarized. This policy should now be reinstated.

Such a policy would be more credible today than in 1981–88. Pakistanis knew that the United States was less concerned about *their* security than their role in containing the Soviet Union; now that containment is a declining issue, U.S. commitments to Pakistan as a regional partner may, paradoxically, carry more weight than links to Pakistan as a partner in containment. American policy should provide Pakistan with a choice: a reduced, but long-term relationship with the United States on the one hand, or further movement down the nuclear path on the other. The latter policy might, ironically, worsen its own security situation.[18] Should it move far enough down that path, it will also encounter American sanctions. If Pakistan were willing to freeze its nuclear program at existing levels, then the limited strategic partnership between the two states could be extended.

On the other hand, hard evidence of a standstill in the Pakistani program, and progress towards a regional freeze should be rewarded. In 1989 there were rumors of a Pakistani proposal to trade concessions on their nuclear program for the supply of civilian nuclear reactors. This was not the first time this proposal was floated: In late 1985 President Zia proposed what he called a "wild idea" to senior U.S. officials. An unimaginative, negative U.S. response only referred to obligations to meet U.S. law, and so forth. If Zia's successors are serious the issue should be pursued further.

There are several other arguments that the United States can deploy in dealing with Pakistan. One pertains to the internal political role of nuclear weapons in Pakistan itself. When Zulfiqar Ali Bhutto began the bomb program he saw nuclear weapons as one way of trimming the size of the military budget and reducing the importance of the army in Pakistan. Today, however, it is clear that the bomb program itself has little to do with controlling the generals, but it has created a powerful political lobby. Further, nuclear weapons might themselves become caught up in Pakistani domestic politics during a crisis—central policy-makers will not only have to worry about the loyalty of army units deployed around Rawalpindi, but the loyalty of PAF units that would, presumably, have operational responsibility for these devices.

To India. The core of American policy towards India should be to link strategic accommodation with New Delhi in exchange for its continued non-nuclear status. Indian ambitions, while still poorly defined, extend well beyond South Asia. But India is not an Iran, a Vietnam, or even a China. Delhi does not have messianic or dangerous hegemonic ambitions. India seeks to be a great power, although it is unsure exactly what that means. The United States should not try to challenge or "contain" India, but it does want to see a newly-powerful India emerge as a responsible regional leader.

A condition for American support can be the continuation of India's non-nuclear status. India, like Japan, should be encouraged to enter that class of states which combine military power and moral stature—the latter in part because they have renounced nuclear weapons, not because they intend to acquire them.[19]

There are many ways the United States can convey to India its broad, strategic support. One symbolic act would be to back India's admission to the UN Security Council; another would be totake seriously Indian interest in disarmament. Rajiv Gandhi, from the beginning, saw himself as pursuing some of Jawaharlal Nehru's broader disarmament goals. Through disinterest and neglect, the United States has angered senior Indian officials by their studied disregard of well-intentioned Indian disarmament proposals. Even American regional experts were cynical about Gandhi's "six nation" initiative, or his later "three tier" scheme for global disarmament, or his statements to American officials that India was seriously interested in the disarmament elements of U.S.–Soviet talks. Some of these Indian proposals contain ideas that can be turned to the advantage of a non-proliferation policy—for example, India has expressed a willingness to allow verification devices to be placed on its territory in order to detect violations of a test ban agreement.[20] Could such devices be used to verify a regional nuclear agreement? The United States needs to attack directly the widespread Indian view that regional arms control agreements cannot be verified. Recent agreements with the Soviets, and Gandhi's own proposals provide the ideal opportunity to join the issue with Indian officials and strategists.

While a policy of positive incentives that helped India achieve its broader ambitions might just make an Indian nuclear program unnecessary, the United States should also be willing to increase the costs of an Indian nuclear program, especially one that destabilizes regional or Asian nuclear balances. America should consider assisting those countries—especially non-nuclear states—that might be threatened by offensive Indian nuclear forces. Washington should make it clear that its goal is not to contain or surround India—but that the United States has legitimate interests in the security of other major states, especially those that have foresworn a nuclear weapons program. The positive way to put this argument (which applies with even greater force to conventional arms balances) is that we want to assist India in avoiding an arms race with itself: If Islamabad, in particular, wants to maintain a 1:3 arms balance, it will be New Delhi, not Islamabad (which has number of external supporters) that will be faced with a disproportionate defense burden.

V. IMPLEMENTATION

While the policy outlined above will not require much in the way of financial resources, it is very demanding in terms of time, thought, and management. In particular, it will require very close contacts and discussions with a wide range of states. Chief among these are India and Pakistan: The United States must revive the dialogue on proliferation issues with both countries— the first step towards solving the regional proliferation problem must be taken in South Asia, not Geneva or Vienna. But this policy will also require extended discussions important non-regional states—especially Japan—and even with some of the smaller states of South Asia.

In all of this, the guiding principle should be to exploit existing elements found at the regional, Asian, and global levels to reinforce and strengthen a regional non-proliferation strategy.

India and Pakistan: Establishing a Dialogue

Because of ten years' close cooperation on Afghan-related matters, there are excellent contacts between American and Pakistani officials. While anti-Americanism still runs deep in Pakistan, a dialogue has been achieved. This is not the case with India. For a number of reasons—including cultural and stylistic differences—Washington has been unable to sustain an extended dialogue on proliferation and nuclear matters with

Delhi, let alone foster discussions between Islamabad and Delhi. Ironically, random visits by individual Americans (e.g. Congressman Stephen Solarz) have been helpful at times, but they are not part of any larger strategy. As noted earlier, the Armacost-Fortier trip of 1985 was to be the first of several visits to the subcontinent, but Fortier's death and anxiety over the aid package to Pakistan limited the number and effectiveness of subsequent trips.

This is the moment to encourage a sustained regional discussion on nuclear proliferation between the United States and both India and Pakistan.[21] This can be achieved through a number of channels: in conjunction with the next NPT review conference, at talks about a regional freeze or verification agreement, and as part of a discussion about the spread of many types of advanced weapons and technologies.

Ironically, the essential ingredient now missing is effective coordination and management of the American side of this dialogue. Non-proliferation is a subject divided among many bureaus and departments, and its recent transfer from the Undersecretary of State for Political Affairs ("P") to the Undersecretary of State for Security Assistance ("T") moves it further from the Department of State's regional experts, although it does bring non-proliferation policy closer to one of the few effective forms of leverage, arms aid. A region-specific working group that included Defense, ACDA and other bureaucratic interests would be helpful in coordinating policy, and even in remembering what that policy is.[22] Equally important would be close consultation with Congress, if only to reduce the opportunities for India and Pakistan to exploit differences between executive and legislative branches.[23] But no organizational arrangement can substitute for sustained, high-level administration interest in the linked tasks of advancing American non-proliferation and regional security and political interests.

Japan, The Soviet Union, and China

The most effective long-term innovation in present U.S. policy would be to associate Japan with our regional non-proliferation efforts in South Asia. For years American officials, fixated on the

Soviet Union, have pointed to Moscow's "good" record on non-proliferation and have waited for a significant Soviet effort in the region. In fact, the Soviets have been only marginally helpful on proliferation issues (beyond their NPT obligations), and, in my judgment, positively harmful in past nuclear threats to Pakistan and unrestrained supply of military hardware to India.

There are also good reasons to be skeptical about the role that China might play in freezing a regional nuclear arms race. While it makes sense to include China when talking about "regional" South Asian nuclear matters (a position always taken by the Indians, and now just being accepted in Washington), China is more likely to be part of the problem than part of the solution. The road to obtaining Chinese cooperation (especially vis-à-vis India) runs through Islamabad; Beijing is likely to be guided by Pakistani wishes on such matters as an Asian INF agreement, negative assurances, and restraint concerning provocative or threatening statements.

In an increasingly multipolar world, the United States should cast around for partners whose interests match up closely on important issues. In the case of South Asian proliferation, Japan is well-suited to become such a partner. It is an Asian state, it has been subjected to nuclear attack, it is unlikely to ever acquire nuclear weapons, it has unquestioned status as a world power, and it now plays an important economic role in both India and Pakistan. From Japan's strategic perspective, a more active role on non-proliferation is potentially rewarding and non-threatening to significant friends and neighbors. However, associating Japan with a regional non-proliferation strategy is not a one-time effort. It will require patience and expertise, but it would be the most promising long-term step the United States could take.

Other South Asian States

India and Pakistan's smaller regional neighbors should not be neglected. None want to see the region go nuclear, several (Nepal and Bangladesh) have publicly spoken out against a regional nuclear arms race, all (except India-dominated Bhutan) have signed the NPT, and all think that as hard as it is now to live with New Delhi, a nuclear neighbor would be a more difficult neighbor. Proliferation, testing, and nuclear war would affect several of these states directly, they might even be dragged into a nuclear arms race if India or Pakistan wanted to use its territory to deploy nuclear weapons.

The diplomatic weight of these states may not individually amount to very much but both India and Pakistan are sensitive to their concerns. The new South Asian Association for Regional Cooperation (SAARC) should not be burdened with a regional security issue—it lays outside the scope of the organization—but regional leaders can be encouraged to speak publicly and privately with India and Pakistan. They might be the key to a regional agreement that allows these two states to level off or even reduce their nuclear programs.

VI. CONCLUSION

Summary of Recommendations

To summarize our analysis and argument, the following points are central:

- An enhanced South Asian non-proliferation policy, supplementing the NPT regime, fits both American non-proliferation and regional interests;

- A *short-term* strategy should emphasize a regional nuclear freeze or standstill, possibly in conjunction with other nations that might join the United States in monitoring it; *long-term* strategies directed towards India and Pakistan should emphasize the net decrease in regional security of weaponization or an arms race;

- As a half-way house outside the NPT regime, the United States should encourage India and Pakistan to join the prohibition against the transfer of sensitive materials and technologies; a reasonable quid pro quo would be resumption of discussions on nuclear safety;

- to encourage a regional dialogue we might begin with subjects where there is congruence between regional and American views (chemical and biological weapons); this would also further the development of a common language and terminology and facilitate further arms control discussions;

- To Pakistan, the United States should restore its 1981 policy of proportionate incentives and disincentives; the United States should also emphasize the changed domestic political implications of a runaway nuclear program;

- To India, the core of American policy should be the linkage of strategic accommodation with New Delhi to continued non-nuclear status; while the United States should pay greater attention to recent Indian proposals for arms control, it should also confront directly the Indian argument that regional arms control agreements cannot be verified;

- The internal U.S. government mechanism for development and coordination of an enhanced regional non-proliferation policy needs to be strengthened;

- We must plan for 1995 and beyond. If India and Pakistan do go nuclear, there will still be important regional and non-proliferation interests that will engage the United States in South Asia;

- In the long run, active Japanese support for a South Asian arms control regime would be especially significant; Soviet and Chinese support is likely to be contingent and partial;

- The smaller regional states–Nepal, Bangladesh, and Sri Lanka–should not be overlooked: they have moral, if not military leverage over India and Pakistan, and would be adversely affected by a nuclear arms race, nuclear accident, or nuclear war.

South Asia, American Policy, and the Future

This essay has only outlined a comprehensive proposal to cope with nuclear proliferation in South Asia. There is no certainty that it will work but it is unlikely to do harm, whereas doing nothing may be damaging to important American interests.

We have emphasized that in the long run that what counts the most are the deeply felt feelings of Indian and Pakistani leaders about their own nation's security. The United States must focus upon those feelings in a manner that draws upon rather than rubs against the regional context in which they are made. We will need the cooperation not only of the Soviet Union, but of major Asian powers, notably Japan, and South Asia's weaker states, to erect and preserve a South Asian security regime which makes unnecessary the need for nuclear weapons.

If India and Pakistan do not go nuclear, it will be in part because of U.S. encouragement and policies; if they do, there is no less need for American influence on regional nuclear decisions, including those that might affect proliferation and nuclear strategy elsewhere. Over the past ten years South Asia has attracted U.S. attention and anxiety as it has moved from a pristine non-nuclear status to that of the nuclear option. This concern will greatly intensify if and when the region makes the transition from option status to weaponization and from weaponization to doctrinal development and deployment. There are better and worse ways of managing each stage. U.S. experience may not be relevant to the South Asia case, but South Asia is likely to be important for other states and regions that proceed down the nuclear path.

Whether or not the policies discussed in this essay are seriously considered, the United States will be tied to nuclear decisions in South Asia for many years to come. Regional proliferation is a long-term problem that affects U.S. national security. The United States should not be confident that it can do very much to halt the process, but also should not let ambivalence concerning nuclear weapons incapacitate its thinking and behavior.[24] Nuclear proliferation in South Asia is not a function of supplier policy, nor is it a technical problem, nor is it even an "arms control" issue. It is a process that will be increasingly central to vital U.S. national security interests and to the interests of many states around the world. The spread of chemical weapons will, in several years, be seen as a sideshow compared to the acquisition of true instruments of mass destruction by fragile and even irresponsible states.

The United States is learning how to cope with issue-complexity in a world of many parts and of powers of unequal size. It has proposed a "mix and match" strategy to deal with proliferation in South Asia. This is not an exceptional suggestion. Regional proliferation is typical of the complex challenges that will face American diplomacy in years to come. In this sense, as the United States grapples with the Indian and Pakistani bombs it has already put one foot into the future.

NOTES

1. For an analysis of the spread of advanced missile technologies, particularly improvements in accuracy, see Janne Nolan and Albert Wheelon, "Ballistic Missiles in the Third World" (Appendix Three of this report).
2. The Soviets have had to defend the Yalta agreement during Indo-Soviet discussions on nuclear arms control. See K. Subrahmanyam and Jasjit Singh, eds., *Security Without Nuclear Weapons: Indo-Soviet Dialogue* (Delhi: Lancer International, 1986), p. 212.
3. The response of a generation of regional scientists and engineers is exemplified in the remark of a Pakistani nuclear scientist to his former teacher at my university. Upon returning to Urbana for a short visit in the late 1970s, he boasted: "Ah! You thought that you were the only ones who could do this—but we can also. You'll see what we are capable of—we'll show you how good we are."
4. House of Representatives, Committee on Foreign Affairs, *Hearings*, April 27, 1981, pp. 118 ff.
5. This also had a strategic dimension. At the same moment, American policy-makers saw the regional approach as a chance to reduce Indian dependence upon the Soviet Union, while Indians claim credit for their "opening to Washington." Both views are correct, both sides were driven by the logic of a complex, five-sized strategic game and might have moved in this direction even if the nuclear factor had not existed.
6. One senior American official has told me that the difficulty of keeping any long-term plans secret was also a factor in the absence of long-term planning.
7. There were actually several other opponents to the regional approach. A memo circulated in 1987 likened the opposition of various government bureaus to the story of the five blind men trying to describe the "elephant" of regional proliferation: each saw a different, and partial view of the problem; none could agree on a common strategy that combined nonproliferation interests and their own special concerns.
8. Inder Malhotra writes that the language of the joint communique invalidates Soviet obligations to aid India against China, since it commits the Soviet Union and China not to use force or the threat of force against each other in any manner including through the use of the "territory, territorial waters and air space of any third country adjacent to the other." *India Abroad*, June 16, 1989.

9. For discussions of Pakistani nuclear objectives, see the two books by Akhtar Ali, *Pakistan's Nuclear Dilemma* (Karachi: Pakistan Economist Research Unit, 1984), and *South Asia: Nuclear Stalemate or Conflagration* (Karachi: Research on Armament and Poverty, 1987); and Stephen P. Cohen, *The Pakistan Army* (Berkeley: University of California Press, 1984).

10. The similarity between the Pakistani and the Israeli programs is by design. Whereas India defended its program and their option, on principles of self-reliance and national sovereignty, Pakistani officials closely studied the Israeli–U.S. connection and utilized the loopholes created for Israel to shield their own program.

11. Even Nehru left the option open by approving an experimental reprocessing facility; this facility produced the plutonium used in the 1974 Pokhran test.

12. For a discussion of alternatives subsumed under the option strategy— ranging from genuine uncertainty about the future to a specific end-point, after which weaponization would occur—see Stephen P. Cohen, *Perception, Influence, and Weapons Proliferation in South Asia* (Washington, D.C.: Department of State, Office of External Research, Bureau of Intelligence and Research, 1979).

13. This position has been most fully articulated by Pierre Gallois, Kenneth Waltz, and, in South Asia, K. Subrahmanyam.

14. See Michael Intriligator and Dagobert Brito, "A Possible Future for the Arms Race," in N.P. Gleditsch and O. Jnolstad, eds., *Arms Races: Technological and Political Dynamics* (London: Sage Publications, 1989), Intriligator and Brito, "Nuclear Proliferation and Stability," *Journal of Peace Science*, Vol. 3, No.2, Fall 1978, 173–183 and Brito and Intriligator, "Proliferation and the Probability of War: Global and Regional Issues," in Brito, Intriligator, and Adele Wick, eds., *Strategies for Managing Nuclear Proliferation: Economic and Political Issues* (Lexington: Lexington Books, 1983).

15. For one estimate, widely discussed in India and Pakistan, see Rashid Naim, "Asia's Day After," in Stephen P. Cohen, ed., *The Security of South Asia: Asian and American Perspectives* (Urbana and Chicago: University of Illinois Press, 1987).

16. Of course, consistency is important in dealing with foreign governments as well. Shifting policies towards Pakistan have made that state very distrustful of American motives and have confused other important states such as India. Washington ignored Pakistan's regional strategic role because of its opposition to Islamabad's bomb; after the Soviet invasion, this was reversed, and we began to tolerate the bomb because of Pakistan's regional importance. Now, in 1989, because Pakistan's bomb program is so delicately poised (and a nuclear Pakistan would create many problems in and out of the region), Washington seems to be willing to tolerate and support Pakistan's regional policies to retain some leverage over its nuclear decisions.

17. These mileposts include: the impending certification of the Pakistan nuclear program (October 1989) which will require the president to assure Congress that Pakistan does not possess a nuclear weapon; the next NPT review conference (1990); and the expiration of the U.S.–Indian agreement

on Tarapur (1992), which places restraints on India's use of the vast stocks of plutonium contained in Tarapur's unreprocessed spent fuel.

18. There are conditions which would make a Pakistani nuclear force highly vulnerable. Dispersing Pakistani nuclear weapons will create real problems of command and control, as Zia acknowledged to me in mid-1988. Under conditions of internal disorder dispersed nuclear weapons may become the target of factions in one or more of the armed services. This scenario may be intolerable for Islamabad's neighbors, and Pakistan's lack of depth means that its nuclear facilities, airfields, and missile fields will be vulnerable to accurate conventional attacks (India may have, or will soon have, target location through use of satellite imaging).

19. There are other elements of this policy. American support must also be conditional upon India continuing to pursue a generally non-confrontational policy towards Asia's other nuclear and near-nuclear states.

20. *Washington Post*, October 29, 1985.

21. It might begin with talks about containing or preventing the proliferation of chemical and biological weapons. Indian firms have sold chemical precursors to Iran, and the Indian government has reacted strongly and negatively. *New York Times*, July 1, 1989.

22. There should be no surprise at the reported statement of a U.S. official who did not know where the 5% restriction on Pakistani enrichment had come from. Because of the fragmented nature of the U.S. record-keeping system, no single bureau or office has a complete record of regional non-proliferation policy. *Washington Post*, June 15. 1989.

23. One problem with enhanced executive-Congressional consultation is that so few members of Congress are either interested in proliferation or knowledgeable. The best-informed and most articulate senator (John Glenn) is also a strong critic of recent regional non-proliferation efforts. See *Congressional Record, Senate*, December 11, December 18, 1987, and May 16, 1989, for Glenn's remarks and other significant materials.

24. This ambivalence—being alternatively fascinated and terrorized by these devices—communicates itself to the strategists of India and Pakistan. They skillfully exploit our qualms about our nuclear programs to justify their own.

Appendix 7

"SOLVING" THE PROLIFERATION PROBLEM IN THE MIDDLE EAST

Geoffrey Kemp

THE PROBLEM

Most of the countries in the Middle East are engaged in major military procurement programs involving some of the most sophisticated weapons in the world including weapons of mass destruction. Experts, by and large, agree that there is something inherently troubling about the unregulated spread of advanced military technology into an area beset with traditional sources of conflict. However, like most complex phenomena of international relations, the arms race and its impact on regional conflicts generates different perspectives as to what the problems are and what to do about them.

This paper focuses on the dilemmas facing American policy. The paper begins with a review of the different perspectives of the key supplier countries and the regional actors. It then discusses the various multilateral efforts to put restrictions on weapons capabilities. This is followed by an analysis of the impact of the arms race on regional security, including U.S. security. The paper concludes with a discussion of the requirements for arms control and its linkage to the efforts to reduce the fundamental sources of conflict in the Near East and South Asia (NESA) region. The premise of this paper is that although U.S. interests would be best served if there were more qualitative controls on the Middle East arms race, reasserting arms control as an American priority will require difficult policy choices. Even under the most favorable circumstances, including U.S.–Soviet cooperation, negotiating or implementing successful arms control agreements on some or all of these high technology items cannot in the last resort be decoupled from the peace process.

There are two sets of circumstances when arms control limitations make sense prior to conflict resolution: First, in those specific cases where arms transfers or weapons developments themselves are likely to increase the risks of war; second, cases where interim arms control agreements may be part of confidence-building measures that can improve the atmosphere for conflict resolution.

CURRENT U.S. POLICY

Every decade the Middle East arms race catches the attention of Congress and the arms control advocates within the Executive Branch. The Reagan administration appeared less concerned with the arms race than its predecessors. The primary emphasis was upon military cooperation with friendly countries. There was no major effort made to talk to the Soviet Union about conventional arms transfer controls and while there was concern about nuclear proliferation, nuclear activity in Israel, Pakistan and India continued. It was not that the administration was indifferent to these problems but rather that other, at the time more pressing strategic questions such as the Iran-Iraq war, and the Soviet invasion of Afghanistan, took precedence over conventional arms control and nuclear non-proliferation policy.

However, towards the end of the Reagan administration, increasing concern was expressed over the use of chemical weapons in the Iran-Iraq war, and the spread of ballistic missiles, especially the Chinese sale of *East Wind* surface-to-surface missiles to Saudi Arabia. Criticism of Iraq was muted so long as the war continued and it remained in U.S. interests not to see Iran win. Once hostilities ended in August 1988 and reports of subsequent use of chemical weapons by Iraq against its own Kurdish population were confirmed, U.S. activism against chemical weapons increased and it was as a result of President Reagan's initiative that the Paris Conference on Chemical Weapons was convened in January 1989.

Interest at the executive and congressional levels in chemical weapons has continued since George Bush has become president. Secretary of State Baker announced a plan in February to consolidate responsibility at the State Department for the spread of chemicals, missiles, and nuclear weapons under one office, to be headed by the new Under Secretary of State for security assistance, science and technology, Reginald Bartholomew. At the most recent count, at least four bills have been tabled in the Senate and House to provide sanctions against countries and companies that violate U.S. laws with regard to chemical weapon and ballistic missile proliferation.[1] In June 1989, a bipartisan group of 75 senators urged the president in a letter to work harder for the conclusion of a global chemical weapons ban.

In testimony before Congress, representatives of the administration have expressed a growing concern with the spread of chemical weapons and ballistic missiles to terrorist countries, such as Libya, and unstable regions, such as the Middle East. CIA Director, William Webster stated that "chemical weapons are thought to offer a cheap and readily obtainable means of redressing the military balance against more powerful foes." He also included the spread of biological weapons and ballistic missiles within the scope of his concern. During his testimony, Webster expressed support for sanctions against companies that provide assistance to these programs. The director of the Arms Control and Disarmament Agency, Major General William Burns, stated during testimony that "if the United States and the Soviet Union, and the other three veto powers of the Security Council, decide on sanctions, then the world, for the first time can do something. I think there are a number of things that can be done, everything from economic pressure to economic ostracism, to military action. I think it's about time we consider these things."[2]

SOVIET VIEWS

The Soviet Union is also concerned with political and military developments in the Middle East, and specifically with the threats posed to the region and to its own territory by chemical weapons and ballistic missiles there. In his speech before the United Nations General Assembly in December, 1988, Soviet President Gorbachev cited the conclusion of a chemical weapons convention as a primary item on the agenda for U.S.–Soviet cooperation. To further underline the Soviet commitment to a chemical weapons ban, Soviet Foreign Minister Shevardnadze announced Moscow's plan to begin the destruction of its chemical weapons stocks at the Paris Conference on chemical weapons in January 1989.

Moscow's interest in resolving the Middle East conflict was highlighted by Shevardnadze's high-profile, ten-day tour of the region in February 1989. In Damascus, Shevardnadze noted that while the rest of the world is working toward disarmament, the Middle East arms race is escalating and includes nuclear and chemical weapons. In Cairo, the Soviet foreign minister met with both the Israeli foreign minister, Moshe Arens, and PLO leader Yasir Arafat, and argued for security guarantees for Israelis and Palestinians alike. In a major foreign policy address in Cairo on February 23, 1989, Shevardnadze stated that the Middle East "is threatened by an arms race which, sooner or later, may grow into a nuclear catastrophe," and argued against Israel and the Arabs "repeating the path along which East-West nuclear rivalry developed." He argued that the arms race in the Middle East is now transcending its traditional boundaries and that the deployment of ballistic missiles in the region "represent[s] a threat both to the Soviet Union and to the countries of Europe, and to the interests of the United States."

In response to this growing threat, Shevardnadze argued for "a dual parallel process: of curtailing the arms race, and, at the same time, a process of peaceful settlement removing the causes of the conflict situation." He went so far as to propose a system of mutual, on-site inspections to remove suspicions of nuclear or chemical weapons production, the declaration of a nuclear and chemical free zone in the Near East, the creation of a regional center for the reduction of military danger, and greater use of fully and partially demilitarized zones throughout the region.

ISRAELI STATEMENTS AND COMMENTS

In early January 1989, an Israeli official stated that the use of chemical weapons in the Iran-Iraq war and their possession by Israeli's fiercest enemies, Syria and Libya, has led Israel to view itself as a prime target for a future chemical weapons attack. At the Paris chemical weapons conference, an Israeli representative intimated that Israel may be prepared to respond in kind to a chemical attack.[3] And while Israel still maintains that it will not be the first to introduce nuclear weapons into the Middle East, Defense Minister Yitzhak Rabin threatened in January that any nations using chemical weapons against Israel "will be clobbered 100 times harder, if not more."[4]

Israel's fear of Arab chemical weapons is compounded by the introduction of ballistic missiles, with ranges sufficient to reach Israel, into Arab arsenals. Saudi Arabia's purchase in March 1988 of Chinese nuclear-capable CSS-II *East Wind* ballistic missiles only served to heighten the existing tension in Israel regarding the growing high technology arsenals of Arab countries. Yosi Ben-Aharon, director of the Israeli prime minister's office, went so far as to issue a veiled threat of an Israeli strike against the Saudi missiles, noting in reference to the Israeli strike against Iraq's nuclear reactor in 1981 that Israel has a reputation for taking swift action against potential threats.[5] One Israeli analyst stated that "the Saudi-Chinese missile deal is an unprecedented development in the missile threat facing Israel. It involves the introduction of an entirely new class of missiles into the Arab confrontation-state arsenals."[6] Israeli Defense Minister Yitzhak Rabin called the Saudi acquisition "a new strategic threat with which we have to cope in the future in case of war," and argued for new impetus on joint defense projects between the United States and Israel to defend against the missile threat.

Furthermore, some Arab states developing chemical weapons and missile capabilities, specifically Syria and Libya, also have strong ties to the most radical Palestinian terrorist organizations. In addition, Egypt, which has recently been rehabilitated into the Arab League after a ten-year absence because of its separate peace with Israel in 1979, is well on its way to an independent ballistic missile capability, through work with Argentina and Iraq, and is also believed to be upgrading its chemical weapons production capabilities. Egypt's renewed closeness with the Arab world, combined with its new military capabilities, make Israel uneasy when contemplating potential renewed Arab-Israeli hostilities.

EGYPTIAN STATEMENTS AND COMMENTS

Egypt, however, has its own concerns regarding the spread of high technology weapons in the Middle East, primary among which is its concern with Israel's nuclear weapons capability. While never openly admitting to its ballistic missile and chemical weapons development programs, a number of Egyptian officials have pointed to Israel's nuclear weapons as the real danger in the region against which the Arabs need their own form of deterrent.

In July 1988, the former head of Egypt's chemical warfare department, Mamdouh Ateya, argued that the Arab countries should acquire chemical and biological weapons as a counter to the Israeli nuclear threat, and should indeed strive for an Arab nuclear capability as a longer-term goal. He stated, "A chemical and biological Arab force could provide a temporary protective umbrella until we can achieve nuclear parity with Israel," and argued that the resulting balance would be stable.[7] In October 1988, then-Defense Minister Abu Ghazala responded to a question regarding the spread of ballistic missile systems to the Middle East by noting that the missiles are only the means of delivering a weapon. "The arguments should revolve around the nuclear warheads in the region. These are the destructive force [sic] that should not be deployed in the region in order to protect world peace and stability."

At the Paris conference on chemical weapons, Egypt's Foreign Minister Esmat Abdel-Meguid stated, "Any progress on banning chemical weapons is tied to the conclusion of a parallel ban on nuclear arms." However, he elaborated during a subsequent interview that "the main thing is to concentrate on regional problems. A peaceful solution to the Near East dispute would relegate the arms problem, particularly chemical weapons, to a secondary level. We do not want an arms race which would be destructive to all."

U.S. officials, while expressing concern about Egypt's missile and chemical programs, and specifically about Egypt's attempt to smuggle key missile technology out of the United States, have acknowledged that they believe Egypt's chemical weapons are directed principally against its longtime enemy, Libya, rather than against Israel.[8] However, legitimate Arab-Arab conflicts do not lessen the potential risk to Israel posed by Arab missiles and chemicals.

IRANIAN, IRAQI, SYRIAN, AND OTHER ARAB STATEMENTS AND COMMENTS

Iran. Iran was both the victim of chemical and missile attacks, and used chemical weapons and ballistic missiles itself in its war with Iraq, and thus has taken an obvious interest in the future of both systems worldwide. On the one hand, Iran has taken the lead in criticizing Iraq for its massive use of chemical weapons against Iranian territory and against Iraq's own Kurdish minority both during and after the war. Then-Iranian President, Ali Khamenei, in his speech before the United Nations General Assembly in September 1988, said that the chemical and nuclear arms race represent "a serious threat to international peace and security," and called the use of chemical weapons "one of the worst inhuman acts, and a grave issue which deserved special attention." In December 1988, Iranian Foreign Minister Ali Akbar Velayati expressed his consternation at the world's silence in the face of Iraqi chemical use, stating: "We wish humanitarian issues would never be sacrificed for political considerations. . . ."[9] During the Paris Conference, Velayati stated his hope that the conference would lead to a comprehensive chemical weapons ban, and a report by the Islamic Republic News Agency (IRNA), called chemical weapons "the most threatening of man-made weapons."

At the same time, however, Iran has been working steadfastly to expand its own production of chemical weapons and ballistic missiles. According to a report by IRNA in October 1988, Hashemi Rafsanjani, speaker of the Iranian Parliament and acting commander-in-chief of the military, argued that "Iran must seriously consider including chemical and biological weapons in its military arsenal," and added that these weapons are "'a poor man's atomic bomb' and would help Iran regain its military strength." In January 1989, the *New York Times* reported that Iran had established an elaborate network of front companies in West Germany, the United States, and Asia to acquire the means to improve its chemical weapons capabilities, and in June 1989, the network was still active with evidence coming to light of new shipments of chemicals to Iran.

With regard to ballistic missiles, Iran has again used the threat it faces from Iraq as the impetus for its expanded production program. During the height of the "war of the cities" between Iran and Iraq in February and March of 1988, Rafsanjani stated that Iran's prime method to deal with the Iraqi missile threat is to bolster Iran's missile industries. The goal, he said, was that "the very thought of an attack with missiles will be eliminated from our neighbor's minds."[10] Iran has reportedly received Chinese assistance in missile production, and has also been active worldwide in its attempts to acquire missile technology and materials.

Iraq. Iraq has also expressed concern for the growth of the arms race in the Near East region, however, like Egypt, Iraq views Israel's nuclear weapons as the primary cause of concern and sees chemical weapons and missiles as a means of countering the Israeli threat. In his speech before the Paris chemical weapons conference, Iraqi Foreign Minister, Tariq Aziz, stated that Israeli nuclear weapons pose a threat to Arab security and the security of the region as a whole, and argued that "efficacious and speedy international measures are required to remove nuclear weapons from this region in order to promote peace and security and a balance of forces there." He added, "Iraq thinks that any call for a total ban on chemical weapons must be coupled with a call for a complete ban on nuclear weapons."[11] Later in an interview Aziz argued that both Israel and Iran are hostile states in the region and "It is therefore unrealistic to ask the Near East states to abandon a particular type of weapon until there is a real prospect of peace. . . . We just hope that parallel disarmament efforts will be developed in both spheres—nuclear and chemical weapons."

In April 1989, at the United Nations disarmament talks in Geneva, the head of the Iraqi delegation, Rahim Abdal Katl, called for the creation of a nuclear and chemical free zone in the Middle East and for the signing of all relevant treaties, including the Nuclear Non-Proliferation Treaty, by all states in the region.

Iraq thus portrays its own production of chemical weapons and ballistic missiles as a requirement to defend the Arab states against Israeli and Iranian aggression. Using this rationale, Iraq is continuing to expand its chemical weapons capability, its indigenous missile production capability, and is believed to be working with Egypt and Argentina on the production of a sophisticated, 1,000 km range surface-to-surface missile commonly known as the *Condor* II which will be nuclear-capable. Iraq claims to have succeeded in developing and testing an anti-missile missile, named *Al-Faw* I which it believes will be effective in neutralizing the Israeli missile threat.

Syria. Syria is believed to have the most advanced chemical weapons capability in the Arab world, although details are difficult to come by. According to William H. Webster, director of the Central Intelligence Agency, Syria has been producing chemical weapons since the mid-1980s, including nerve agents, and has kept the program highly secret.[12] Syria has also acquired a number of ballistic missile systems from the Soviet Union, including the 300 km range *Scud*-B and the highly accurate SS-21, with a range of 100 km.

However, Syria, like the majority of Arab states, has also adopted the policy that chemical weapons should be seen as a counter to Israel's superior nuclear forces. In anticipation of the

Paris chemical weapons conference, one Syrian commentator urged the world community not to allow the conference to become "a cover for the dangers posed by the proliferation of nuclear weapons, especially when this proliferation involves states whose intransigence and indifference to world security and peace have been experienced by the international community."[13] And in his statement before the conference, Syrian Foreign Minister Farouk Charaa stated, "We support any international effort to eliminate weapons of massive destruction—chemical, biological, nuclear—but we think there is a link among all these arms. . . . That is why we will demand that a paragraph of the Paris conference final declaration make a link between chemical arms and nuclear arms."[14]

Libya. Considered potentially the most dangerous of Arab confrontation states by virtue of its unpredictability, Libya is striving to make its entry into the high technology arms arena in the region. According to CIA chief William H. Webster, Libya is attempting to build the largest chemical weapons plant in the Third World outside of Tripoli, and has also been active in its attempts to acquire ballistic missiles.[15]

As expected, Libya joined the chorus of Arab states at the Paris conference calling for a link between bans on chemical and nuclear weapons, stating that Israel had developed both nuclear and chemical weapons and arguing that "agreed international rules must be applied to all parties without discrimination. . . ."[16]

The Arab community as a whole seems to agree with the principal Arab states that chemical and nuclear weapons must be dealt with together, both as threats and in terms of the search for arms control mechanisms. At the Paris conference, Kuwait linked chemical and nuclear weapons in its approach and called for the international community to prohibit both kinds of weapons.[17] The Arab League, itself, issued a statement prior to the Paris conference indicating that "Israel brought destructive and internationally banned arms to the region, among them chemical and nuclear weapons. . . ."[18] The view that the great powers had no right to call on others to ban chemical weapons while they continue to produce and stockpile them was expressed in Dubai, just prior to the conference, when one commentator stated, "Those who set themselves up as legislators of the ethics governing the use of weaponry should practice what they preach," and by Algeria at the conference when its Foreign Minister, Boualem Bassaih, chastised the United States for denying Third World countries the right to advance their chemical industries while producing chemical weapons itself.

MULTILATERAL ACTIVITIES

On the multilateral level, in January 1989, a UN-sponsored meeting in Paris reaffirmed the international community's desire to prevent further weapons proliferation. The meeting, first proposed by President Reagan in his out-going speech to the United Nations General Assembly and taken up by French President François Mitterand, had the goals of confirming support for the 1925 Geneva Protocol banning the use of chemical weapons in war and providing renewed vigor for the on-going talks at the UN Disarmament Conference in Geneva on a global chemical weapons convention.[19] While the final statement of the conference failed to call for stricter measures to be taken against those who use chemical weapons, 149 nations present in Paris for the talks signed the document pledging their continued support for the 1925 ban and urging an early conclusion of a global ban on production and stockpiling. The final document also reasserted the goal of general and complete disarmament.

An informal group of Western states has also taken shape recently to deal with chemical weapons from the angle of export policy. Currently, the United States, eighteen other countries and the European Commission are joined in what is known as the Australian Group. The purpose of the group is to coordinate chemical export controls in order to deny the relevant technologies to those Third World states that are trying to acquire a chemical weapons production capability. However, the Australian Group has suffered from its informal status, essentially a gentlemen's agreement, and thus from the different interpretations and degrees of enforcement of existing laws in the member states.

The other multilateral efforts of note include the continuing efforts to restrict nuclear proliferation through the mechanism of the Nuclear Non-Proliferation Treaty (NPT) and the newly created Missile Technology Control Regime. Details of these regimes and how they compare to the efforts to secure chemical disarmaments, together with other arms control options, are listed in Tables 1 and 2.

SUMMARIZING THE PROBLEMS

With such a complex set of issues and so many different perspectives on the causes and consequences of the arms race and what is necessary for its control, neat and easy solutions do not spring to mind. For this reason it seems at first glance much easier to focus efforts on restricting certain types of weapons rather than attempt comprehensive arms control arrangements. However while there is more consensus among the suppliers about the dangers of certain weapons, especially nuclear and chemical weapons, there are strong differences among the regional powers as to the equity of selective arms control measures.

While most regional powers agree that arms control arrangements are feasible, and indeed essential, *following* a resolution of basic sources of conflict and agreements to make peace, most insist that in the absence of peace settlements, arms control arrangements must take second place to more traditional security goals including arms acquisitions. Furthermore, the record of the past 30 years suggests that so long as adversaries are convinced that their security is at risk, they will defy attempts by the major external powers to dictate to them their security requirements by denying them certain categories of arms. How to achieve the acquiescence of the regional powers in arms control arrangements con ceived by the external powers is the most difficult task facing the United States as it attempts once more to revisit the problem of weapons proliferation.

Table 1 Comparison of Nuclear/Chemical/Missile Control Regimes

Regime	Purpose/Background	Content	Status	Reactions
NPT	To halt the spread of nuclear weapons beyond the 5 powers possessing them in 1968. Originally negotiated with Japan and West Germany in mind.	Divides world into nuclear and non-nuclear states based on status in 1968. Obliges non-nuclear states to refrain from acquiring nuclear weapons and to accept IAEA safeguards on their nuclear energy facilities. Obliges nuclear states to refrain from providing nuclear weapons to non-nuclear states and to assist in the development of nuclear energy in non-nuclear states. Obliges nuclear states to work toward global nuclear disarmament.	Signed July 1, 1968. Entered into force on March 5, 1970. 139 states are currently full parties to the treaty including 3 of the official nuclear weapon states: U.S., USSR, U.K. are parties; France and the PRC are not parties. Last review conference held in Geneva in 1985; next review conference to be held in 1990. The treaty comes up for formal renewal in 1995.	The countries of primary proliferation concern world-wide—Israel, India, Pakistan, Argentina, Brazil, and South Africa—are not parties to the treaty and have been, by and large, critical of the treaty's discriminatory nature and its failure to recognize the regional security motivations for acquiring nuclear weapons.
CWC (Chemical Weapons Convention)	Purpose of the 1925 Geneva Protocol was to avoid any further use of chemical weapons in war. This stemmed from the heavy use of chemical weapons by all sides during WWI. Purpose of the proposed CWC being negotiated in Geneva	Geneva Protocol of 1925 prohibits the *use in war* of chemical and biological weapons. CWC will prohibit the possession, production, stockpiling, use of provision of chemical weapons.	As of January 1989, 123 states are signatories to the Geneva Protocol. 149 states were represented at the Paris conference on chemical weapons in January 1989 and reaffirmed their commitment not to use chemical weapons and to	Estimates of states with chemical weapons stocks are now at 15-20 with only the U.S., USSR, and France as major powers with chemical weapons. In 1984 the U.S. introduced a new draft treaty in Geneva. The Soviet Union recently removed one

Regime	Purpose/Background	Content	Status	Reactions
CWC continued	is to eliminate chemical weapons completely from the world's arsenals. The negotiations began in the 1960s to strengthen the Geneva Protocol and were reinvigorated in the wake of extensive use of chemical weapons in the Iran-Iraq War.		work for a speedy conclusion of the CWC negotiations in Geneva.	of the major hurdles to successful conclusion of the treaty negotiations by accepting the U.S. concept of onsite challenge inspections of chemical facilities. In 1987 the Soviet Union announced that it was ceasing the production of chemical weapons and would begin the destruction of its existing stockpile. The U.S. and France have both planned to renew production of chemical weapons. The spread of chemical weapons is being increasingly tied to the spread of nuclear weapons, expecially in the Middle East where chemical weapons are seen as a deterrent to Israeli nuclear weapons. At the January 1989 Paris conference, virtually every Arab state represented linked the spread of chemical weapons to nuclear weapons.

Regime	Purpose/Background	Content	Status	Reactions
Australian Group	Formed in January 1987 to coordinate chemical export controls. Grew out of Gulf War-related export controls beginning in spring of 1984. The group is based on the assumption that "relevant technologies are so highly developed, or rare, that they can be controlled by a relatively small number of governments through their export-control policies" (SIPRI yearbook, 1988, p. 104).	8 chemicals are subject to certain formal export-licensing requirements in every member country. Some countries apply restrictions to more than the official 8 chemicals. Additional chemicals are drawn from Group's warning list of 30 chemicals.	Membership includes 12 members of EEC, Australia, Canada, Japan, New Zealand, Norway, U.S., Switzerland, and the European Commission. Several members of the group have recently been accused of exporting technology for chemical weapons plants to a number of countries, including Libya, Iraq, Iran, and Egypt.	Several members of the group, specifically West Germany, Switzerland, and Japan, have recently come under attack for disregarding their obligations under the Australian Group and selling technology and materials to Third World countries for the production of chemical weapons. This had engendered a certain skepticism as to the effectiveness of coordinated export controls in controlling the spread of national technologies.
BWC (Biological Weapons Convention)	Purpose is to reinforce prohibition against use of biological weapons contained in Geneva Protocol of 1925.	Prohibits the development, production, stockpiling, or other acquisition of biological weapons and toxins. Also places prohibition on delivery systems for biological weapons. All prohibited material should be destroyed or diverted to peaceful purposes 9 months after entry into force of treaty.	Signed on April 10, 1972, entered into force March 26, 1975. As of January 1988, 110 states are parties to the BWC.	The BWC has been criticized from its inception for having no requirement for inspection or verification. The BWC is currently threatened by recent advances in the development of toxin weapons (i.e., producing biological poisons such as rattlesnake venom on large scale in labs for use as weapons).

Regime	Purpose/Background	Content	Status	Reactions
MTCR (Missile Technology Control Regime)	Formed in April 1987 to coordinate export controls for nuclear-capable ballistic missile technology. Grew out of concerns that new front on combatting nuclear proliferation is in area of delivery systems and that ballistic missiles are the most destabilizing.	Set of parallel export controls to slow the development of nuclear-capable ballistic missiles defined as having a range of at least 300 km and a payload capability of at least 500 kg. The agreement prohibits the transfer of conventional SSMs, space launch vehicles, key subsystems for SSMs, and facilities and equipment to produce SSMs. Other items to be limited are on-board computers, inertial navigation systems, liquid and solid rocket fuel, testing equipment, flight control equipment, materials for rocket body parts and engine parts, and technology and know-how for above items. Any of these items sold must be accompanied by assurances that they won't be diverted to rockets.	Agreed to on April 16, 1987, by U.S., Canada, France, Italy, Japan, the U.K., and West Germany. Agreement appears to have been bypassed with regard to U.S. collaboration with Israel on the Arrow ATBM system.	Major problem has been that not all of the principle suppliers are members of the regime—specifically the Soviet Union and the PRC are not members of the regime. Nuclear-capable definition leaves out a number of smaller missile systems that have a lower range but a higher payload, or that are chemical weapons-capable. There have also been complaints that the regime is unverifiable and unenforcable.

Table 2 Matrix of Arms Control Arrangements in the Near East and South Asia (NESA)

E=Existing
P=Potential

		Formal	Informal
Multilateral	External powers only	London Nuclear Suppliers Club (E)	MTCR (E) Australian Group (E) NEACC (Defunct)
	Regional powers only	Notification of missile tests (P) Warhead/weapon ceilings (P)	Arab–Israeli "understanding" on missile deployments and uses of air power (P)
	External and regional powers	NPT (E) Biological Weapons Convention (E) Geneva Protocol (E) Chemical Weapons Convention (under negotiation) Egyptian–Israeli Sinai Agreements (E) Syrian–Israeli Golan Disengagement (E)	
Bilateral	External powers only		U.S.–Soviet "understanding" on missile deployments (P) U.S.–PRC "understanding" on missile sales (E)
	Regional powers only	Indo–Pak joint military commission (E) Indo–Pak no-attack agreement (E) Indo–Pak chemical weapons treaty (P)	Syrian–Israeli "red lines" in Lebanon (E)
	External and regional powers		
Unilateral	External powers	U.S. laws on nuclear proliferation and munitions control (E) Pending legislation on CBW and missiles (P)	U.S. restraint on arms sales (E)
	Regional powers		Israel, India, Pak restraint on nuclear testing (E)

IMPACT OF ARMS RACE
ON REGIONAL SECURITY

The arms race in the NESA region threatens the interests of the two superpowers, as well as the Europeans and the regional countries in direct and indirect ways. It poses different threats to different parties. These need to be explained, for unless the different threat perceptions are identified in some detail, efforts to reach common goals on arms control and conflict limitation will flounder.

Impact on U.S. security

As long as the United States has important strategic interests in the NESA region, it will need to be able to deploy forces to forward areas such as the Persian Gulf and engage in military operations ranging from surveillance to direct combat. To sustain a forward based presence requires that the United States continue to have strategic access to the region. This, in turn, puts a premium on secure lines of communication and rear base areas for support.

During the Reagan administration the United States deployed forces on many occasions to the region. In some cases the interventions were quick, successful, and involved no hostile military engagements and no loss of life. On other occasions, especially in Lebanon and the Gulf, U.S. forces were deployed at high risk and sustained considerable casualties for very mixed results.

To assure access to both the forward and rear areas, the United States must remain sensitive to the security requirements of the local states. This means taking seriously their requests for sophisticated military capabilities and their desire to work alongside the United States in building up a credible defense force. In the case of the Gulf and the U.S. desire to retain a residual capability to intervene to secure oil supplies, it means helping the GCC countries with their defense needs, which means selling them arms and providing training. Since it is U.S. policy to undertake operations in the Gulf in concert with local countries, it is in American interests to assure that our local partners be capable of operating sophisticated equipment in the event of hostilities. Unfortunately, in most cases these countries face multiple threats. In the cases of Saudi Arabia and Jordan, this includes threats from Israel. Over the years the Israeli air force has flown with impunity over Jordanian and Saudi airspace, sometimes for deliberate provocation, sometime to take a short cut en route to another Arab country.

Aside from arms sales dilemmas, the most important military problems for the United States relate to the changing threat environment in key forward areas such as the Gulf. Consider the experience of the U.S. navy during the Iran-Iraq war. The Iraqi attack on the USS *Stark* demonstrated that surface warships are extremely vulnerable to missile strikes. For a period during the Gulf operations there was concern that Iran would use its newly acquired Chinese *Silkworm* missiles against U.S. ships. While the *Silkworm* is a first generation missile and was vulnerable to preemptive strikes by U.S. naval attack aircraft, the next generation of SSMs may be more difficult to attack at source and will certainly be more difficult to defend against if armed with chemical warheads.

Missiles and chemicals are only two of the new weapons that could create difficulties for an American military presence. New generations of aircraft, submarines and missile patrol boats that are being purchased by regional powers also pose potential threats.

Impact on Soviet security

High technology weapons proliferation worries the Soviets for several reasons. The region, with all its rivalries, competitions, and unstable alliances, borders on the Soviet Union. In the con-text of planning for a global war with NATO forces the Soviet Union must take into account the threats to its southwestern flank posed by the presence of U.S. and allied forces in the eastern Mediterranean. To the extent that Israel, in addition to the traditional NATO countries, could contribute to NATO forces in a general war, the ability of the Israeli air force to project power into the Mediterranean is formidable. Since the Soviet Union's exit from Egypt in the early 1970s, Syria has assumed great military importance as Moscow's chief ally in the Middle East.

The proximity of the region to important Soviet cities and Soviet industrial infrastructure cannot be ignored either. While it requires considerable imagination to believe that Israel or any other local power would threaten to attack Soviet cities, one can imagine the uproar in the United States if a Soviet client in Central America had forces as powerful as Israel's. Thus, the Soviets inevitably take into account the strides Israel has made in the development of surface-to-surface missiles.

Impact on European Security

The unchecked proliferation of advanced long range delivery systems to the North African countries would eventually have to be taken seriously by the southern Europeans. One only has to recall Libya's use of SSMs against the Italian island of Lampedusa following the U.S. bombing raid against Tripoli and Bengazi in April 1986. At the time, the Libyan attack was seen as something of a joke—it did no damage—but as a portent of things to come the idea that Libya could fire missiles against a northern neighbor did not go unnoticed.

If other North African countries and Israel gradually build up an inventory of long range missiles, it will have an impact on de-fense planning in Greece, Turkey, Italy, France, Spain and Portugal and perhaps further to the north. While it takes imagination to believe that missiles themselves could have much impact on regional security, the possibility that they might be armed with chemical, biological or nuclear warheads is enough reason to expect some form of reaction for the European states most directly concerned. Whether this would take the form of unilateral or multilateral efforts at arms control, de-fense preparedness or both would depend on circumstances not yet foreseeable.

Impact on the Arab-Israeli Balance

Israel-Syria. Israel's ability to exploit its "high tech" advantage over Syria will remain a cornerstone of its defense program. Both Israel and Syria have radically different conceptions of what they seek in a military relationship. As the Israelis see it, they are surrounded by hostile, or potentially hostile, Arab countries and must therefore have a qualitative military edge over all potential adversaries. To maintain it they need two ingredients: well-trained and highly motivated military forces, and open and guaranteed access to high technology. The latter can only come from the United States, which is pledged to maintain Israel's qualitative edge. Thus, there is a built-in, upward and escalatory dynamic to the arms supply process which is a cornerstone of official Israeli and American policy and runs counter to calls for greater arms control and weapons restraint.

Syria is pledged to overcome its permanent inferiority to Israeli military power and argues that Israel has been able to dominate the Mideast, both on the battlefield and in the conference halls, because of its military superiority. Thus, the Arabs, rather than traipsing cap in hand to Jerusalem like the late President Anwar Sadat, need to build up their military power and confront Israel from a position of strategic parity.

Although Syria faces major problems in planning an offensive strategy against Israel, including strong Soviet admonitions not to try to use force to resolve the conflict, the premises are clear; since Israel has superiority, Syria must strive to redress the imbalance. The Syrians have an objective, a benchmark against which they can measure their progress vis-à-vis Israel.

Israel, on the other hand, has achieved strategic superiority over its neighbors. Now, however, the Israelis see Syria struggling to catch up militarily while offering no meaningful political bait. Hence Jerusalem feels pessimistic about long-term relations with Syria and worried that a war, at some point, may be inevitable.

The 1982 war in Lebanon upset Israeli calculations about strategic use of military power. This confrontation was not fought to protect Israel from a danger that threatened the existence of the State. (There had been an effective cease-fire along the border for a year.) It was, instead, an attempt to redraw the strategic map of Israel's northern borders, while, at the same time, removing the serious manageable threat posed by PLO military forces in Southern Lebanon. The war was a disaster because it had no clear objectives and resulted in high Israeli casualties.

The Lebanon experience and, more recently, the Intifada in the occupied territories, have convinced some Israeli strategists that Israel's most bitter enemies cannot be defeated with high technology. If new generations of Shi'ites and Palestinians are prepared to die to liberate the land of Palestine and are able to continue to find recruits in the West Bank and Gaza, internal security could become a much greater problem.

Israel's superiority in its wars with the Arabs has been based on a combination of better technology, more motivated and better trained manpower, superior tactics and battle field management. While there is no evidence that Israel is losing its superiority in any of these categories, it may be losing the *degree* of superiority it has enjoyed for the past 30 years or so. This must include the all-important factor of motivation as well as the more technical questions relating to the performance of different weapon systems. The build-up of the Syrian and other Arab arsenals since 1982 lends credibility to the thesis that, over time, the Arab armed forces may be able to improve their technical competence to the point where they will be able to reduce the edge that Israel has always insisted it needs to overcome any combination of hostile powers.

Israeli strategic deterrence has long depended on a "preemptive counterforce" capability to limit the enemy's ability to use air and ground forces in the early days of an operation, thereby carrying the brunt of the war to Arab territory. Some argue this strategic capability is being systematically undermined not only by the Arab "offensive" build-up—aircraft and missiles— but by the strengthening of Arab defenses, for air, anti-air, and anti-tank operations.

There are different nuances as to what "deterrence" means in the Israeli context, but in practice this has meant the development of forces capable of preemptive operations designed to keep the war zone as far away from Israeli population centers as possible. Given the emphasis that Israel places on its citizen army and the ability to call up reserve forces quickly, the air force has played a key role in the evolution of Israeli strategy and is the chosen instrument in the early hours of a war. Hence, any trends that threaten the superiority of the Israeli air force undermine the concept of deterrence.

One effect of the Arab, especially Syrian, build-up may be to blunt the edge of the preemptive counterforce capability. This makes it less likely that Israel could win a war quickly and decisively. The Israeli—and presumably the Syrian—calculation is that the longer a war lasts, the greater the number of casualties on both sides and the increased likelihood of some sort of superpower intervention. Unless Israel can achieve a decisive victory that would make the costs of high casualties more bearable, a long war would raise the possibility either of escalation to new levels of violence or of external intervention.

For Syria, an all-out war carries enormous risks, not the least of which is the expectation that Israel would eventually win. Given the costs Israel is likely to face, the Syrians have to assume that Israel would only stop if military victory were total. That would mean the destruction of the key units of the Syrian army, the crippling of the Syrian economic infrastructure (which is one of the more enduring achievements of the Assad regime), and a direct military threat to the regime itself.

A Syrian worst-case scenario would be the destruction of its army units by Israel and no Soviet assistance. Almost as bad for Syria would be a military defeat that had no compensatory political benefits. If an Israeli military victory over Syria were the precursor to better Israeli relations with Jordan and the Palestinians, it could lead to serious peace talks. If these *excluded* Syria, the al-Assad regime would be in deep trouble.

The scenario that most worries Israeli planners is a Syrian preemptive or surprise attack. Depending upon what indicators are counted, it might take the Syrian army twenty minutes to two hours to launch a preemptive strike against Israeli positions in the Golan Heights. If such an attack were accompanied by all-out missile and air strikes against Israeli forward mobilization bases in Galilee, as well as airfields and oil refineries throughout the country, a Syrian breakthrough could conceivably occur within the first twenty-four hours of the war, leading in turn to occupation of Israeli-held territory in the Golan. Israel would need forty-eight to seventy-two hours to mount an offensive against the Syrian positions in the Golan. It might take another forty-eight hours to repel Syrian forces to the pre-war DMZ lines. Battle casualties on both sides would be very high.

To be able to repel such an attack, but then to find itself back where it started, would raise grave political questions for any Israeli government. Hence, Israel would have to move beyond such a *status quo ante* position and either inflict such damage on Syria as to "compensate" for the loss of casualties or to occupy more Syrian territory.

There are several ways Israelis can up the ante against the Syrians. Each alternative carries high risks. They could, for instance, launch an amphibious assault against Syrian territory north of Lebanon along the coast, hoping to take an important piece of Syrian real estate as a bargaining chip. Alternatively, they could mount an offensive against Syria through Lebanon, along the lines of advance taken by General Sharon in 1982. This is technically feasible but would take time and almost certainly cost lives. They could also engage in massive aerial attacks or even airborne commando raids against Syria's rear position. Again, from a military point of view, the Israelis could do this, but the price would be major casualties and could provoke a Soviet response.

The other great fear of Israel is that under certain circumstances Syria might use chemically-armed missiles to strike at Israeli cities. Some have argued that the fear of such an attack acts as an Arab deterrent and causes Israel to pause before embarking on preemptive attacks on Arab targets, such as missile and weapons factories, for fear of retaliation.

How justified is the Israeli fear of chemical attacks on cities? Assuming that Syria was able to launch its missiles against, say Tel Aviv, and assuming some of them reached the target and the chemical warheads detonated correctly, the effects against an unprotected population in the heavily built up areas of the city would be devastating. While not comparable to even a very low yield nuclear attack, chemical agents such as Soman could cause hundreds and possibly thousands of deaths from one 500kg warhead plus an even larger number of the population would be left moderately ill. (It is impossible to be precise about casualties since they will depend on many variables including the size of the warhead, the type of chemical agent, the wind speed at the time of attack, the time of day, the protection of the population etc.) Nevertheless, using conservative figures it is not unrealistic to estimate that two or three warheads on the city could well cause more casualties than Israel has suffered in all its wars and encounters with terrorism since the creation of the state.

Given Israel's extraordinary sensitivity to casualties, such an event would be catastrophic—the worst nightmare since the holocaust. What makes Israelis particularly fearful of Syria is the knowledge that its leaders were quite willing to kill thousands of their own citizens in the city of Hama in 1982 to quell the fundamentalist uprising. In short, it is fear of massive Israeli reprisals that keeps Syria from such actions, not the morality of its leadership.

Israel vs Arab Alliance. It is a matter of considerable debate whether, in the context of a wider Arab-Israeli conflict, new technologies help Israel or the Arabs the most. As long as Israel has a monopoly on nuclear weapons it is unlikely that any combination of Arab countries would use chemical weapons except either in the case of a last resort, or unless they were convinced that Israel would never use nuclear weapons against them, but would, instead, rely on its own chemical arsenal and its formidable conventional power projection capabilities.

Regarding the overall developments in weapons technologies, Israel's highly sophisticated defense industries are at the forefront in innovation and adaptation and have made great progress in modernizing Israel's ground and air forces to meet the new challenges posed by the steady build up of Arab inventories. But in the long term, and discounting for the moment Israeli nuclear weapons, the outlook for Israel is not rosy. The Arabs have money, population, geography, and, increasingly, world opinion on their side; and since the Iraqi victory over Iran, some of them have a new sense of military pride. It is true that Syria remains isolated within the Arab camp, but the return of Egypt to the fold lends credence to the argument that in the last resort the Israeli's may have to fight Egypt again. There are many scenarios that could bring this about; few of them have to do specifically with the military balance. Yet if relations were to deteriorate precipitously between Israel and what are presently grouped as the moderate Arabs, perceptions about the balance of power might influence the nature and timing of a new war.

By far the most serious contingency would be one that pitted Israel against Syria, Jordan, Egypt and Iraq. In a one-on-one against Syria, Israel has force superiority and strategic depth. Against an Arab coalition its strategic depth and force superiority is drastically weakened. It is for this reason that any future resolution of the West Bank that involved Israeli withdrawal from most of the territory would have to include a *cordon sanitaire* extending into Jordan with strict ground rules concerning the presence of Iraqi forces in Jordan.

Impact on Arab-Arab and Arab-Iranian Conflicts

One of the strongest motivations for the Arab countries to upgrade their arsenals with the most modern equipment is their own internecine conflicts which have frequently erupted into violence over the past two decades, and the threat to many of the regimes posed by the Iranian revolution. In recent years, intra-Arab conflicts have included: Algeria-Morocco; Libya-Egypt; Libya-Sudan; Libya-Chad; Syria-Jordan; Syria-Lebanon; and Syria-Iraq. Indeed, if one looks at the entire postwar history of the Near East, it can be shown that in the 1950s and 1960s intra-Arab conflicts were the most important factors in determining the demand for arms. It was the Iraqi-Egyptian rivalry as much as Arab-Israeli competition that motivated much of the pressure on Baghdad and Cairo to break out of the restraints of the Western arms rationing schemes. And in the 1960s, it was Egypt's intervention in Yemen and its use of chemical weapons and bomber aircraft, including attacks by bombers on Saudi villages, that motivated the Saudis to negotiate the huge air defense agreement with the United States and Britain in 1965.

The impact of the Iranian revolution on the local military balance has been most obvious in the Iran-Iraq case, but it has also been the strongest reason for the development of the Gulf Cooperation Council (GCC) and its increasing efforts to forge cohesive defense policies for the region. Until such time as the internal situation in Iran stabilizes, continued defense preparedness by the smaller Gulf powers is inevitable irrespective of the course of the Arab-Israeli conflict.

PROSPECTS FOR ARMS CONTROL:
THE POLITICAL ENVIRONMENT

During the past two years three political developments, in addition to the arms control initiatives listed earlier, have occurred which could pave the way for more cooperation between external and regional powers concerning the dangers of the arms race. The three developments are the improvement in U.S.-Soviet relations, the hope that some resolution to the Palestinian problem may be possible, and the end of the Iran-Iraq war.

However a better political environment does not necessarily mean improved prospects for weapons reductions. For instance, steps that move in the direction of a resolution of the Palestinian problem are invariably going to revolve around the complicated issue of "land for peace." If the previous record of Arab-Israeli negotiations on this subject is a reliable guide, it can be assumed that Israel is unlikely to agree to *both* territorial withdrawal *and* arms limitations agreements unless the latter are part of an extremely complicated arms control regime that would have to include demilitarization and verification measures at least as substantive, if not more so, than those that currently pertain in the Sinai as a result of the Egyptian-Israeli peace.

Arms Control and the Peace Process.

The complicated process of reconciling arms control and peace objectives with strategic realities is highlighted in the case of Israel's occupation of the Golan Heights, the West Bank and Gaza district, and the lessons from the withdrawal from Sinai which lead to peace with Egypt and the Golan disengagement agreement with Syria in 1974.

In examining these agreements several interesting facts emerge. First, the trade-off for Israeli withdrawal from the Sinai, and Egyptian and Israeli compliance with the subsequent Peace

Treaty, was a massive *increase* in U.S. military assistance to both countries. Second, the success of both the Sinai and Golan agreements has been based on force separation and restrictive force *deployments* rather than *overall reductions* in forces levels and weapons inventories. Third, a key component to the success to date of these agreements is the physical presence of international peacekeeping forces.

The linkage between Arab-Israeli arms control initiatives and the peace process can be shown in matrix form (see Table 3). It must be noted that the types of practical arms control measures that either have worked in the past or will be needed in the future will depend according to the stage of peace negotiations. It is only when we reach the post-negotiations phase that comprehensive arms control limitations on entire categories of weapons are likely to be acceptable.

It seems clear that if there is to be any further Israeli withdrawal from occupied territory, and an agreement between Iran and Iraq over the Shatt al Arab is to be reached, some variant on the above options will have to be negotiated.

Table 3   Arab-Israeli Arms Control Initiatives and the Peace Process

Pre-Negotiations	• "Red-lines" • Deployment limitations • Weapons testing limitations • Multilateral talks on CBW/Nuclear • External restraints on supply
Trans-Negotiations	• Demilitarized zones • Peacekeeping forces • Deployment limitations • Enhanced surveillance and verification • Possible *additions* to force inventories
Post-Negotiations	• Conventional force reduction • CBW/Nuclear agreements • Inspection of arms production • Regional arms supply agreements

Similarly, improved relations between Iran and the outside world will almost certainly be followed by requests by Iran for access to more advanced weaponry to replace the enormous losses it suffered in the war and the great effectiveness of the American led arms embargo. A major refurbishment of the Iranian armed forces would assure that Iraq will also seek to upgrade its own forces and in the absence of a peace treaty with parallel arms control strictures, Iraq will continue to upgrade its own armed forces by putting increasing reliance on high technology items to offset Iran's inherent geographic and demographic advantages.

U.S. INTERESTS

It is against this changing but uncertain backdrop that current American policy in the region and the role that arms control plays in furthering American interests must be examined. The United States has several clear interests in the region. These include continued access to reasonably priced oil, the security of key friends and allies, especially Israel, the absence of a major hostile presence in the region which poses a threat to these interests, and the termination of acts of terrorism against American personnel and facilities in the region.

However, stating interests by themselves is of little use to policy-makers. To translate interests into operational concepts requires a statement of goals, as well as the realistic policy options and the trade-offs the United States should be prepared to make when competing priorities present themselves.

U.S. Policy Goals

The most clear-cut goal for American foreign policy in the region must be to work for the peaceful resolution of regional conflicts, in cooperation with the major external and regional powers. The purpose will be to strengthen political, economic and cultural ties with individual countries, and to work to defuse and control the most dangerous components of the arms race. More specific goals include the following:

- A comprehensive Arab-Israeli peace including a resolution to the Palestinian problem. This would include guaranteed security arrangements between Israel and its neighbors. It would probably have to include the United States and Soviet Union as guarantors of the peace.

- A peace treaty between Iran and Iraq and the renewal of diplomatic relations between the United States and Iran.

- Continued economic ties between the United States and the region including assured access to Persian Gulf oil at reasonable prices.

- Initiatives to limit the dangers of weapons proliferation in the Near East and South Asia.

The last goal—the focus of this paper—is phrased in a deliberately general manner and does not explicitly use the term "arms control." The reason is that this term has become so identified with Western thinking on conflict, that for some regional powers it cannot be separated from broader attempts by the external powers to manipulate the regional powers' military capabilities in ways that are detrimental to their perceived security requirements.

It is necessary to be very precise about the meaning of arms control before making recommendations as to its viability as a policy goal. If we limit the definition of arms control to refer to steps taken to reduce the risks of war—including if necessary increases in qualitative weapons supplies—then arms control may be a powerful tool for furthering U.S. interests without necessarily arousing the ire of friendly regional powers.

This assumes the United States can play the role of honest broker. To be a credible broker the United States must seem fair. However, compounding the exasperation of many concerning American policy is the complex and unique decision-making process in Washington. Not only are executive branch agencies frequently at odds with each other over arms transfer policies, but in virtually all cases the approval of the U.S. Congress is needed before weapons and other military assistance can be provided.

Unlike other major high technology supplier countries, the United States has a true separation of powers on decision-making that has an important bearing on transfer policies. This is both a source of confusion and strength. Confusion arises because Congress and the administration often have different agendas for different audiences and this can lead to widely different interpretations of what policies are in the best American interests.

Legislative tactics by the Congress have an important impact on the nature and direction of U.S. policy on technology proliferation. Congress can pass laws and, equally important, *threaten* to pass laws. In the former case Congress can literally tell the administration what to do; in the latter case it can often influence how the administration negotiates with foreign governments.

Most legislation on foreign technology transfers, especially military transfers, contains sufficient latitude in the language to allow the president to override specific constraints of the law if U.S. national security interests warrant. But in these cases the onus is put on the president to demonstrate why exceptions should be made. In the case of arms sales this means that most administrations will think twice before recommending to the president that he use his override powers; this encourages caution and careful analysis before approving such measures.

Congressional actions on arms sales and other technology transfer items are invariably less structured and analytical than most specialists would like to see. One reason is that senators and representatives work for a broad constituency of interests, that often have either very specific or very general goals in mind, when arguing in favor of new legislation. Thus lobbying efforts by the supporters of, say, Greece or Israel or Pakistan will make efforts to assure their clients get certain items or that their enemies do not get certain items. Global initiatives by Congress are equally prevalent: for instance, proposals calling for a ban on sales of all surface-to-surface missiles or Mach 2.0 aircraft to the "Third World."

Despite all the contradictions and frequent hypocrisy of Congress on technology transfer issues, its role in determining U.S. policy is a necessary counter balance to the enthusiasms the executive branch will frequently display for particular clients. And in reality the dichotomy between the Hill and the executive is never so clear cut. Within the byzantine labyrinths of the bureaucracy, coalitions between Congressional committees and agencies in the executive branch can work to put limits on or override current policies being pursued by the White House. In the mid-1970s the Office of the Secretary of Defense and the Senate Foreign Relations Sub Committee on Foreign Assistance worked together to put curbs on U.S. arms sales to Iran which were being feverishly pursued by the White House, the Secretary of State, and the U.S. armed services. Executive agencies frequently seek allies on the Hill to undermine the policies of rival agencies. While this can lead to anarchy, it can often help to clarify issues and put pressure on the White House to decide what is really important in terms of U.S. priorities.

In the Middle East, the goal of American policy must be more stable regimes which reduce the risks of war. As noted above, the problem is that a stable military balance is not in the interest of the revanchist countries, particularly Syria. The Arab countries believe that the *status quo* is unacceptable and therefore ways must be found to change it. The peace conference is one method; but improving their military capabilities is another. Thus, to expect symmetrical arms control in the absence of a peace settlement while revanchism remains a key component of policy adds to the difficulty of envisaging a realistic model for the military balance.

PRIORITIES FOR
THE BUSH ADMINISTRATION GOALS

The United States must articulate more clearly what its goals in the Middle East are and what price it is prepared to pay to achieve them. If it wants to reduce the risks of war, encourage stability and the traditional resolution of conflict, the means by which this has been achieved in the past has been the balance of power and formal force separation and reduction agreements. This has involved arms transfers, support of friends through military assistance, and elaborate peacekeeping operations.

If arms control, as a goal unto itself, is believed to supersede these regional objectives—because, for instance, of universal concerns over nuclear and chemical weapons—then a new set of priorities has to be articulated.

The purpose of arms control initiatives in the region should be to reinforce those trends which err towards peace rather than contribute towards war. Since the primary sources of conflicts among the regional actors have different origins and demonstrate different tendencies, it is very difficult to establish a universal set of arms control principles which can be applied within the same time-frame to each conflict.

It follows that arms control initiatives need to be tailored to the needs of each conflict. In practical terms this means that the initiatives that make most sense for the Iran-Iraq case may have little in common with what makes sense and is practical in the Arab-Israel case.

It is well to remind ourselves of the conditions that have enabled the NATO and Warsaw Pact forces to reach the point when serious progress on arms control in Central Europe appears pos-sible. The two superpowers achieved approximate strategic par-ity in key weapons categories, especially nuclear weapons: years and years of negotiation provided some basis for making assessments about the needs for mutual reductions in conventional forces within clearly defined areas; above all else the political climate in Europe and between the superpowers had stabilized and there was agreement over the most basic issue of all—the status of geographical borders between the parties. Even with all these positive developments, arms control proposals remain highly complicated and politically divisive among the parties.

In the Near East and South Asia none of these conditions presently pertain: there are significant asymmetries in weapons capabilities; many of the parties are still in a state of hostility with each other; and, above all else, unresolved geographical disputes separate the parties. Furthermore, the new strategic reach of modern weapons systems, especially surface-to-surface missiles and combat aircraft, has made it increasingly difficult to restrict the focus of arms limitation efforts to specific regions.

The administration should maintain a two track approach. First, it should continue to seek international agreements to limit nuclear, chemical, and missile proliferation, bearing in mind this will be a slow and complicated process. Second, and equally important, it should undertake several ad hoc initiatives designed to address near term practical problems raised by specific developments. These include:

- Work with the Soviet Union to hold down the numbers of Soviet surface-to-surface missiles in Syria and try to delay the upgrading of the existing missiles to be armed with chemical submunitions. Discuss with the Soviet Union the dangers of rebuilding the Iranian airforce with top of the line equipment.

- Persuade Israel to defer deployment of surface-to-surface missiles that can reach Soviet targets,and to desist from deploying chemical warheads. Request that Israel not transfer missile technology to any country except the United States. In this context encourage Soviet-Israeli discussion on missile proliferation.

- Continue to talk to China about its arms transfer policies, especially in the context of possible missile sales to Iran and Syria. Make future U.S. high tech cooperation with China contingent upon agreed rules of engagement regarding arms sales to U.S. adversaries in the Near East.

- Focus continued attention on Libya's quest for chemical weapons and make it clear that in the event that Libya begins full scale production of chemical weapons, the United States will urge whatever measures are necessary to prevent those weapons entering active Libyan inventories. Libya must be isolated as a radical power that has used and encouraged terrorism against American citizens. Continue to give widest publicity to Western companies who help Libya in its chemical weapons program.

- Recognize that there is a danger that Israel and Iraq may miscalculate each other's strategic intentions and come to blows over weapons capabilities. Help to broker indirect talks between the two about possible "red lines" concerning each others military activity, especially relating to preventive or retaliatory attacks on each others facilities.

- Begin low-keyed but substantive discussions with Israel and its Arab neighbors and the Soviet Union about hypothetical arms control regimes to be part of a peace settlement. While these talks should not presume any specific territorial boundaries, they should explore a range of options including enhanced peacekeeping operations and restricted deployment zones.

NOTES

1. A partial list includes: H.R. 696, introduced by Rep. Levine calling for sanctions against countries that use chemical or biological weapons; S. 8, introduced by Sen. Dole calling for sanctions against companies that have assisted in the spread of chemical or biological weapons; S. 238, introduced by Sen. Helms to impose sanctions against firms that provide assistance to chemical weapons programs to terrorist states; and H.R. 963, introduced by Rep. Berman requiring sanctions against companies that assist in the spread of ballistic missile technology. For more information, see Kyle B. Olson, "Feasibility of a Chemical Weapons Control Regime," and Paul Doty, "Policy Issues in Chemical Weapons Control" (Appendices Four and Five of this report).
2. For more details see Elisa D. Harris, "Chemical Weaons Proliferation: Current Capabilities and Prospects for Control," and Janne Nolan and Albert Wheelon, "Ballistic Missiles in the Third World" (Appendices Two and Three of this report).
3. See Edward Mortimer, "Israel hints it keeps chemical weapons as defensive measure," *Financial Times*, January, 1989.
4. Quoted in Kenneth Kaplan, "Concern over Arab chemical, germ arms," *Jerusalem Post International Edition*, January 28, 1989.
5. See, "Shamir Aide Discusses 'Removing' Saudi Missiles," Jerusalem Domestic Service, 0505 GMT, 20 March 1988, translated in Foreign Broadcast Information Service–Near East and South Asia (FBIS-NESA), March 21, 1988, p. 26.
6. Dore Gold, "The growing missile threat," *Jerusalem Post International Edition*, April 2, 1988.
7. Quoted in, "Egyptian Says Arabs Should Acquire Chemical Weapons," Reuters, July 27, 1988, PM cycle.
8. See, "U.S. Concerned By Cairo CW Capability," *Defense and Foreign Affairs Weekly*, April 10–16, 1989, p. 4.

9. Quoted in, "Velayati Invited to Chemical Warfare Conference," Tehran, Islamic Republic News Agency (IRNA), 1835 GMT, 1 December 1988, FBIS-NESA, December 2, 1988, p. 50.
10. See "Hashemi-Rafsanjani Visits Missile Factory," Tehran Television Service, 1705 GMT, 28 March 1988, translated in FBIS-NESA, March 29, 1988, pp. 56–57.
11. Quoted in "Tariq 'Aziz Addresses Chemical Weapons Conference," Baghdad, IRNA, 1550 GMT, 8 January 1989, translated in FBIS-NESA, January 9, 1989, pp. 31–33.
12. See "Statement of the Honorable William H. Webster, Director, Central Intelligence Agency, Before the Committee on Governmental Affairs, Hearings on Global Spread of Chemical and Biological Weapons: Assessing Challenges and Responses," U.S. Senate Committee on Governmental Affairs, February 9, 1989.
13. "Commentary on Attempts To 'Exploit' Paris Talks," Damascus Domestic Service, 1230 GMT, 6 January 1989, translated in FBIS-NESA, January 11, 1989, pp. 50–51.
14. Quoted in R. Jeffrey Smith and Edward Cody, "U.S. Drive To Censure Libya Lags," Washington Post, January 7, 1989.
15. On Libya's chemical weapons plant, see David B. Ottaway, "CIA Chief Says Libya Builds Massive Chemical Arms Plant," Washington Post, October 26, 1988, and Carleton A. Conant, "Libya's CW Gamble," Defense and Foreign Affairs, January 1989, pp. 30–32; on Libya's attempts to acquire ballistic missiles, see Robert D. Shuey, et. al, "Missile Proliferation: Survey of Emerging Missile Forces," Congressional Research Service Report for Congress, Congressional Research Service, October 3, 1988, pp. 61–63.
16. Quoted in Michael R. Gordon, "Libya Says It Can Make Chemical Arms if Others Do," New York Times, January 10, 1989.
17. See "Foreign Minister Addresses Chemical Warfare Talks," Kuwait, KUNA, 1210 GMT, 9 January 1989, in FBIS-NESA, January 13, 1989, p. 28.
18. See "Arab League Concerned Over U.S. Threats on Libya," Tunis Domestic Service, 1600 GMT, 26 December 1988, translated in FBIS-NESA, December 27, 1988, p. 3.
19. See Julie Johnson, "U.S. Asks Stiff Ban On Chemical Arms," New York Times, September 27, 1988; John H. Cushman Jr., "Reagan's Plan for Chemical Arms Parley Is Called a Stopgap," New York Times, September 28, 1988; and Paul Lewis, "France Plans Meeting on Chemical Weapons," New York Times, October 21, 1988.

Appendix 8

FOUR DECADES OF NUCLEAR NON-PROLIFERATION: SOME LESSONS FROM WINS, LOSSES, AND DRAWS

Lewis A. Dunn

For more than four decades, the United States has opposed the spread of nuclear weapons to other countries. This basic policy has rested on the belief that nuclear proliferation would result in new threats to American security, heighten global and regional instabilities, and quite possibly lead to the use of nuclear weapons. That assumption continues to guide U.S. policy today and there is little reason to question it here.

To serve that objective, U.S. nuclear non-proliferation efforts have relied on three broad sets of specific policies over the years. Initiatives have been launched and measures taken to reduce the political incentives that could lead countries to acquire nuclear weapons; to make it technically more difficult for them to do so; and to put in place international non-proliferation institutions. These, too, remain the basic building blocks of U.S. nuclear non-proliferation policy.

It is especially timely now to step back to consider the record of the past decades of nuclear non-proliferation efforts. With heightened pressures for open or unacknowledged nuclear proliferation in all of the world's regions, such an analysis can provide useful insights for renewed attempts to head off a world of many nuclear weapons states. Of equal importance, with growing policy attention to the problems of chemical weapons and missile proliferation, examination of that nuclear non-proliferation experience can provide lessons for those two areas.

With those two objectives in mind, the following paper offers some reflections on nuclear non-proliferation wins, losses, and draws. It focuses on both the policies pursued and the results achieved. In some cases, whether to categorize given policies and their results as wins, losses, or draws is open to differing interpretations; readers will undoubtedly strike their own balance. By way of conclusion, some lessons are drawn from that nuclear non-proliferation record for chemical weapons and missile non-proliferation.

NUCLEAR NON-PROLIFERATION WINS

There are now five acknowledged nuclear weapons states—the United States (1945), the Soviet Union (1949), the United Kingdom (1952), France (1960), and China (1964). In addition, India detonated a nuclear explosive device in 1974 but claimed it was only for peaceful purposes, while Israel is publicly reported to have manufactured nuclear weapons.[1] Top officials in both South Africa and Pakistan have stated publicly that their countries have "the capability" to make nuclear weapons.[2]

This proliferation situation is quite different from what many officials and observers in the late 1950s and early 1960s thought would be the case by now. Back then, it was widely feared that 15–20 states, if not more, would possess nuclear weapons by the mid-1970s. Behind the difference between past predictions and current outcome are a series of nuclear non-proliferation wins.

Decisions by Western European Countries
Not to Acquire the Bomb
In thinking about steps to slow overt or unacknowledged nuclear proliferation, we rightly focus on the "problem countries" of today, countries such as Pakistan and India, North and South Korea, Taiwan, Israel, Iran and Iraq, Libya and Syria, and South Africa. Two decades ago, however, the list of "problem countries" was quite different. Rather than Third World countries, high on that list were West European countries, including

France, West Germany, Italy, Switzerland, and Sweden. Japan also should be put in this category of early potential "problem countries," despite the fact that there was considerably less open (or serious) discussion of nuclear weapons acquisition there. With the exception of France, all of these countries eventually chose not to acquire nuclear weapons.[3]

The decisions of these Western European countries and of Japan to renounce nuclear weapons is a clear, and often forgotten, nuclear non-proliferation success. It also was not a foregone conclusion. Acquisition of nuclear weapons was at differing times in the 1950s or 1960s an open question in virtually all of them. Several of these countries had nuclear weapons programs, including Sweden and Switzerland. Particularly for West Germany and Japan, moreover, later adherence and ratification of the 1968 Nuclear Non-Proliferation Treaty (NPT)—rather than keeping the option open—was not an open and shut issue.

Many considerations explain this nuclear non-proliferation win, some tied to U.S. policies but others not. Perhaps most important, for countries such as West Germany, Japan, and Italy, the U.S. alliance connection provided a necessary and credible foundation for their security. By contrast, the security costs of seeking nuclear weapons in terms of disruption of that alliance and possible Soviet threats would have been quite high. For Japan, domestic politics and its "nuclear allergy" also provided strong disincentives. As for Sweden and Switzerland, both countries had their own reasons not to acquire nuclear weapons. Military leaders in each came to question whether nuclear weapons would be useful to support their postures of armed neutrality. In the Swedish case, shifting domestic politics and a new emphasis on Sweden's role in the forefront of disarmament efforts in the late 1950s also ran counter to acquisition of nuclear weapons.

Third World Incentives and the Norm of Nuclear Non-Proliferation

Establishment and strengthening of a norm of nuclear non-proliferation is another closely related success. It has helped to contain the spread of nuclear weapons to the Third World, while reinforcing the decisions of most Western countries to renounce nuclear weapons.

This norm encompasses several changes in thinking about nuclear weapons and nuclear proliferation. As demonstrated over a decade ago by India's claim to have carried out only a peaceful nuclear test—as well as by the reluctance of current problem countries to acknowledge nuclear weapons activities— global opinion has increasingly rejected the legitimacy of acquisition of nuclear weapons. Equally important, there is a widespread belief that the spread of nuclear weapons would add to regional and global insecurity. Unlike the early 1960s, moreover, the current perception is that a world of dozens of nuclear weapons states is not the wave of the future. Similarly, acquisition of nuclear weapons no longer is seen as a main route to international prestige and recognition.

U.S. nuclear non-proliferation policy contributed in several ways to emergence of this norm. Most important, the United States took the lead first in successful negotiation of the Nuclear Non-Proliferation Treaty, and then in encouraging decisions by over 135 non-nuclear weapons states to adhere to the NPT, including virtually all Western European countries. This treaty now embodies and demonstrates the norm of nuclear non-proliferation. Presidential anti-nuclear rhetoric has also strengthened perceptions of the illegitimacy of nuclear weapons.

This norm probably has been most important in containing proliferation incentives in those Third World countries that are not today's "problem countries" but which could have been driven to seek nuclear weapons by fear of their neighbors' long term intentions, by prestige, or by simply a belief that sooner or later all important countries would have nuclear weapons. This group includes, for example, Indonesia, the Philippines, Singapore, Venezuela, Mexico, Chile, Egypt, Algeria, Nigeria, and Yugoslavia. At the same time, the norm of nuclear non-proliferation, as discussed more fully below, also appears to have constrained the nuclear weapons activities of Third World problem countries. In particular, concern about hostile foreign reaction undoubtedly partly explains, for instance, decisions not to move to open nuclear weapons programs in several oft-remarked problem countries. Finally, this norm has helped to prevent reopening of earlier decisions by most Western countries to opt for non-nuclear status.

The Nuclear Supply Regime: Making it Harder to Get the Bomb

Beginning in the mid-1950s, U.S. policy-makers also took the lead in putting in place a set of international institutions, procedures, and agreements to regulate peaceful nuclear cooperation and the supply of nuclear materials, facilities, and technology to other countries. This nuclear supply and export control regime now comprises bilateral U.S. agreements for cooperation (setting conditions on cooperation with the United States); International Atomic Energy Agency (IAEA) safeguards (to monitor the peaceful uses of nuclear energy); the so-called Zangger "trigger lists" (which specify items that NPT nuclear suppliers can export only under safeguards and which have in effect become the basis for rejecting export requests from problem countries); the London Nuclear Suppliers Guidelines (which extend controls to technology and include commitments to restraint in the transfer of sensitive reprocessing and enrichment equipment or technology). At present, efforts are underway to extend the nuclear export control and supply regime to meet the challenges posed by so-called dual-use exports, items with both nuclear and non-nuclear uses, and by new enrichment technologies.

At one level, successful U.S. efforts to foster multilateral agreement to this set of institutions and procedures governing peaceful nuclear supply and cooperation is a definite nuclear non-proliferation win. Consider their impact respectively in regulating and permitting legitimate peaceful nuclear cooperation and in impeding problem country nuclear weapons programs.

International Atomic Energy Agency safeguards have been the main means whereby recipients of peaceful nuclear equipment and materials could reassure both suppliers and their neighbors that such support was not misused for manufacture of nuclear weapons. Though problems have arisen and challenges remain, on balance, IAEA safeguards have done a credible job in providing that assurance. In their absence, neighboring countries' suspicions could well have fueled pressures for steps toward nuclear weapons, as indeed has occurred in regions (e.g., Latin America) in which countries have not accepted such safeguards on all of their peaceful nuclear activities. Similarly, the London Nuclear Suppliers' Guidelines restrictions on transfers of sensitive reprocessing and enrichment technology have helped head off the global spread of "mom and pop" sensitive facilities. This, too, avoided comparable pressures for proliferation.

Nuclear export controls and supplier restraint have also significantly complicated, slowed, or increased the costs of efforts by problem countries to acquire nuclear weapons. Pakistan, for example, is publicly estimated to have begun its nuclear weapons activities in the early 1970s. In so doing, export controls have bought time for diplomatic initiatives to be taken. But they also have bought time simply for unexpected domestic political changes to occur (e.g., Indira Gandhi's assassination and Rajiv Gandhi's election or President Zia's death and Benazir Bhutto's election.) Moreover, in some important cases, quite possibly Libya, such export controls probably have and can continue to block acquisition of nuclear weapons for many years.

However, at another level, the limits of export controls and nuclear supplier restraint must be frankly acknowledged. Problem countries have increasingly developed sophisticated methods to circumvent controls. Implementation of regulations by some key U.S. allies is often weak, while high level U.S. officials have sometimes been reluctant to expend political capital on export control diplomacy. Not least, as discussed more fully below, it has been clear since the Soviet detonation of an atomic bomb in 1949 that export controls, secrecy, and denial of technology cannot alone prevent additional spread of nuclear weapons.

Winning Widespread Adherence to the Nuclear Non-Proliferation Treaty

Widespread adherence to the Nuclear Non-Proliferation Treaty also stands out as a non-proliferation success. As already suggested, this adherence has helped to establish a norm of nuclear non-proliferation. In adhering to the NPT, moreover, nearly 140 countries have renounced the right to manufacture or acquire nuclear weapons. While in a few cases this undertaking may be open to question, for virtually all others it both significantly binds their future policy and provides reassurance to their neighbors. In addition, the legal obligations assumed by parties under Article III of the NPT have been a major foundation for nuclear supplier restraint and export controls. Similarly, for many countries, their acceptance of IAEA safeguards on all of their peaceful nuclear activities rests on their NPT obligation also under Article III.

Nonetheless, several countries' commitment to the Treaty is increasingly open to question. This includes most importantly Iraq, Iran, and Libya in the Middle East and North Korea in Asia. If these countries eventually acquire nuclear weapons, that would damage the NPT's credibility. In addition, it will be necessary in 1995 to extend the NPT. At that time, the parties to the Treaty must decide by majority vote whether ". . . the Treaty shall continue in force indefinitely, or shall be extended for an additional fixed period or periods." The adherence of many small third world countries with potentially little direct security interest in (and reason to support) the NPT could prove a problem in mustering that majority vote.

Regularizing U.S.-Soviet Non-Proliferation Bilaterals

Also exemplifying successful institution-building, a pattern of regular bilateral discussions between the United States and the Soviet Union on nuclear non-proliferation matters has been established. Ranging across the nuclear non-proliferation agenda, these exchanges have taken place approximately every six months since 1983. They also have proved relatively insulated from the ups and downs of the broader political relationship. For example, even as the Soviet delegation was walking out of the Geneva nuclear negotiations in 1983, the Soviet Union was proposing a new round of non-proliferation talks. This, too, falls into the win category for several reasons.

These U.S.–Soviet discussions have proved most useful for discussions of policies toward multilateral nuclear non-proliferation institutions, from how to handle challenges to Israel's right to participate in IAEA meetings to cooperative efforts to ensure success at the five-yearly review of the NPT in 1985. They also have helped to coordinate U.S.–Soviet efforts to buttress nuclear export controls, by upgrading the Zangger "trigger lists" to include additional items. Over time, sufficient habits of cooperation were built up to make it possible to use these bilaterals for non-polemical consideration of what steps either side might take to head off problem country nuclear weapons programs. In some instances, actions resulted. Nonetheless, both sides' reluctance to use available influence with such countries (due to other political interests) as well as the limits of influence frequently stood out.

NUCLEAR NON-PROLIFERATION LOSSES

The record also contains a number of nuclear non-proliferation losses. These losses suggest the limits both of what U.S. nuclear non-proliferation policy can accomplish and of U.S. readiness to pay a political or domestic price for that goal.

Additional Nuclear Weapon States: Could More Have Been Done?

Failure to prevent additional countries from acquiring nuclear weapons is the most obvious nuclear non-proliferation loss. In addition to the five acknowledged nuclear weapons states, four other countries are widely assumed publicly either to possess a nuclear weapons capability or to be sufficiently close to do so within a limited period of time. At the same time, the pattern of this additional proliferation activity has changed. Since China detonated a nuclear weapon in 1964, no other country has openly opted for nuclear weapons status. Instead, a new group of neither acknowledged nuclear weapons states nor questioned non-nuclear weapons states has emerged.

Brief consideration of the record with regard to both sets of countries is useful. That record makes clear that if a country has strong incentives to acquire nuclear weapons and a sufficiently broad industrial base, it will not be possible to prevent it from achieving that goal eventually. This became evident at the very start.

The early postwar U.S. policy of secrecy and denial, written into law in the 1946 Atomic Energy Act, was clearly aimed at preventing early Soviet acquisition of the atomic bomb. As already noted, it was unsuccessful. The Soviets' 1949 atomic bomb test demonstrated for the first but not the last time the limits of technology controls in the face of a country determined to acquire nuclear weapons.

Though not necessarily aimed at Great Britain, rigid application of the strictures of the Atomic Energy Act—on top of the postwar breakdown of U.S.–British Manhattan Project cooperation—again served only to delay the first British atomic bomb test. However, U.S. legislation was later revised in 1954 and 1957 to permit increased assistance to Britain's nuclear weapons program. From the 1960s on, U.S. sale of submarine launched ballistic missiles also was essential to maintenance of Britain's nuclear deterrent. Both developments reflected a primacy of alliance concerns over more diffuse nuclear non-proliferation interests.

By contrast, quite extensive U.S. efforts were made by the Kennedy administration in the early 1960s to convince the French that an independent nuclear force was illusory and dangerous. This partly reflected the broader pressures from the administration to raise the nuclear threshold in Europe and shift toward more reliance on conventional forces. These efforts came on top of previous U.S. refusal to amend restrictive legislation to permit aid to France's nuclear weapons program. Not surprisingly, U.S. arguments against French acquisition of nuclear weapons fell on deaf ears. Along with the legislative restrictions, they served mainly to antagonize the French who were firmly committed to becoming a nuclear weapons power.

In the early 1960s, Israel's first steps toward a nuclear weapons capability became a matter of concern. The United States learned that Israel had purchased a research reactor (the Dimona reactor) from France, which would eventually provide that country with access to unsafeguarded plutonium for weapons. The Kennedy administration obtained Israeli agreement for regular visits to the site in exchange for sale of *Hawk* surface-to-air missiles. But these visits gradually became pro forma and then ended in the Johnson administration.[4] In the years that followed, attempts were not made to bring U.S. influence decisively to bear in an attempt to contain Israeli nuclear activities. Other considerations, speculated on below, clearly took precedence.

A decade later, both Canada and the United States sought unsuccessfully to use their diplomatic influence to head off India's 1974 detonation of a nuclear explosive device. In carrying out that test, India took advantage of a loophole in the terms of its agreement covering nuclear cooperation with Canada and the United States to go ahead. (The agreement did not explicitly ban peaceful nuclear explosions.) However, the strong adverse foreign reaction, especially from the Canadians, that followed India's test probably contributed to the Indian government's decision not to test again. Nonetheless, by the mid to late 1980s, heightened concerns about Pakistani nuclear weapons activities led the Indian government to warn publicly of the dangers of stepped up Indian nuclear weapons activity. Outside calls for restraint appear to have had little impact, nor have export controls due to India's technical capabilities.

The case of South Africa is somewhat similar. In 1977, combined pressure from the United States and the Soviet Union was brought to bear in response to indications of possible South African preparations for a nuclear test; no test occurred. It remains uncertain whether South Africa or some other country secretly tested a nuclear device two years later in the South Atlantic. In any case, as official South African statements make clear, neither renewed external political pressure nor export controls have stopped that country's advance to the point of possessing a capability to make nuclear weapons.

Based on statements by Pakistani officials, including former President Zia, it is widely assumed that Pakistan now has the capability to make nuclear weapons on short notice. (Prime Minister Bhutto has stated that Pakistan does not possess a nuclear weapon.) Pakistan's nuclear weapons advances over the past 15 years since India's test have entailed concerted and successful efforts to circumvent nuclear export controls. Nonetheless, these controls did slow Pakistan's advance and buy time for diplomacy to be brought to bear. U.S. willingness to use military assistance as a lever to pressure Pakistan to stop its nuclear weapons activities, however, was tempered by both the continued need to work with Pakistan to funnel arms to the Afghan rebels and the real risk that to cut-off assistance would remove the last Pakistani disincentive for an open nuclear weapons program. Besides, even had the United States cut off assistance, past experience with a comparable cut-off in the late 1970s suggests that Pakistan's nuclear weapons activities would not have stopped.

Taken together, these brief sketches suggest that it may be useful to distinguish nuclear non-proliferation losses from policy failures. Some losses are unavoidable regardless of what the United States and other like-minded countries attempt to do. Export controls can only slow a determined country; U.S. influence may be too little or unavailing. At the same time, several cases highlight the limits of U.S. readiness to pay a domestic or foreign policy price for nuclear non-proliferation. In those cases, it will continue to be debated whether the United States could have "done more" and whether policy failed.

The NPT Holdouts

The presence of a group of countries that have refused to sign the Nuclear Non-Proliferation Treaty, despite U.S. efforts to convince them to do so, is another nuclear non-proliferation loss. Some of these NPT holdouts fall into the group of neither acknowledged nuclear nor unquestioned non-nuclear weapons states, e.g., Pakistan, India, Israel, and South Africa. Others appear to be further removed from possession of a nuclear weapons capability, including prominently Argentina, Brazil, and Chile in Latin America and Algeria in the Middle East. France and China, also hold-outs, are nuclear weapons states.

U.S. diplomacy has continued to seek these countries' adherence to the NPT in recent years, working closely with like-minded countries. Sometimes, key holdouts have changed their position. Spain, Saudi Arabia, and North Korea all have done so. But the odds seem very low that any of the remaining key holdouts, with the possible exception of South Africa, will change policy.

The reasons for non-adherence vary. For virtually all of them, refusal to adhere partly is a means to keep open the option to make nuclear weapons. Rejection of adherence also is buttressed in some cases (e.g., India, Argentina, and Brazil) by arguments that focus on the NPT's discriminatory character. These arguments emphasize that nuclear weapons states are not required to renounce their nuclear arsenals, nor do they have to accept IAEA safeguards on their peaceful nuclear activities. For China, non-adherence is a residue of earlier attitudes which stressed the benefits for communism of nuclear weapons spread. French non-adherence is tied up as much with Gallic pride and the logic of independence as with French criticism of the NPT's discriminatory elements. The French also claim to be concerned that adherence to the NPT would make it more difficult for them to continue testing of nuclear weapons.

Widespread Civilian Use of Plutonium

The growing prospect of widespread commercial use of plutonium is a somewhat different nuclear non-proliferation loss. Although estimates vary, upwards of 40–50,000 kilograms of separated plutonium could be in international commerce by the year 2000. Most of this plutonium will be used as nuclear fuel in light water reactors in Japan, France, West Germany, Switzerland, and some other Western European countries. With time, South Korea could again seek access to plutonium for use in its good-sized civilian nuclear power program.

A series of developments over the past decade explain this growing commercial use of plutonium. Efforts by the Carter administration in the late 1970s to convince the Europeans and Japan not to use plutonium failed. These countries argued that such use was necessary for their energy security, particularly in then planned programs for breeder reactors. They also moved to reprocess nuclear spent fuel to ease the problems of managing nuclear waste.

The Reagan administration shifted away from Carter's opposition to reprocessing and plutonium use. This shift partly reflected the belief that better nuclear supply relations with our key Western European nuclear trading partners would pay-off with non-proliferation cooperation elsewhere. It also rested on a less skeptical attitude toward nuclear power generally and use of plutonium in breeders specifically. A possible compromise position between Carter and Reagan, acquiescence in use of plutonium in breeders joined to active efforts to discourage plutonium recycling, was never tried.

By the mid-1980s, the growing storage costs for plutonium that had already been separated led to countries' decisions to recycle that plutonium in light water reactors. It was cheaper to use up the plutonium than to store it.

Increased commercial use of plutonium and its frequent international shipment will place new strains on countries' ability to ensure adequate physical security for it. The risk of theft of this material, whether by terrorists, extortionists, radical governments, or thieves for resale could well be high. Problems with tracking and accounting for large shipments and stocks of plutonium—especially since some amount will be normally unaccounted for in use—will open up the possibility of insider collusion in any such thefts.

Failures of Nuclear Supplier Cooperation

Overall, most nuclear suppliers, most of the time have taken their responsibilities for nuclear export controls quite seriously. Nonetheless, periodic failures of nuclear supplier cooperation comprise yet a different type of nuclear non-proliferation loss, one with implications for other areas of non-proliferation export controls. Two types of supply failure have occurred: specific export control breakdowns; broader inability among the major nuclear suppliers to agree to hold regular multilateral discussions of non-proliferation.

At one time or another, the export control system in virtually all nuclear suppliers has failed to block exports of concern to a problem country, despite good faith efforts by the supplier. There also have been instances in which the nuclear export control bureaucracy of a given country has not paid sufficient attention to potentially troublesome exports or to entreaties to stop particular exports of non-proliferation concern.

In addition to specific breakdowns of the nuclear export control regime, it has not proved possible since 1977 to convene a meeting of all of the London Nuclear Suppliers' Group, which brought together both East bloc and Western major nuclear suppliers. Particularly France and West Germany have opposed that meeting on the grounds that it is likely to antagonize Third World countries. Despite U.S. and Soviet counter-arguments, neither country has been prepared to shift position. Lack of regular meetings of all of the nuclear suppliers has made it harder to reach consensus on new supply initiatives (e.g., to deal with the problems posed by so-called dual use exports with both nuclear and non-nuclear uses.) It also has impeded more general discussion of nuclear supply problems, exchanges of information on problem country efforts to circumvent controls, and consideration of possible common responses to violations of nuclear supply conditions.

NUCLEAR NON-PROLIFERATION DRAWS

Still other developments of the past decades fall into the category of nuclear non-proliferation draws. For them, the jury is still out. Or else, there were both positive and negative consequences, a mixture of both success and failure.

Containing the Openness and Scope
of Nuclear Weapons Programs

While U.S. policies have not been successful in preventing all additional nuclear weapons proliferation or nuclear weapons programs, they have contributed to constraining the openness and scope of nuclear weapons activities in current problem countries. This comprises a nuclear non-proliferation draw in both of the above senses. These countries still may proceed to open nuclear weapons programs and deployments; their current unacknowledged moves toward or apparent acquisition of a nuclear weapons capability are less damaging than open proliferation.

There are several reasons to believe that this outcome is less dangerous. On balance, unacknowledged possession of nuclear weapons is likely to have a less corrosive impact on the perception that widespread proliferation still is avoidable. It also probably will have less impact on incentives of countries other than regional rivals to acquire nuclear weapons. In turn, constraining the size of a country's nuclear weapons program—in terms of amount of nuclear weapons materials and weapons—can help reduce the threat of nuclear theft or nuclear gifts. Scarce nuclear assets are easier to keep track of and too dear to give away for political, ideological, or economic reasons. Most broadly, to the extent that new nuclear weapons states move beyond small unacknowledged capabilities, crisis instability and the risk of accidental, unintended, or intentional use of nuclear weapons would likely increase.

Decisions by current problem countries to stop short of acknowledged nuclear weapons activities partly reflect the impact of the more general norm of non-proliferation. Nuclear jaw-boning by the United States and other countries also has helped. Still other regional concerns, including fear of neighbors' and outsiders' reactions, probably have had an impact as well.

In addition, export controls probably have affected the size, sophistication, and character of problem countries' nuclear weapons capabilities. U.S. ability to block Pakistan's purchase of high quality steel for use in uranium enrichment centrifuges, for example, could not but have impeded future production of that material. Global constraints against nuclear weapons testing, both the Limited Test Ban Treaty and the broader anti-testing norm, also would affect problem countries' ability to produce more sophisticated nuclear weapons—rather than a first fission device—that probably need to be tested.

Some Nuclear Weapons Program Shutdowns: For Now?

It is well known that in the mid-1970s both South Korea and Taiwan had active nuclear weapons programs. Under political pressure from the United States, both countries shut down these activities. Nonetheless, this must be considered only a nuclear non-proliferation draw. Under certain circumstances both programs could spring back to life.

Within South Korea, pressures may again be growing to reconsider a nuclear weapons option, given both reports of nuclear weapons related activities in North Korea and rumblings in the United States about withdrawal of some U.S. troops from the South. (Withdrawal of one U.S. division from South Korea in the early 1970s was a major precipitant of its earlier nuclear weapons activities.) Despite the shutdown of its activities, Taiwan is publicly reported to have sought in the mid-1980s to resume steps that would have provided it access to weapon-usable plutonium. U.S. influence apparently again convinced it not to do so.

Comparison of the U.S. approaches to South Korea and Taiwan with that to Pakistan and then to Israel is instructive. In the two East Asian cases, U.S. nuclear diplomacy is reported to have stressed to both countries in the mid-1970s and to Taiwan in the mid-1980s that further steps towards nuclear weapons would call into question the basic U.S. security tie (for South Korea) and residual political, economic, and security links (for Taiwan). Both countries apparently took that warning seriously. By contrast, U.S. nuclear diplomacy clearly has been less effective against Pakistani nuclear activities.

To speculate briefly about why this may have been so, the relatively greater dependence of Seoul and Taipei, compared to Islamabad, on the U.S. connection may partly explain the different outcomes of U.S. intervention in these cases. In addition, Washington's greater stake in avoiding the spread of nuclear weapons to the Korean Peninsula (with the U.S. military presence and possible impact on Japan) may have been a consideration affecting both the credibility of U.S. nuclear diplomacy and the readiness to exert it. Indeed, as noted, in South Asia, the main driver behind U.S. policy toward the region in the 1980s has been to convince the Soviet Union to withdraw from Afghanistan.

Turning to the Israeli case, other than attempts in the early 1960s to gain access to Israel's Dimona reactor (and periodic appeals continuing until the present to Israel to join the NPT), the public record is blank in terms of high level intervention to constrain that country's nuclear activities. This was so despite Israel's high dependence on the U.S. connection and the danger that a nuclear Middle East is the most likely source of a future super-power nuclear confrontation. Any explanation of this approach is highly speculative, not least since different individuals probably had quite different ways of thinking about the problem. Initially in the mid- to late-1960s, however, overall lack of high U.S. priority to nuclear non-proliferation probably was an important element. Over time, a reluctant acceptance of a possible but unacknowledged Israeli nuclear weapons capability as a sunk cost for U.S. nuclear non-proliferation policy—as a given that could not be changed— may have been increasingly important. An assumption of overall stability—that the Arabs would always be far behind and that Israel's capability would remain uncertain and unacknowledged—is likely to have played a role. It also is difficult not to presume that domestic political considerations were at work as well, along with the view that the Israeli government would have rejected out of hand U.S. attempts to rein in its nuclear activities.

The Treaty of Tlatelolco: An Almost Nuclear Free Zone
The Treaty of Tlatelolco provides the legal framework to make Latin America a nuclear weapons free zone. Nonetheless, it can only be considered a nuclear non-proliferation draw. Chile and Cuba have not signed; Argentina has not ratified; and, having signed and ratified, Brazil has yet to waive it into force. As such, the Treaty of Tlatelolco remains as much nuclear non-proliferation promise as reality.

The United States and the neighboring Latin American countries have repeatedly urged Argentina, Brazil, and Chile to take the needed steps to bring Tlatelolco fully into force. In response, they have made various arguments, from calling into question whether the United States was abiding by its obligations as a protocol party to calling for a special Tlatelolco (not an NPT) IAEA safeguards agreement. But the underlying explanation of their reluctance to bring the Treaty fully into force has been a desire to preserve a nuclear weapons option.

Nonetheless, the Treaty does serve to constrain their activities to a degree. Brazil, for example, has stressed that in accordance with international law it will take no action inconsistent with Tlatelolco. The Treaty also adds to the norm of nuclear non-proliferation. Moreover, at some point both Argentina and Brazil for their own reasons could decide to adhere. For instance, if fears of a nuclear arms race fueled by mutual suspicions grow in Buenos Aires and Brasilia, full adherence to Tlatelolco would offer a ready-made vehicle to provide needed reassurance. Here, too, then the jury is still out and some measure of success has occurred.

Non-Use of Nuclear Weapons

Though not the direct result of U.S. nuclear non-proliferation policy, the non-use of nuclear weapons over the past four decades also has had important nuclear non-proliferation benefits. For that reason, it deserves brief mention.

In particular, non-use contributed significantly to the emergence and widespread acceptance of the belief that nuclear weapons were not simply advanced conventional weapons. This oft-remarked nuclear taboo, in turn, affected the calculations of some of the first generation "problem countries" regarding the benefits and need for nuclear weapons. It also supported the growth in the 1960s and 1970s of the norm of nuclear non-proliferation.

More widespread nuclear weapons proliferation, however, could lead to future use of nuclear weapons. Depending on the specifics, such use could either greatly strengthen the nuclear taboo and associated non-proliferation norm, or undermine it. For that reason (and because it had little to do with non-proliferation per se), non-use is considered a draw.

SOME IMPLICATIONS FOR CHEMICAL WEAPONS AND MISSILE NON-PROLIFERATION

Within the past several years, the United States and other countries have begun to place greater emphasis on measures to control the spread of ballistic and cruise missiles and chemical weapons. A Missile Technology Control Regime, with a list of sensitive items and guidelines for their control, has been agreed to by the United States, the United Kingdom, France, West Germany, Japan, Italy, and Canada. (China and the Soviet Union remain outside, though the Soviets have indicated interest in creation of a "new" multilateral control regime.) In turn, under the auspices of the Australia Group a list of chemical weapons precursors have been identified and steps taken by individual countries to control the export of some or all of them. Negotiations also are underway at the Geneva Conference on Disarmament (paralleled by U.S.–Soviet talks) on an international convention to ban the development, stockpiling, production, transfer, and use of chemical weapons.[5]

There is a series of lessons for missile and chemical weapons non-proliferation from the nuclear non-proliferation record. By way of conclusion, these lessons are sketched briefly, with some thoughts on the similarities and differences of nuclear weapons, chemical weapons, and missile non-proliferation.

First, a key to longer-term success is likely to be establishment of an international consensus or norm in favor of control. The norm of nuclear non-proliferation significantly influenced the calculations and decisions both of potential nuclear weapons states and of suppliers of nuclear technology. It provided the legitimacy for all other non-proliferation measures. No comparable norm now exists in the area of missiles. The Geneva Protocol's norm against use of chemical weapons was badly undermined by repeated successful and unpunished Iraqi use of chemical weapons in the Gulf war.

A second lesson is that export controls and technology denial can make it harder, more time consuming, and complex for countries to develop advanced military capabilities. They can buy time for other measures to be implemented. But with some exceptions, they cannot alone prevent proliferation and should not be called on to do so. The impact of export controls, moreover, is likely to be even weaker in the chemical weapons area. Legitimate civilian chemical activities are more widespread, the number of firms and countries involved greater, and the unique constraints of radioactivity to assist control are lacking. For missiles, export controls again seem most useful to slow the process and buy time. While access to guidance technologies could be a key bottleneck, this applies only to countries seeking more sophisticated capabilities.

Third, technical characteristics aside, the nuclear non-proliferation experience suggests that ensuring effective export controls will be a continuing political not only technical struggle. Problem countries will continue to find new ways to circumvent their impact. More important, other supplier countries will often lack the will, the mechanisms, or the personnel to implement effective export regulations. A growing number of suppliers will compound the problem. Recent experience with both chemical weapons and missile export controls serves only to demonstrate this point again.

Fourth, the existence of a legally binding international obligation to enforce export controls can be especially helpful in obtaining other countries' support to alleviate some of the preceding weaknesses. In the nuclear non-proliferation area, the fact of the NPT made it easier for governments to convince legislatures to place restrictions on trade. A legally binding obligation under the NPT also provided a valuable handle for U.S. arguments with these countries about the need to put in place export control systems and to implement them effectively. NPT membership also could be cited as part of nuclear diplomacy aimed to head off specific exports. In neither the chemical weapons nor missile technology control fields is there now a comparable legally binding obligation. One of the main benefits of a complete and total chemical weapons ban would be its creation of that obligation, via the ban on transfer.

Fifth, the nuclear non-proliferation record also drives home the importance of influencing incentives to acquire advanced military technologies. Steadily growing skepticism about the utility of nuclear weapons, backed up by strong U.S. alliances, have been most critical in the nuclear field. By contrast, Iraq's recent successful uses of chemical weapons have sent the opposite signal, while the problem of assistance to countries threatened with chemical weapons has yet to be addressed. With regard to missile proliferation, it may be feasible to take measures via tactical missile defenses to negate directly the benefits for Third World countries of acquiring missiles. Absent that, perceptions of the utility of missiles also are likely to rise over time, again partly boosted by Iraq's use of these weapons in the war of the cities as well as by recent Afghan government use of SCUDs.

Sixth, four decades of nuclear non-proliferation clearly demonstrates that non-proliferation efforts in any area must be placed into a broader national, regional, and international political perspective. Consider each briefly.

Nationally, nuclear non-proliferation has traditionally been but one piece—and often in practice a subordinate one—of overall national security and foreign policy. This already has been evident from the start in the chemical and missile non-proliferation areas. It is unlikely to change, barring a dramatic proliferation threat to the United States itself.

In turn, the key to long-term regional nuclear non-proliferation success increasingly seems likely to be political initiatives to defuse the underlying conflicts. In South Asia, the Middle East, the Gulf, and the Korean Peninsula, nuclear non-proliferation cannot be pursued only in its own terms.[6] This increases the difficulties and complexities but also may open up new opportunities. Even here, however, the more traditional non-proliferation measures can buy time. Similarly, both missile and chemical weapons non-proliferation need to be put into such a broader regional political context. Equally important, the relationships between all three types of proliferation need to be factored into policy development.

Finally, the nuclear non-proliferation record reflects both the benefits and the limits of U.S.–Soviet cooperation. Cooperation between the two countries was essential to put in place a strong nuclear supply regime, buttress the NPT, support the IAEA, and defuse at least some problem country hotspots. But U.S.–Soviet regional interests also have differed on occasion, restricting the possibility of common non-proliferation action. Similarly, limits even on their joint influence have been evident. These same strains can be expected in trying to put together a parallel approach to chemical weapons and missile non-proliferation.

CONCLUSION

Looking back at the four decades' record of nuclear non-proliferation wins, losses, and draws makes clear both the potential influence and the continuing limits of U.S. efforts to prevent the further spread of nuclear weapons around the globe. Both what we can realistically hope to do and what we cannot do need to be taken into account in revamping our nuclear non-proliferation policies in the decades ahead. Those lessons of the past decades' record need to be reflected, as well, in the new measures now rising to prominence to prevent the spread of chemical weapons and missiles. To do so could measurably increase the prospects for their success.

NOTES

1. For a detailed discussion of recent revelations about Israeli capabilities, see Frank Barnaby, *The Invisible Bomb* (London: I.B. Tauris & Co., 1989).
2. For an overview of the current non-proliferation situation, see Leonard S. Spector, "Nuclear Proliferation in the 1990s: The Storm After the Lull" (Appendix One of this report).
3. A clear nuclear proliferation loss, the French case is discussed below.
4. See McGeorge Bundy, *Danger and Survival* (New York: Random House, 1988), p. 510.
5. On chemical weapons arms control see Kyle B. Olson, "Feasibility of a Chemical Weapons Control Regime," and Paul Doty, "Policy Issues in Chemical Weapons Control" (Appendices Four and Five of this report).
6. On Regional Proliferation problems see Stephen Philip Cohen, "Proliferation Problems in a Regional Context: South Asia," and Geoffrey Kemp, "'Solving' the Proliferation Problem in the Middle East" (Appendices Six and Seven of this report).

Appendix 9

RETHINKING NON-PROLIFERATION POLICY: INCREASING EFFICIENCY AND ENHANCING STABILITY

Thomas W. Graham

I. INTRODUCTION

The international "landscape" of nuclear proliferation has been transformed with the advent of four *de facto* nuclear weapons states and four advanced threshold states who all could use nuclear weapons in any conflict that takes place during the first Bush administration. As a result, pursuit of U.S. non-proliferation policy, as presently defined and implemented, will become increasingly dysfunctional over the next decade and could weaken U.S. national security as the world moves into the 21st century. To prevent this from happening, the administration will have to double its efficiency in implementing policy, and it will have to plan a major new initiative to reverse the trend where sensitive countries increasingly perceive that a substantial number of relatively sophisticated nuclear weapons are essential to their security. Otherwise, just as the Bush administration may be able to stabilize U.S.–Soviet nuclear relations with a START agreement, it could easily face a series of events that stimulate one of eight nations to test, openly deploy, or threaten to use nuclear weapons. If either of these actions occur, important taboos will have been broken, and one might "lose" the entire non-proliferation ball game. Even though the probability of a total system failure is low, administration officials must realize that continuation of a non-prolieration policy that automatically takes second place to other national security objectives has the possibility of destroying everything that has been accomplished in arms control over the last 40 years.

Three assumptions have been made in writing this paper. First, nuclear proliferation is a serious national security problem which deserves some attention of the president, secretaries of state, defense, and energy, the director of Central Intelligence, and the director of ACDA. While day-to-day decisions concerning implementation are best made at the assistant secretary or under secretary level, no significant "victories" will occur if senior American national security decision-makers continue to delegate this issue to subordinates. Second, effective policy requires a comprehensive evaluation of the current state of nuclear proliferation in approximately a dozen "sensitive" countries. Building an effective U.S. non-proliferation policy should emphasize developments in these dozen countries and should not over-emphasize the nuclear fuel cycle or elements of the NPT regime which attempt to treat all countries alike. Third, given budget constraints, a revitalized non-proliferation effort will have to be achieved with no increase in financial resources. This is possible if genuine bi-partisanship is restored and if cooperation among executive branch agencies reaches the level achieved in previous administrations.

II. THE TRANSFORMED POLICY SETTING

On the surface, the international non-proliferation regime—built around the Non-Proliferation Treaty (NPT)—seems in reasonable shape. In the last decade no country has used or threatened to use nuclear weapons. No additional non-nuclear weapons state (NNWS) has overtly tested a nuclear device or deployed nuclear weapons. No additional country has initiated a new covert nuclear weapons design & development program. No violations of the NPT have taken place.[1] The growth in nuclear power-related facilities which produce weapons-usable plutonium or highly-enriched uranium has been slowed. The dire predictions made in the 1960s and 1970s about the large number of countries that could possess nuclear weapons have *not* come true.

Despite the potential for a major failure in the NPT regime, the American political system seems to have accepted the basic conclusion either that nuclear proliferation is under control or that it is beyond the influence of the United States. The spread of nuclear weapons to additional countries was not an issue in the 1988 presidential campaign, and congressional interest is limited to a handful of staffers and members. The relative priority of non-proliferation in the national security agenda during the Reagan administration was lower than it had been in both the Ford and Carter administrations. Awareness and concern over proliferation has increased in the Bush administration, but no successes have yet been achieved.[2] Over the last ten years, encompassing parts of three presidential administrations, only moderate attention given to the issue by senior officials has not produced any dramatic, politically salient policy failures.[3]

How can one reconcile this perception of stability and calm with the dire prediction that the spread of nuclear war fighting capabilities to volatile regions will diminish U.S. security in the 1990s? Four reasons help explain this phenomenon. First, even though the non-proliferation regime is a *patchwork* of treaties, bilateral agreements, international institutions, and ad hoc national policy decisions, the regime is firmly in place and has restricted the proliferation problem to less than a dozen "sensitive" countries.[4] The fact that the scope of the contemporary proliferation problem has been bounded is extremely important but insufficiently appreciated by senior national security policymakers. Second, despite important differences in public rhetoric, actual United States non-proliferation policy has been rather consistent in the last four administrations. The intensity of policy implementation has varied, not the basic policy. Over the fifteen years since India's nuclear explosion, an adequate numbers of well-qualified, mid-level experts in all executive branch agencies have been trained.[5] As a result, rarely does a major problem "slip through the cracks" and generate the type of controversy that attracts presidential attention. Third, progress continues in incrementally improving the non-proliferation regime (e.g., upgrading of the nuclear export control trigger lists, improving safeguards, and expanding the NPT). While these improvements are important, they have given a stronger appearance of progress than is warranted.

A fourth, more unsettling, reason helps to explain the perception of stability. While things appear calm on the surface, major problems exist just below the surface. There are strong, but subtle, incentives for both the official nuclear weapons states (NWS)—including the United States—and for the NNWS to keep the exact nuclear weapons status of the dozen most sensitive countries ambiguous. A comprehensive review of the state of nuclear proliferation shows that a *very* serious regional nuclear crisis could occur *at any moment*.[6] Nuclear weapons production and delivery capabilities have been growing. Today four NNWS are *de facto* nuclear weapons states: India, Israel, Pakistan, and South Africa. These countries either have nuclear weapons or could build them in a short time (days or weeks). Four others—Argentina, Brazil, South Korea, and Taiwan—are advanced threshold states which could become *de facto* nuclear weapons states in one to three years, that is during the first Bush administration. In the 1990s, conflict involving any of these eight countries could involve the credible use or threatened use of nuclear weapons. Potential threshold states are at least a decade away from nuclear weapons status (see Table 1).

Currently, the United States is incapable of dealing with the security challenge presented by a potential nuclear conflict

Table 1 The Dozen Most Sensitive Countries of Proliferation Concern

De Facto *Nuclear Weapons* *States*	*Advanced* *Threshold* *States*	*Potential* *Threshold* *States*
Israel	Argentina	Iran
India	Brazil	Iraq
Pakistan	South Korea	Libya
South Africa	Taiwan	North Korea

among either the *de facto* or advanced threshold states. The two central actors in the development of U.S. defense policy—the Joint Chiefs of Staff and the Office of the Secretary of Defense—do not give nuclear proliferation very high priority in terms of U.S. defense planning.[7] Low priority is assigned to this issue because the most important military implications of proliferation occur outside North America, Europe, or Japan. Today, the direct military threat of proliferation to the United States is small and much less serious than the nuclear threat presented by the Soviet Union. However, given the expansion of nuclear weapons capability in several countries around the world, the proliferation of ballistic missile capability in several Third World countries, and the possibility that new nuclear countries might threaten to use their weapons in a crisis, the direct national security threat from proliferation to the United States or to our deployed forces overseas will increase substantially before the year 2000.[8] As a result, over time, the direct military component of the nuclear proliferation problem will grow for the United States.

III. CURRENT POLICY

Broadly speaking, current U.S. non-proliferation policy is divided into four functional areas: export control, improvement in the NPT regime and its associated safeguards, intelligence collection and analysis, and bilateral diplomatic, economic and military pressure exerted on each of the dozen sensitive countries. On balance, the first three of these functional areas have been moderately successful. (However, improvements are needed to maintain this relative success.) With the exception of bilateral policies adopted toward Taiwan and South Korea, bilateral diplomacy with sensitive proliferating states has been less successful.

Export controls have been moderately successful given the limited resources devoted to the task. Export controls are the primary policy tool responsible for slowing the rate of proliferation among the dozen sensitive states. Improved export controls can play a major role in keeping the least technically advanced sensitive countries from acquiring a nuclear weapons capability for several *decades.*[9]

Improvement in the NPT regime has been substantial, and maintenance of the NPT and the IAEA safeguards system is essential to keep the problem from getting worse.[10] However, an infinite amount of money and diplomatic pressure to strengthen these institutions will not directly influence the dozen sensitive countries.

The most consistent and successful element of the current U.S. non-proliferation effort focuses on the collection and analysis of intelligence. The U.S. government has consistently obtained sufficient "timely warning" (from one to several decades) that a country has decided to produce unsafeguarded weapons grade nuclear material or nuclear explosive devices. However, a problems exists in this area because the bulk of the resources for non-proliferation intelligence *analysis* is spent by the Department of Energy while the primary consumer of that information (the State Department) has no formal ability to set priorities or to insure that intelligence data flows to the appropriate analysts. To make matters worse, the continued disintigration of DOE headquarters staff, scattered non-proliferation responsibilities throughout the department with no assistant secretary in charge, and the perceived lack of interest in the subject by the secretary has produced inadequate DOE leadership in this area.

The disfunctional nature of the current policy system is that while export controls, strengthening the NPT regime, and intelligence analysis might be sufficient to deal with the proliferation problem in four of the least technically sophisticated sensitive countries, the most destabilizing elements of proliferation (use, threatened use, open deployment, or testing nuclear weapons) are more likely to occur among the four *de facto* nuclear weapons states and the four advanced threshold states. For these eight countries, "winning" in the non-proliferation area will require that the United States mobilize substantial diplomatic, economic, and military resources and linking U.S. bilateral relations with these countries demonstrating nuclear restraint.[11]

IV. INCREASINGLY DISFUNCTIONAL POLICIES

By failing to back up its non-proliferation rhetoric with action, the United States now lacks credibility with the eight sensitive countries it needs to influence most. For example, Pakistan has repeatedly violated various assurances given to the president of the United States concerning its nuclear program, continued to produce nuclear weapons-grade uranium, and has maintained its covert nuclear purchasing effort. At the same time, Pakistan has received large amounts of economic and military aid.[12] This pattern of U.S. government non-action, taken over the last *three* administrations, has seriously undermined American credibility in South Asia.

Consequently, there is little reason for any Pakistani government to take seriously American statements or diplomatic initiatives on non-proliferation. The United States has become the country that has cried "wolf" too many times.

The lack of U.S. credibility is not limited to Pakistan. Presently, the United States is not able to engage Indian leaders in a serious discussion of South Asian nuclear issues. Indian officials believe that the United States will do nothing to restrain Pakistan's nuclear weapons program. As a result, India's policy has focused on completing its program to acquire technical independence which could allow it to deploy a French style nuclear force by the late 1990s. Once India masters delivery technology and acquires certain technologies needed to produce sophisticated boosted or thermonuclear weapons, and if Pakistan continues to pursue its nuclear program without restraint, there will be few incentives for India to continue to keep its nuclear weapons program in the basement.

The lack of U.S. credibility in South Asia will continue to be a very serious problem as the United States tries to initiate confidence-building measures between India and Pakistan. There is a significant chance that neither Pakistan nor India would listen to U.S.-led non-proliferation initiatives even if such efforts were taken in a crisis. Past experience has shown that neither Indian nor Pakistani leaders have ever placed constraints on their nuclear programs as a result of bilateral discussion between themselves or as a result of international initiatives. They have learned that U.S. non-proliferation initiatives can be successfully resisted. Thus, in a crisis both countries might be extremely reluctant to take difficult diplomatic or military steps needed to diffuse a potential nuclear conflict.[13]

The lack of U.S. credibility is not limited to South Asia. Many governments have concluded that the United States *talks* a great non-proliferation line, but rarely uses its leverage to obtain a non-proliferation benefit. Our European allies have listened to hundreds of American requests to control their nuclear exports to sensitive countries only to see the United States unwilling or unable to fully enforce its own export control laws. Since the visits to Dimona in the early 1960s, the United States has ignored the potent Israel nuclear weapons program. The flip-flop of American foreign policy toward South Africa from the Carter policy of confrontation to the Reagan policy of constructive engagement has had the net effect of abandoning any serious effort to constrain South African development of significant quantities of nuclear weapons grade material. In Latin America, over the last 10 years, no major initiatives involving both the president and the secretary of state have been taken to encourage Argentina and Brazil to place additional constraints on their nuclear programs.

V. INCREASING EFFICIENCY OF POLICY IMPLEMENTATION

Until the United States and Soviet Union complete a START agreement and thereby free-up presidential and national security advisor time, the top priority for non-proliferation policy should be to improve implementation of policy. The following dozen initiatives can strengthen present non-proliferation policy and help lay the ground-work for a major initiative later in the administration.

U.S.-Soviet Diplomacy

Even though the two superpowers have had an extensive set of bilateral discussions on non-proliferation, a serious discussion has not yet focused on key sensitive country issues. Three topics should be raised in the near future. First, the Soviet Union should be encouraged to use its extensive economic and military assistance to North Korea to get the Koreans to place all of their nuclear facilities under IAEA safeguards and to terminate activities that would give the North Koreans the ability to produce nuclear weapons. In exchange, the U.S. should commit itself to using similar leverage over South Korea and Taiwan to keep those countries from developing the ability to produce nuclear weapons.[14] Only this type of extreme pressure, which brings with it extensive outside interference in the indigenous nuclear programs of Taiwan and the Koreas, will keep Japan from being forced to re-evaluate its currently strong commitment to non-proliferation.

Second, the Soviet Union should be encouraged to press Cuba to ratify the Latin American nuclear weapons free zone treaty.[15] In exchange, the United States should commit itself to opening dis-cussions with the Cubans to establish diplomatic relations. Paying this diplomatic price will signal to the world American interest in bringing this treaty into force.

Third, the United States should inform Pakistan that continuation of economic and military aid is dependent on Pakistani nuclear restraint in the following areas: no testing, no transfer of nuclear equipment and technology without safeguards, no deployment of nuclear weapons. In exchange for "controlling our client" in South Asia, the United States should ask the Soviet Union to make a parallel commitment to India.[16]

Recall of Ambassadors and Senior Staff

Upon completion of the non-proliferation National Security Review, ambassadors, science councilors, and political councilors from the American embassies in the dozen sensitive states should be recalled to Washington to be briefed on the policy decisions which have been taken with respect to non-proliferation. If meetings were conducted on a regional basis (i.e. with U.S. diplomatic staff from India and Pakistan attending the same meeting in Washington), it would assure that the entire U.S. team is working with the same instructions. In the past, constant bureaucratic fighting has occurred between the various regional bureaus and the non-proliferation staff in the State Department. Such a meeting in Washington is needed so that each player is aware of what the United States wants to accomplish in terms of non-proliferation and what it is willing to pay to reach that goal. In addition, such a meeting would demonstrate to the sensitive countries the increased level of U.S. concern with non-proliferation.

De Facto Reorganization

Currently extensive duplication of staff effort exists with several bureaus in the State Department and ACDA each maintaining staffs that follow issues in the dozen sensitive countries. However, because each staffer has responsibility for several countries, all reach only a moderate degree of expertise on any one particular country. To change this, informally the staffs of ACDA and State should be combined, and one staff member in State/ACDA should be assigned primary responsibility for a *single* sensitive country. That person should receive all appropriate clearances, accesses, and need to know authority. In addition, this person should be assigned primary drafting responsibility for all diplomatic cables, policy papers, and intelligence assessments done at Foggy Bottom that deal with his/her country. Such an organization would significantly improve the level of expertise that can be brought to bear on sensitive country issues. If a crisis were to develop, senior policy-makers could call on one person and have reasonable confidence that such a person would be able to quickly answer factual questions.

Rebuild Bipartisanship

Over the past fifteen years, developing a U.S. government consensus on non-proliferation has been difficult because the executive branch and Congress often have taken opposing policy positions, and new administrations often have purged former officials who have had extensive non-proliferation experience. For a number of reasons, the Bush administration has not followed this history and thus has an opportunity to rebuild a

bipartisan consensus concerning non-prolieration. One concrete step that could help improve this situation would be to
appoint 1 or 2 members of Congress with significant interest in
non-proliferation and 1 or 2 former senior administration officials with non-proliferation responsibility as members to
ACDA's General Advisory Committee. Since this body reports
to the President, and since it has rarely been taken seriously on
issues of U.S.-Soviet arms control, this existing committee could
focus on non-proliferation and provide an additional communication channel where experts on non-proliferation can articulate
the need for a strong policy.

Systematic Intelligence Sharing

European economic integration scheduled for 1992 will present the current international system of nuclear export controls with a severe challenge. Even though national expert
controls are scheduled to continue beyond 1992, less restrictive
monitoring of exports within Europe means that sensitive proliferation countries are likely to move their covert purchasing
networks to countries like Greece and Italy with the least developed export control and custom systems. This means that
the United States will have to provide non-proliferation intelligence information to a wider number of European countries if
it wants to attempt to limit sensitive nuclear exports. In addition, in the past, few countries that were provided with such
U.S. information initiated their own domestic investigations
that could produce evidence which could be used in eventual
prosecution if an export could not be stopped. To help solve this
problem, before the United States initiates systematic intelligence sharing, agreement must be reached by the heads of
state that intelligence sharing will take place, and that each
country will commit itself to initiate investigations and report
back its findings.[17] Since the United States also faces constraints
in using intelligence information to monitor relevant nuclear-
related exports out of the United States, such a systematic
exchange of information and a commitment to conduct follow-
on inquiries would help improve America's export control
system. In the past, information provided to the United States

by foreign governments was essential to trigger extraordinary efforts to stop several sensitive exports. In addition, other major supplier governments (the U.K., France, and Germany) should be encouraged to share relevant intelligence information with their European allies. This would reduce the perception that the United States is the only country that is concerned about sensitive nuclear exports.

Inter-Agency Intelligence Analysis Priorities

Currently, while intelligence collection requirements are discussed on an inter-agency basis, priorities for assigning staff time to analyze that information are made by each separate agency. The department with the largest resources, the Department of Energy, is currently implementing procedures that explicitly reject serving the needs of other agencies as a basis for establishing priorities. Implementation of these procedures would cripple the non-proliferation policy community's access to technically sophisticated analysis on issues of policy relevance.[18]

JCS Staff Assignment

A position on the staff of the Joint Chiefs of Staff should be created to develop and coordinate military contingency plans in the case conflict breaks out involving *de facto* nuclear weapons states. Currently, the professional military staff devotes almost no time to thinking about the spread of nuclear weapons.[19] At some point in the near future, a president may have to decide whether U.S. military or covert action is needed to keep a regional conflict that is on the verge of going nuclear from escalating. At this point, no clear military options have been developed to provide the president with the ability to contain such a crisis. Given the fact that a nuclear war starting in a regional context is judged by some experts as more likely than nuclear war originating from any other scenario, it seems ironic that so many resources are devoted to developing a SIOP focused on general nuclear war, and so little effort on conventional or nuclear options that might be needed in a regional context.

Historical Awareness

It is a truism that the United States has difficulty maintaining a historical perspective in conducting its foreign policy. This proclivity is a particular problem for nuclear proliferation because it takes a country decades, not years, to create a nuclear weapons capability. Thus, it is important that U.S. non-proliferation staffers have access to information on the complete history of a sensitive country's nuclear program. To complicate matters, one of the challenges of working in the non-proliferation area lies in the need to integrate information from a diverse source of diplomatic, intelligence, and technical fields. Much of this information is extremely sensitive and must accordingly be distributed to very few people. However, the result of this information dissemination system is that no comprehensive set of files exists which can be used to write detailed histories of the nuclear programs in sensitive countries. One agency should undertake to develop such a set of historical files which would contain all source information from all agencies that is at least four years old. By this time, the extreme sensitivity of documents will have diminished to the point where appropriately cleared staffers should be able to gain access to a complete set of historical files.

NSC Staff Slot

A tentative decision has been made not to fill an NSC slot with a mid-level expert responsible for nuclear proliferation and ballistic missiles. The logic for this decision might have been to try and keep the NSC staff relatively small and to organize non-proliferation issues around the Under Secretary of State's office. The problem with this decision is that for an effective non-proliferation effort, resources will have to be coordinated among several agencies and disputes will arise where agency positions differ. In such a circumstance, the senior State Department non-proliferation official will be a partisan by definition. In addition, if the president is to make any initiatives in the non-proliferation area, effective implementation requires an NSC staffer. For these reasons, the administration might consider filling a non-proliferation slot either now or later on into the administration.

Role of Non-Government Expertise

The U.S. government can encourage non-government action and initiatives which supplement official initiatives. The first involves utilizing United States Information Agency–funded speakers programs to make sure that a range of U.S. non-government nuclear experts travel to countries of non-proliferation concern and discuss related security issues. For example, people who are knowledgeable about U.S.–Soviet nuclear command and control and superpower threats to use nuclear weapons in the 1950s and 1960s should talk in India and Pakistan so that the local press and academic experts are aware that relative stability in U.S.–Soviet nuclear relations did not develop quickly or automatically. The U.S.–Soviet balance was delicate and was the product of a massive technical effort, some luck, and difficult learning by leaders of both countries. Other speakers could discuss the ability to verify safeguards without compromising indigenously developed nuclear technology. Such a speakers program can be used to initiate a non-government dialogue on these and other issues in which for one reason or another the U.S. government may not want to participate directly.

Second, informally government officials can communicate to senior foundation officials concerning the importance of non-proliferation research which is being conducted by the non-profit sector. This unofficial feed-back can help foundations evaluate programs and maintain a priority for nuclear proliferation.

VI. ENHANCING STABILITY

Even if all of the steps outlined above are implemented, one major problem will not be addressed: the four *de facto* nuclear weapons states are all developing nuclear weapons that are increasing in number and sophistication.[20] If these states continue with their programs, each could have produced a substantial number of nuclear weapons over the next decade. In addition, technological and bureaucratic momentum has already encouraged military officials in these countries to perceive these weapons as militarily useful, not just as symbolic weapons to be used only as a last resort. For these reasons, the United States must spend some time thinking about a major initiative involving these four countries. Two specific policy decisions could be part of such an initiative.

Sanctions Regime
Over the last fifteen years, during which time the United States has attempted to apply sanctions in the context of nuclear proliferation, one lesson is clear: linkage only to nuclear trade, economic, or military assistance rarely produces results. If the United States wants to have a major impact on a sensitive country's program, it has to pay a *significant* price. This has been the case with Taiwan and South Korea. If the United States wants to get sensitive countries to take positive steps in the non-proliferation area, trade sanctions worth hundreds of millions of dollars must be utilized.[21] This type of sanction should be triggered only for the most severe proliferation actions: openly deploying nuclear weapons, testing nuclear devices, and NNWS use of nuclear weapons. Using trade as a sanction should be raised by the United States with other countries in the context of a meeting of the Nuclear Suppliers Group. Current agreements made among these countries call for discussion of sanctions, but serious discussions have never been held on this topic. While the United States is likely to find that no country will commit itself to specific sanctions in advance, discussion of this issue could facilitate consultations among suppliers in the event a nuclear crisis takes place. Inside the United States, the Congress could play a very useful role by holding hearings on the issue of past effectiveness and future development of sanctions. In the past, strong U.S. legislation has encouraged the executive branch to take the lead on international negotiating issues which would not have otherwise been true.

STOP: Simultaneous Termination of Production
Realists argue that the United States does not have the power or willingness to keep the four *de facto* nuclear weapons states from maintaining their nuclear weapons status. Since these

countries have decided that it is in their national security interest to possess nuclear weapons and these countries have acquired the capability to produce such weapons, realists often argue that nothing the United States does can reverse their nuclear weapons status. While this logic is difficult to contradict, it does not automatically follow that these nations would be unwilling to stop their nuclear weapons production at some point in the future once they felt they had a finite deterrent capability. This is the essence of a STOP initiative. If production of weapons-grade material were to stop simultaneously in all four *de facto* weapons states and if it were preceded by a U.S.–Soviet START agreement, such an initiative could be a major step to "solve" the proliferation problem.

By the mid-1990s each of the four *de facto* weapons states will have some nuclear capability to meet their perceived national security needs. However, if these nations continue to produce more nuclear weapons with longer delivery systems and possibly more sophisticated designs, the direct national security significance of advanced proliferation will increasingly affect the United States. Thus, it might be worth the United States leading a multilateral initiative to cap these nuclear programs. A STOP proposal also could be supported by national security experts in these affected states. While virtually no domestic political actors in these four countries are against their country's effort to gain a nuclear weapons capability, the same may not be true if an initiative would allow these countries to keep what they have already produced.[22]

The most common criticisms of this type of freeze proposal relate to the precedent that this would establish for the NPT regime and the technical difficulty of verifying a STOP agreement. On the first issue, of the dozen sensitive countries, only Argentina, Brazil, South Korea, and Taiwan have the technical capability to reach the position of being a *de facto* nuclear weapons state if a STOP initiative is proposed within five years. In the case of South Korea and Taiwan, what keeps nuclear weapons out of their hands is not a lack of interest but strong actions taken by the United States. This policy is likely to continue and also to be effective regardless of a STOP initiative.

Thus, for a STOP initiative to be successful, only Argentina and Brazil would have to be included even though they have not yet reached *de facto* nuclear weapons status. However, a STOP treaty might meet Argentina's and Brazil's needs because the basic incentive for both programs is not to fall behind in the technology race. At this time neither country wants to develop nuclear weapons. In fact, both countries have initiated confidence building measures and have agreed not to enrich uranium above twenty percent. Thus, a STOP initiative would reinforce restraint that has been exercised by these countries. If combined with entry into force of the Treaty of Tlatelolco, a STOP treaty would "solve" the proliferation problem in Latin America and assure that the United States will not face a nuclear threat from a country in its own hemisphere.

If the focus of verification procedures was to determine whether weapons-grade material was being produced, rather than fully accounting for past nuclear production, many technical issues would become much easier. Such a STOP initiative would require some form of safeguards, but construction of various systems is technically feasible and need not duplicate the current IAEA system.

Initiating a STOP proposal would be a major initiative and would open up the obvious question whether the United States and Soviets would accept a similar freeze. For these reasons, it might not be the best initiative for the United States to take. However, if no similarly ambitious initiative is made, by the year 2000, Israel, India, Pakistan, and South Africa will be medium nuclear powers similar to France. In addition, the four current advanced threshold states might become *de facto* nuclear weapons states by the next century. Thus, in the not too distant future, these countries will have to be brought into the international nuclear arms control arena one way or the other. It would be better from the U.S. perspective to think hard about making a STOP initiative immediately after a START agreement has been signed rather than to wait for a decade during which time the proliferation problem will only have gotten worse, not better.

NOTES

1. Despite the fact that the NPT has not been violated, Libya, Iraq, and Iran's participation in the treaty in no way indicates that these countries are of little non-proliferation concern.
2. While policy coordination in the State Department has been improved under the direction of an under secretary and cabinet officers have focused on the proliferation issue, in other areas progress has been slow. Both the Departments of Energy and Defense continue to treat this issue on a third priority basis, the NSC has not filled its non-proliferation slot, and 8 months into the administration the non-proliferation review (NSR 17) has not been completed.
3. De-emphasis of nuclear proliferation began toward the end of the Carter administration, especially after Soviet forces invaded Afghanistan. Since 1979, U.S. non-proliferation policy has emphasized export controls and preserving the NPT.
4. Contemporary policy makers should remember that when the NPT regime was established in the 1950s and 1960s, it was never designed to deal with contemporary 1990s proliferation problems. The regime was designed to keep indigenously developed nuclear weapons out of Germany and Japan, to constrain the overt production and deployment of nuclear weapons by Nth countries, and to *facilitate* the international diffusion of nuclear power technology and facilities.
5. However, few current officials have experience initiating major improvements in the NPT regime which took place in the 1960s and 1970s.
6. For an expansion on this point, see Leonard S. Spector, "Nuclear Proliferation in the 1990s: The Storm After the Lull" (Appendix One of this report).
7. Throughout the entire federal government (and weapons laboratories), only approximately 100 professional staff work on the non-proliferation issue. In budget terms, less is spent for non-proliferation than for verification of the INF agreement.
8. For an excellent review of the issues associated with the spread of ballistic missile capabilities, see Janne Nolan and Albert Wheelon, "Ballistic Missiles in the Third World" (Appendix Three of this report).
9. Export controls can be especially effective to constrain nuclear capability in Iran, Iraq, and Libya.
10. See Scheinman, Lawrence, *The International Atomic Energy Agency and World Nuclear Order* (Washington, D.C.: Resources for the Future, 1987).
11. These eight countries include Argentina, Brazil, India, Israel, Pakistan, South Africa, South Korea, and Taiwan.
12. The argument that U.S. military and economic aid has encouraged Pakistan not to test or deploy nuclear weapons is questionable given the lack of technical incentives for Pakistan to test its nuclear weapon and other strong disincentives to test that are independent of the United States (i.e., the certainty of an Indian test or open deployment after a Pakistani test).
13. Since the United States has reasonably good intelligence in this area, it is more likely than any other country in the world to pick up indications that a crisis was building. Even though some argue that American "leverage"

is weak in South Asia, the Unites States would become a major player in any nuclear crisis in the sub-continent.

14. This is current U.S. policy, and the United States should impress upon the Soviets the great effort that has already been exerted to achieve this goal. Thus, unless the Soviets want a nuclearized Japan, they should not require an explicit new quid pro quo to restrain the North Koreans.

15. Known as the Treaty of Tlatelolco, the final steps needed to bring this treaty into force require action to be taken by Cuba, Argentina, and Brazil.

16. More ambitious U.S.–Soviet initiatives for South Asia are described in section IV.

17. This is one example where some presidential involvement is essential, but to be effective it must be preceded and followed up with substantial staff work. Usually, making sure that this occurs requires an NSC staff member. Unfortunately, this administration has not filled such a slot to date.

18. This is only one of many examples that illustrate the high cost of having no senior official at the Department of Energy who is assigned primary responsibility for non-proliferation. While the department will undergo some type of reorganization which could solve some of these problems, it is not clear that the secretary is aware of the serious management problems in this policy area.

19. The small staff that works on non-proliferation for DIA could support a military officer who works for the JCS.

20. This statement does not reflect a legal judgment that nuclear weapons have actually been assembled in all of these states, only that weapons design work, production of weapons-grade material, and fabrication or purchase of weapons parts has taken place.

21. Congressional interest in using such sanctions in the context of chemical weapons is discussed in Elisa Harris, "Chemical Weapons Proliferation: Current Capabilities and Prospects for Control," and Kyle Olson, "Feasibility of a Chemical Weapons Control Regime" (Appendices Two and Four of this report).

22. For discussion of a proposal for South Asia with some similar features, see Stephen Philip Cohen, "Solving Proliferation Problems in a Regional Context: South Asia" (Appendix Six of this report).